MAPLE LEAFS

TOP 100

TORONTO'S GREATEST PLAYERS OF ALL TIME

MIKE LEONETTI

ESSAYS BY JOHN IABONI

Raincoast Books gratefully acknowledges the financial support of the Province of British Columbia through the BC Arts Council and the Book Publishing Tax Credit and the Government of Canada through the Canada Council for the Arts, and the Book Publishing Industry Development Program (BPIDP).

Edited by Brian Scrivener
Cover and interior design by Bill Douglas

Library and Archives Canada Cataloguing in Publication

Leonetti, Mike, 1958–
    Maple Leafs top 100 : Toronto's greatest players of all time / Mike Leonetti.

Includes index.
ISBN 13: 978-1-55192-808-1
ISBN 10: 1-55192-808-6

    1. Toronto Maple Leafs (Hockey team)—Biography. 2. Hockey players—Ontario—Toronto—Biography. 3. Toronto Maple Leafs (Hockey team)—History. I. Title.
II. Title: Maple Leafs top one hundred.

GV848.T6L453 2007   796.962092'2713541   C2007-900489-X

Raincoast Books
9050 Shaughnessy Street
Vancouver, British Columbia
Canada V6P 6E5
www.raincoast.com

In the United States:
Publishers Group West
1700 Fourth Street
Berkeley, California
94710

Printed in China by Book Art.

10 9 8 7 6 5 4 3 2 1

TABLE OF CONTENTS

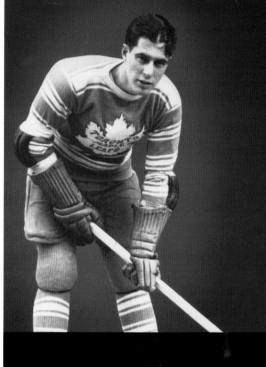

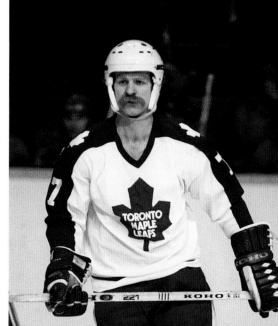

CELEBRATING 80 YEARS OF TORONTO MAPLE LEAFS HOCKEY

★ THE MISSION

The idea for the Maple Leafs Top 100 began in 2002 when the team celebrated its 75th anniversary. A selection committee chose the top 25 Maple Leafs of all time but gave them no ranking. After discussing this with my colleague, John Iaboni, who was part of that selection panel, we thought it would be fun not only to list the top 100 Leafs but also to tabulate them in order from 1 to 100. We believed that it would be a neat way of celebrating 80 years of Maple Leafs hockey.

We knew it would not be an easy task because there are so many things to consider, not the least of which is: how does one compare a Leaf from the 30-team NHL to one from the Original Six? However, we both felt that naming the top 100 Leafs was a mission that could be completed reasonably if each selector gave it some careful consideration. We also thought it would be a fun task that would ultimately generate some interesting debate and discussion among all Leafs fans. It was also determined that this process would only be for Maple Leafs players. This of course excluded the two NHL teams in Toronto that preceded the Leafs — Arenas and St. Patricks — and the many fine players who played for them (including Babe Dye, Harry Cameron, Hap Holmes, Jack Adams, Corb Denneny, Frank Finnigan, Reg Noble and John Ross Roach).

★ A JURY OF 14

To help compile the top 100 Maple Leafs, our panel consisted of 14 individuals with extensive Maple Leafs knowledge, including the authors of this book. The dozen who joined us were Mark Askin, Howard Berger, Joe Bowen, Milt Dunnell, Doug Farraway, Paul Hendrick, Lance Hornby, Harry Neale, Frank Orr, Paul Patskou, Frank Selke and Bill Watters. (For more on each member of the selection committee, please see page 233.) Each selector was given a ballot consisting of 140 Maple Leafs (in alphabetical order covering the years 1927 to 2007). Each of us then ranked 100 players starting from number 1 (the player each of us believed the top all-time Leaf) to 100. Selectors were free to write in names on their ballot if they felt a player was overlooked. The voting took place in the summer and fall of 2006 with the results being finalized early in 2007. All were assured that their individual results would be kept confidential and everyone was informed of the final tabulation at the same time.

John and I are eternally grateful for the contributions from our panellists. This project would not have been possible without them.

★ KEEPING TABS

The first tabulation from the ballots submitted by the 14 selectors was to recap which players appeared on the most ballots. Some players were listed on all 14 ballots. They were grouped together and then listed in order based on the score they earned. The scoring was done as in golf — the lower the total for each player, the better his ranking. Any player

ranked number one, for example, received one point; a number two ranking was worth two points and so on all the way down to 100. The next group was 13 ballots, then 12 followed by 11 and so forth all the way to six. The scoring was done in the same fashion for each ballot group until 100 players were listed. Any player appearing in this book was named on at least six ballots.

★ THE STORIES

Each of the top 100 Maple Leafs selected is given equal time in terms of presentation, except for 11 players who have an essay along with their profile. Rather than write the oft-done career summaries for each player, the focus of each profile is a great moment by that player while he was with the Maple Leafs. It could be a story about an important goal, a significant shutout, a terrific playoff performance, a major trade or a team record.

The stories were put together from game reports taken from the date of the event and any quotes used come from the time the game took place. This book celebrates great moments in Leaf history and is not meant to be a critical analysis of any player's career. Since the profiles are based on the players who made the Top 100, not all the great Leafs games are covered but we did find a special moment for each player on our list.

★ THE FINAL SCORE

Maybe it's just pure coincidence but our panel of 14 selectors made the man who made number 14 famous the number 1 Leaf of all time. Dave Keon was ranked first on six ballots, second or third on five other ballots and was never ranked lower than eighth. Keon certainly left a mark on anybody who was lucky enough to see him play with the Maple Leafs.

All the selectors pretty much agreed on who the top 50 players were (a total of 51 players were on all 14 ballots) — it was just a matter of putting them in order.

The next 50 selections, however, saw less consensus and the selectors placed different emphasis on their choices. Some favoured those with better overall NHL careers, many considered being on a Leafs championship team to be more significant, while others focused on particular moments (such as a very good year, winning an award or earning a spot on an All-Star team). Of the 100 players chosen, 12 were goaltenders, 27 were defencemen and 61 were forwards. The top 10 featured (in order) Dave Keon, Ted Kennedy, Syl Apps, Frank Mahovlich, Darryl Sittler, Charlie Conacher, Johnny Bower, Tim Horton, Turk Broda and Borje Salming — a very impressive group of Toronto hockey legends. The selectors did a great job of putting this ranking together and it was a pleasure to write about these players and the significant contributions they made to the long and illustrious history of the Maple Leafs!

1 | DAVE KEON

BORN: MARCH 22, 1940 IN NORANDA, QUEBEC
POSITION: CENTRE
YEARS AS A LEAF: 1960–61 TO 1974–75
SWEATER #: 14
MAPLE LEAF MOMENT: APRIL 9, 1964

CENTRE DAVE KEON always found a way to play well, and in the seventh game of the 1964 semi-finals versus Montreal he found a way to play superbly. It was the first time the Leafs and Canadiens had met in a seventh-game showdown in the postseason. Keon had not contributed much offence to the Leafs' attack during the previous six games in the series, but he scored three times in the last contest, played on April 9, 1964, to help the Leafs take the series 4–3 and assure the defending Stanley Cup champions a shot at keeping their title.

The Leafs started the game with an all-out blitz on the hometown Canadiens but were only up 1–0 after 20 minutes of play. Keon opened the scoring as the Leafs buzzed around Montreal netminder Charlie Hodge. Good plays by Bob Baun, George Armstrong and Don McKenney kept the puck in the Habs' end until it finally squirted out to Keon, who knocked it in. "The little man from Noranda made no mistake," *Hockey Night in Canada* play-by-play man Danny Gallivan told a national audience watching this game on a Thursday evening.

Montreal came out determined to even the score in the second period, but it was Keon who scored the only goal of the middle stanza. Armstrong fed a pass to Keon while the Leafs were short-handed, and the speedy centreman broke away from Montreal defenceman Jean-Guy Talbot to rifle a shot past the startled Hodge. The Habs kept pressing, but Toronto goalie Johnny Bower, who was stellar all night long, kept the Habs off the scoresheet until the third period. Ralph Backstrom scored to make it 2–1 before the third period was eight minutes old, but the Leafs' defence stiffened and did not allow another Montreal tally, despite the fact the Habs had 18 shots on the Leafs' net in the final frame.

Both teams went back and forth during the third period, exchanging scoring chances before a Forum crowd of 14,541 fans. With time running out the Canadiens pulled Hodge from the net, but it was Keon who scored his third goal of the night to end any Montreal hopes. Red Kelly and George Armstrong did most of the work in the Canadiens' end, and the puck coasted out to an unattended Keon who slid it into the cage with just 11 seconds to play. The Leafs poured over the boards to congratulate Keon on his hat trick, the first three-goal performance by a visiting player in the seventh game of a playoff series in NHL history. (In 1993 Wayne Gretzky would equal this mark against the Leafs.) It was also the first career hat trick for Keon. "A big night for a truly great player," Gallivan concluded on the television broadcast. In spite of his great game, Keon was named as the game's third star, with the first two stars reserved for Bower and Hodge respectively.

After the game Keon said, "I'm happy I got three. They came in handy. The Canadiens kept coming at us. They could easily have tied it up playing in that last period." Montreal coach Toe Blake thought Keon's second goal of the night was the backbreaker for his club. "That goal was the winner and that was the break they needed," he said.

The Leafs faced the Detroit Red Wings in the finals. Keon continued his fine play with four goals and one assist in the series. His biggest goal came in the seventh game, played at Maple Leaf Gardens, when he scored early in the third period to give the Leafs a 2–0 lead on their way to a 4–0 victory. It was the third straight Stanley Cup for the Leafs.

MAPLE LEAF CAREER HIGHLIGHTS

★ Member of four Stanley Cup teams
★ Winner of the Conn Smythe Trophy (1967)
★ Winner of the Calder Trophy (1961) and Lady Byng Trophy (1962, 1963)
★ 365 regular season goals (in 1,062 games) and 32 in the playoffs as a Maple Leaf

LEAF FACT:

One of the best penalty killers in NHL history, Dave Keon shares the team record for most short-handed goals in one season — eight in 1970–71. (Dave Reid tied the mark in 1990–91.) Keon was also the first NHL player to score two short-handed goals in one playoff game (vs. Detroit in 1963).

Dave Keon:
A Personal Memory

One day after school when I was about 10 years old I noticed my neighbour, Albert, running down Whitmore Avenue. He had started his sprint from the top of the hill. Obviously, he had some breaking news to tell all of us. All out of breath and still very excited, Albert explained that hockey star Dave Keon had been to his school and that he, Albert, had got his autograph. He unfolded a square piece of paper he held in his hand. There, written in black ink, was "David Keon." Talk about being envious! Keon was my favourite hockey player. How many Toronto kids back then pretended they were Keon when they played a game of hockey? I would go one better by picking one player on my table hockey game and calling him Keon! I would have given anything to meet him and get his signature. Albert wasn't even a hockey fan — he was into music — so why should he have this valuable treasure? It seems that Keon's sister, Pat, was a teacher at Darcy McGee Catholic School, and she had arranged for the visit. Two years later, I was attending the same school, and Pat Keon was one of my grade 8 teachers. I must have bugged her the whole year, but her brother never did get back to Darcy McGee, at least while I was there. But that did not change how I felt about my first hero.

As a youngster, my life seemed to revolve around the fortunes of the Toronto Maple Leafs. I waited for every Saturday night when *Hockey Night in Canada* came on television at 8:30 p.m. Toronto was good back then, winning championships, and for me and many others of that time, Keon stood out as the truest Leaf of them all. Game in and game out, Keon could be relied upon to score a key goal, help kill a penalty, skate miles every night and save his best for when it mattered most — the playoffs — when he would play with a tremendous intensity. Keon was admired for all these qualities, but there was one thing that made him stand out above the pack. He played the game in a special way. It seems to me that Keon's style of play was rooted in the era where character, integrity and hard work were all highly valued.

Keon played the game in a clean fashion, yet he never shied away during a tough contest. He was a renowned checker who did not cheap-shot his opponents or use ugly stick work on them. When he did get a penalty, it seemed that a royal commission was going to be called to find out why. The opposition

had to make a good play to beat the smooth, swift-skating Keon, who was always ready to pounce on a loose puck. If the Leafs needed a goal, Keon was more likely to score it than anyone on the team (with the possible exception of Frank Mahovlich). He could score in a variety of ways: using a terrific backhand drive, a nice deke on the goalie, a snap wrist shot and, if needed, a hard, well placed slap shot that would handcuff the opposition netminder. Keon did all this while standing only 5′9″ and weighing 165 pounds and checking the likes of Jean Béliveau (Montreal), Stan Mikita (Chicago), Norm Ullman (Detroit) and other future Hall of Fame players on the opposing teams. In short, Keon's game was all about skill, speed, finesse and durability — all the attributes we were taught to value in our hockey heroes in those days.

Finding out information about players was not nearly as easy in the sixties and seventies as it is today, but if you collected the right stuff you could learn a great deal about your favourite star. I kept everything I could find about Keon, starting with the December 1963 issue of *Hockey Illustrated* magazine, which featured a photo of Keon trying to score on Detroit netminder Terry Sawchuk. My mom bought that magazine for me. I recall the story on the inside was written by Leaf coach Punch Imlach. The headline read, "I wouldn't take a million for Keon." That sounded about right to me. I remember my dad bought me a pack of the "Tallboy" hockey cards that were issued one year, and when I opened it, there was Keon right on top! What luck, I thought. From then on I tried to get Keon's card first as soon as the new issue came out every year. I probably traded away a few Bobby Hulls and a Gordie Howe or two, but as long as I got my Keon card, I was happy. They always put some interesting tidbits on the backs of those cards. I must have looked at the 1963–64 Leafs media guide thousands of times, and I would read Keon's bio over and over again to make sure I had all my facts right. Included with his NHL record was a photo of Keon accepting the J.P. Bickell Trophy as the Leafs' best player from Prime Minister Lester Pearson.

All of the magazine stories and cards told of his many accomplishments: rookie of the year, two Lady Byng Trophies, 20-goal seasons, All-Star selections, two goals to clinch the 1963 Stanley Cup for Toronto and on and on. But what I remember most was how Keon came through when everything was on the line. The great thing about Leafs TV is that we can see some of the wonderful games of the past. For Keon, no game was better than the one on the night of April 9, 1964, when he scored three goals in a 3–1 Leaf victory over the Montreal Canadiens at the Forum. In the seventh and deciding game of a hard-fought playoff series, Keon was at his best and almost single-handedly got

the Leafs into their third straight final. He was outstanding in the finals versus Detroit and scored a key goal in the seventh game when the Leafs beat Detroit 4–0 to clinch their third consecutive Cup.

If he was good in '64, he was even better in 1967, when the Leafs came out of nowhere to steal their fourth Cup of the decade. Watch any of those games from the final against the Habs and you will see Keon in constant motion from the beginning to the end of each shift. As Leafs broadcaster Bill Hewitt told the television audience, "Keon is here, there and everywhere." He scored an important goal and assisted on another in the fifth game of the series, and then checked the Canadiens relentlessly to help the team close out the series with a 3–1 Leafs win at Maple Leaf Gardens. I was eight years old in '67, and I kept a scrapbook during the playoffs. I can still see the front page of the *Toronto Telegram* the day after the Leafs beat Montreal. It was a colour photo of Keon with the Stanley Cup. Many believe that Sawchuk (who was superb for the Leafs in goal throughout the '67 postseason when called upon) or Jim Pappin (the leading playoff scorer) deserved the Conn Smythe Trophy that year, and you could make those arguments effectively.

Dave Keon

wearing the blue and white of the Maple Leafs.

It was a great thrill for me when I finally got to meet my hero in 2001, when he agreed to do a foreword to a book I was writing on the Leafs-Canadiens rivalry. He was in town to look after the affairs of his sister Pat, who had just recently passed away. He gave me a great interview and signed a few autographs for me (I finally got the autograph I always wanted, and it was personalized — something Albert did not have!), and for my son David. We spoke about family for a few minutes, and he even showed me pictures of his children. What I remember most from my visit was when he told me that he was proud to represent the Maple Leafs, and that he appreciated how Toronto fans had treated him over the years.

Keon stayed away from the Leafs for decades after his retirement. Attempts to get him to return to the fold were not successful. He nearly reconciled with the organization on more than one occasion only to have it fizzle out. Many were critical of Keon for his stance. Everyone is entitled to their point of view. However, some forget that Keon made appearances with the Leaf alumni, and I'll always remember when he was at the Meet the Leafs Luncheon in 1991 and kept everyone's attention during a superb interview he did with his good friend Harry Neale. I was also happy to see that Keon took the time in 2006 to acknowledge Mats Sundin when the classy Swede passed him on the all-time list for most career points as a Maple Leaf. Then, on February 17, 2007, Dave Keon made his triumphant return, not to Maple Leaf Gardens, but to Air Canada Centre, for a ceremony honouring the 40th anniversary of the '67 Cup-winning Leafs team, and the 80th anniversary of the organization.

I have to admit I was a little surprised that Keon topped the list of the Top 100 Leafs of all time. I thought that honour might go to someone like Ted Kennedy, Syl Apps or maybe even Turk Broda or Tim Horton. But when I stop and think about what Keon meant to the team and the loyal Leaf fans, I'd have to say that his number 1 ranking is well deserved. There was one incident that speaks volumes about how Toronto fans felt about Keon. It came after the Leafs clinched the Cup on home ice on April 18, 1963 and the Leafs' centre scored two short-handed goals in the contest. When the game was over and interviews were being done on the ice, the fans chanted "Davey! Davey!" until he appeared on the ice to speak to Ward Cornell. *Hockey Night in Canada* had just signed off but quickly returned when they saw Keon was being interviewed and the crowd was applauding their hero.

Like most Keon fans I hope that he will one day appear at the Air Canada Centre and let the team honour him with a banner raised to the rafters. If he chooses not to do that, even Keon's most ardent fans

But to my mind Keon was a very deserving winner.

The Leafs were never the same after 1967, even though Keon continued to play with his usual brilliance. In 1970–71 while playing on a line with journeymen Gary Monahan and Billy MacMillan, he scored a career-best 38 goals, eight of them short-handed markers, that set an NHL record at the time. In his final year as a Leaf, the 1974–75 season, Keon still managed to record 43 assists and total 59 points, but Leaf owner Harold Ballard decided it was time for the Maple Leaf captain (since 1969) to leave — as long as it was not to another NHL team. That decision forced Keon to the World Hockey Association for the large part of what remained of his career. He was with Hartford when they joined the NHL in 1979 (scoring 62 points in 76 games), but I didn't want to see him in that uniform. It just wasn't right. I always wanted to remember him

will have to accept that he has made that choice. I still have his Beehive photo from his rookie year when the youthful, clean-cut Keon was just starting out his Hall of Fame career. It's a black-and-white shot and he is looking straight into the camera wearing the uniform with the multi-point Maple Leaf on it. For me that photo represents the young star of the Maple Leafs that I will always remember, from a special time in my life when as a little boy I could admire my hero for all the right reasons.

— *Mike Leonetti*

I HAVE TO ADMIT I WAS A LITTLE SURPRISED THAT KEON TOPPED THE LIST OF THE TOP 100 LEAFS OF ALL TIME. I THOUGHT THAT HONOUR MIGHT GO TO SOMEONE LIKE TED KENNEDY, SYL APPS OR MAYBE EVEN TURK BRODA OR TIM HORTON. BUT WHEN I STOP AND THINK ABOUT WHAT KEON MEANT TO THE TEAM AND THE LOYAL LEAF FANS, I'D HAVE TO SAY THAT HIS NUMBER ONE RANKING IS WELL DESERVED.

2 | TED KENNEDY

BORN: DECEMBER 12, 1925 IN HUMBERSTONE, ONTARIO
POSITION: CENTRE
YEARS AS A LEAF: 1942–43 TO 1954–55; 1956–57
SWEATER #: 9
MAPLE LEAF MOMENT: APRIL 19, 1947

TED KENNEDY FIRST attracted the attention of NHL scouts when his Port Colborne team won the Ontario juvenile hockey championship in 1941. The Montreal Canadiens put the 5′11″, 175-pound centre on their negotiation list and invited him to their camp when he was just 16 years old. The youngster never felt comfortable there and decided to go home, knowing he would never wear a Montreal uniform again. Kennedy played senior hockey in the 1942–43 season with the Port Colborne Sailors, scoring 23 goals in 23 games.

The Maple Leafs learned of Kennedy's talented play and had him in for a two-game trial during '42–43. Toronto had to make a trade to acquire Kennedy's NHL playing rights and sent defenceman Frank Eddolls to the Habs to complete the transaction. Leaf manager Conn Smythe was furious when he was made aware of the deal, mostly because his assistant Frank Selke had not consulted him before the trade was made (and because Eddolls was an army man like Smythe). Soon all was forgotten as Eddolls faded away while the determined Kennedy became the Leafs' best player and leader for many years. Never a great skater, Kennedy made up for it by being a fierce competitor who had a good scoring touch and a reputation for being the best face-off man in hockey. He scored 26 goals his first year, 29 in his second and 28 in his fourth year, the 1946–47 season. Kennedy saved his most memorable marker of the latter year for the night of April 19, 1947, when the Leafs met the Canadiens with the Stanley Cup on the line.

The Leafs were up 3–2 in the finals with a chance to win the Cup on home ice before 14,546 fans at Maple Leaf Gardens on this Saturday night. It was not going to be easy to eliminate the defending champions, and the Leafs were a team filled with youngsters. The inexperience of the Toronto club showed itself early as the Canadiens got a goal just 25 seconds into the contest. But rather than fold, the Leafs started to counterattack and pelted Montreal netminder Bill Durnan with a flurry of shots. The Leafs tied the game early in the second period when Vic Lynn scored, assisted by Kennedy and Howie Meeker.

The game remained tied until late in the third period, when Kennedy beat Durnan with a long, low drive that the Montreal goaltender did not see. The Leafs hung on for the remaining five minutes behind the great goaltending of Turk Broda, eking out a 2–1 victory and a Cup win in the 20th anniversary year of the Maple Leafs. Kennedy, Syl Apps of the Leafs and Durnan were named the three stars of the game. The Stanley Cup was not presented to the Leafs after the game because it was back in Montreal. When NHL president Clarence Campbell was asked about it he said, "It's still in Montreal at the request of the Toronto club. They didn't want to jinx themselves by having it brought here for this game."

When someone suggested that Kennedy was the best centre in the league, Toronto coach Hap Day would not disagree: "He won the Cup for us two seasons back. We fell apart when he was shelved by injuries last season, and he came back to lead us home this term. His was as fine an

individual performance as I've seen." Meeker and Vic Lynn hugged Kennedy and told him, "You did it Teeder. You're the guy who tied the can to them." Showing his leadership skills, Kennedy took the time to congratulate teammate Gus Bodnar, who had been called up from the minors for this game. "You gave us that extra zip we needed, just like two years ago, and I hope you're back to stay."

After the Leafs won the Cup in 1948, Kennedy was named captain when Apps announced his retirement. He captained the Leafs to two more championships (1949 and 1951) and won the Hart Trophy for the 1954–55 season, his last complete NHL campaign.

MAPLE LEAF CAREER HIGHLIGHTS

★ Member of five Stanley Cup teams with Toronto
★ Named Toronto team captain in 1948
★ Elected to the Hockey Hall of Fame in 1966
★ Recorded 560 points (231G, 329A) in 696 games played with the Leafs

LEAF FACT:

Ted Kennedy played his entire NHL career with the Maple Leafs. His first contest with the team came on March 7, 1943, against the New York Rangers at Madison Square Garden. Playing on a line with Gaye Stewart and Bud Poile, the 17-year-old Kennedy earned an assist on a goal by Stewart in the first period. The game ended in a 5–5 tie.

Ted Kennedy
Born to Be a Maple Leaf

By John Iaboni

He deserves to be considered the greatest Maple Leaf of all time: a gritty centre who provided character and emerged as a driving force in five Stanley Cup wins during one of the golden eras in the checkered history of the blue and white. Ted Kennedy was more grinder than slick; more determined than smooth; more leader than follower. Major Conn Smythe, the ever-demanding owner and founder of the Maple Leafs, once said if World War III ever broke out, the one Leaf player he'd want by his side would be the indomitable Kennedy, who served as captain of the Leafs from 1948–49 until his retirement in 1954–55 and for 30 games in 1956–57 when he came out of retirement.

Kennedy celebrated Stanley Cup triumphs in 1945, '47, '48, '49 and '51. And he wasn't known as Theodore or Ted. He was simply the admired and beloved "Teeder." The loud cry of "Come on, Teeder!" frequently rained from high atop the hockey shrine known as Maple Leaf Gardens. And he heeded the call, of that there is no denying.

His roots were in a tiny village called Humberstone, nestled in Ontario's Niagara Region about an hour's drive west of Toronto. Amalgamated since as Port Colborne, it is still home to Kennedy. Fittingly, in 1974 Teeder Kennedy Youth Arena was named in honour of Port Colborne's "local hockey hero," emphasizing once more that even long after his career was over, a hockey giant like Kennedy is never forgotten.

Tragically, Kennedy's father (Gordon) died in a hunting accident 11 days before Theodore was born on December 12, 1925. That left Ted's mother Margaret Clarke Kennedy to raise the young family, and she took up working at the local arena snack bar as a means of making some extra money. That arena became another home to Kennedy.

"I was weaned on a hockey stick because we lived a nine-iron shot from the arena, and I was there most of the time," Kennedy said. "I watched some real good old-timers who were playing senior hockey. Some of them were in their early 40s, but you learned a lot by watching their skills."

Initially — and to his chagrin — the Canadiens owned Kennedy's NHL rights, and he headed to Montreal looking to combine his junior hockey skills with a continuing education.

"But I couldn't take a liking to Montreal," Kennedy said. "I was only 16 and they had me billeted at a downtown hotel. Some of the lads I was billeted with couldn't speak English and I couldn't speak French, so I felt I was an alien down there. So I convinced my mother that I would come back home to finish my high school education." It was while in school one day during that winter of 1942–43 that Kennedy was excused from class to take a telephone call in the principal's office informing him that the Leafs had acquired his rights from the Canadiens (for Frank Eddolls). Yet, even after hurrying to catch the late afternoon train to Toronto, meeting with Leaf coach Hap Day and getting a contract offer, Kennedy rejected it at first.

"I said 'no, no, I'm sorry Mr. Day, but I wouldn't think of signing your contract until I talk this over with my mother,'" Kennedy said. "I came back home and mother was very, very upset with me because I had an older brother who was a star athlete at Western University in London [Ontario]. He was a graduate from there and they all wanted me to go on and continue my education so I could do what I'd like after that. And I said 'Oh mother, my heart's made up on playing for the Maple Leafs.' She was Irish and she lost her patience and said 'Well, you'll only do what you want to do anyway, so go ahead and do what you like!'"

Kennedy signed with the Leafs and thus fulfilled his childhood dream. "I wanted it," Kennedy said. "In my day, most kids who were raised in Ontario and the rest of [English-speaking] Canada wanted to be a Maple Leaf player. My hero was (Leafs great right-winger) Charlie Conacher. I always wanted to emulate Conacher. I was a right-hand shot and, ironically, when I went into the National Hockey League with the Leafs, I was a right-winger. But when our centreman Mel Hill received a very serious injury I guess Day felt I could skate well enough and keep in the play, so he tried me at centre and it worked out okay."

For most of his NHL career, Kennedy wore Conacher's number 9. The Leafs saluted both — Kennedy in 1993 and Conacher in 1998 — by raising

banners to honour that number. In 1955, Kennedy became the second Leaf and only Leaf forward to win the Hart Trophy as the NHL's Most Valuable Player. At 5′11″, 175 pounds, his tenacity drew admiration. He played 696 regular season games, scoring 231 goals and 329 assists for 560 points. In the playoffs, he retired as the Leafs all-time leader in goals (29), assists (31) and points (60), marks that have since been surpassed. Kennedy was selected to the NHL Second All-Star Team three times (1950, '51 and '54), and he played in six NHL All-Star Games. He was inducted into the Hockey Hall of Fame in 1966.

No account of Kennedy would be complete without his explanation of just how he obtained his trademark nickname. "My Christian name is Theodore, but nobody among the kids I grew up with could pronounce it," Kennedy said. "They would say almost everything, but it didn't come out as Theodore. When I was playing bantam hockey the local newspaperman thought they were saying 'Teeder.' He printed Teeder — and it stuck." Teeder Kennedy . . . nice ring to it, don't you think?

KENNEDY CELEBRATED STANLEY CUP TRIUMPHS IN 1945, '47, '48, '49 AND '51. AND HE WASN'T KNOWN AS THEODORE OR TED. HE WAS SIMPLY THE ADMIRED AND BELOVED "TEEDER."

3 | SYL APPS

BORN: JANUARY 18, 1915 IN PARIS, ONTARIO
POSITION: CENTRE
YEARS AS A LEAF: 1936–37 TO 1947–48
SWEATER #: 10
MAPLE LEAF MOMENT: MARCH 21, 1948

OUTSTANDING ATHLETE, scholar and gentleman are just some of the words one could use to describe Syl Apps. He was first noticed by Maple Leafs manager Conn Smythe while Apps was playing football at McMaster University. Smythe was so impressed with the athleticism he saw in Apps that he made sure the Leafs put his name on their protected list. The youngster refused to even consider a career in hockey until he competed for Canada at the 1936 Summer Olympics in the pole vault competition, but then joined the Leafs for the 1936–37 season, in which he took the Calder Trophy as the NHL's best rookie with 16 goals and a league-leading 29 assists in 48 games. He scored 21 goals in his second season and had 20 in 1940–41, a year that saw him named team captain.

The six-foot, 185-pound centre had a determination to go to the net, scoring 23 or more goals over the last four seasons of his illustrious career. Apps was a clean player and would rarely display any temper, but woe to anyone who dared to challenge him too strongly. His leadership skills were never more evident than when he led the Leafs back from a three-games-to-none deficit against Detroit in the 1942 finals to win the Stanley Cup, his first of three in a Toronto uniform. He took out two seasons from his hockey career to join the Canadian army during the Second World War but came back to enjoy his greatest years as a Leaf from 1945 to 1948. Apps made it clear he was going to retire after the 1947–48 season, and as the year was coming to a close, he was just two goals short of 200 for his career. He had one more chance to hit the milestone when the Leafs travelled to Detroit for the final game of the season on March 21, 1948.

The game was also important to Toronto goalie Turk Broda, who was hoping to clinch the Vezina Trophy for allowing the fewest goals during the season. The Leafs opened the scoring early when Harry Watson scored before the game was three minutes old. The Red Wings tied it up before the first period was over, but early in the second Apps scored career goal 199 when Max Bentley set him up. Less than four minutes later, Apps scored number 200 when Watson passed up a chance to score himself and slid a puck across to his centre, who slapped it home. The Detroit crowd of 13,591 fans gave Apps a standing ovation as if he were one of their own players. Apps retrieved the puck and was mobbed by his teammates at the Leaf bench. For good measure Apps added another goal in the third period for his 201st and final regular season goal — all as a Maple Leaf. Apps was the first Leaf player to score more than 200 career goals, beating the mark held by the legendary Charlie Conacher. Broda also got his wish by winning the Vezina, since the Leafs gave up only two goals (on 30 shots) in winning the contest, beating Harry Lumley of the Red Wings by five goals for the coveted award. Just a few games earlier, Broda had trailed Lumley by five goals, but the Leafs had a good week while Lumley and the second-place Red Wings struggled in the final games of the campaign.

Following the 5–2 victory by the first-place Leafs, Apps

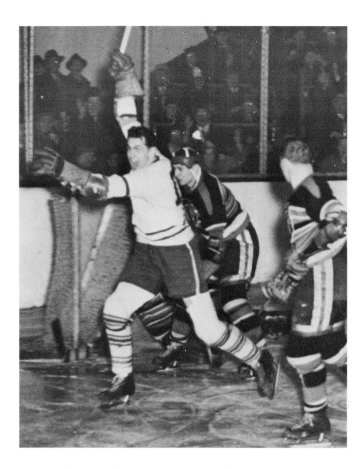

and Broda posed for photos in the Toronto dressing room and received the congratulations of their teammates. Apps commented on Watson's unselfish play that set him up for one of the goals. "It was nice of him all right, but you should have heard the yelling I was doing at him to pass it!" Apps recounted. Broda said he was counting every goal for and against. "When we got the fifth I felt my worries were over," he said.

The Leafs beat Boston and Detroit in the 1948 playoffs, allowing the 33-year-old Apps to retire in a manner fitting a true champion, while he and his team were the best of the NHL.

MAPLE LEAF CAREER HIGHLIGHTS

★ Member of three Stanley Cup teams with Toronto
★ Named to the First All-Star Team twice (1939 and 1942)
★ Elected to the Hockey Hall of Fame in 1961
★ Recorded 432 points (201G, 231A) in 423 games played

LEAF FACT:

Most Leaf captains have done very well in the playoffs, and Syl Apps is no exception with 54 points (25 goals, 29 assists) in 69 postseason games. Of the top 10 all-time Toronto playoff scorers (as of 2007), eight were team captain at some point in their careers with the Maple Leafs. Apps ranks 10th on this all-time list.

4 | FRANK MAHOVLICH

BORN: JANUARY 10, 1938 IN TIMMINS, ONTARIO
POSITION: LEFT WING
YEARS AS A LEAF: 1956–57 TO 1967–68
SWEATER #: 22 AND 27
MAPLE LEAF MOMENT: NOVEMBER 5, 1960

WHEN YOU HAVE the size (six feet, 205 pounds), speed and skill of a left-winger like Frank Mahovlich, much is expected. Add a superior junior career with Toronto's St. Michael's Majors (52 goals in his last season), toss in the Calder Trophy as the NHL's best rookie (in 1957–58), and the messiah label gets slapped on pretty quickly. It was during the 1960–61 season that the Leafs really started to see the 22-year-old Mahovlich reaching his potential. He scored 48 times that year, highlighted by two four-goal games, the first of which came against the New York Rangers in a 7–3 win.

The November 5, 1960, contest at Maple Leaf Gardens saw Mahovlich get the crowd of 13,307 fans out of their seats every time he touched the puck in what was otherwise a routine win for the Leafs over the hapless Rangers. The first goal of the night for "The Big M" came in the first period when Bert Olmstead threw the puck into the middle of the ice in the New York zone and Mahovlich swatted it into the net out of mid-air. The goal evened the score 1–1, but the Leaf star was just getting started.

On his second goal Mahovlich picked up a loose puck behind the Ranger net after teammate Red Kelly had knocked it over the cage. As goalie Jack McCartan scrambled back into position, Mahovlich circled the goal and rammed the puck in before the Ranger netminder could block the attempt. Olmstead assisted on the third marker while the Leafs were on a power-play. Mahovlich took Olmstead's pass and ripped it in early in the third period.

His fourth goal of the night was really an individual effort as he spun and twisted his way down the ice before hitting linemate Bob Nevin with a pass. Nevin's shot was blocked, but he gathered in the rebound and passed it to Mahovlich, who was going strong to the net. The big winger rocketed a 35-foot blast into the net for his second goal of the third period. McCartan, better known as the hero of the United States' gold-medal-winning team at the 1960 Winter Olympics, had virtually no support from his defence, and the whirling Mahovlich was unstoppable on this night.

Leaf assistant general manager King Clancy said Mahovlich reminded him of another great Leaf. "Mahovlich took over like Charlie Conacher used to do in his heyday. He turned those Ranger defencemen inside out with his shifts, change of pace and his stickhandling," Clancy said after the game.

Ranger defenceman and future Hall of Fame player Bill Gadsby was not about to dispute anything Clancy intimated. "He's one of the toughest guys in hockey to defend against," Gadsby said. "He's big, fast, strong and an excellent stick-handler with a two-way shift and an extension-ladder reach. He either just moves that puck out of your reach or bulls you out of the way when you try to trap him along the boards. . . . The guy's murder."

Mahovlich scored four goals against Black Hawk netminder Glenn Hall on December 11 in a game at the Chicago Stadium during a 6–1 Leaf victory. He looked destined to score 50 or more easily, but he tired as the

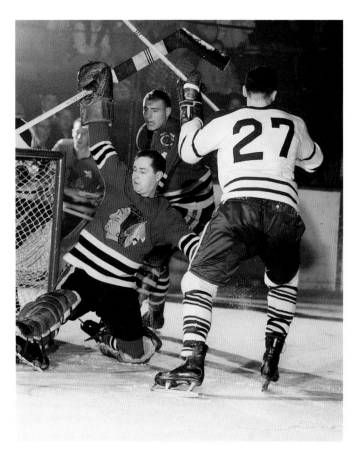

'60–61 season went along and finished two goals short of the coveted mark. His 48th and final goal of the season came against Boston on March 18 in a 6–2 win, and he was shut out in the final game of the season in New York. Montreal's Bernie Geoffrion scored 50 that year to become the first player since Maurice Richard to score that many goals in one season. Mahovlich would score 49 goals for the Detroit Red Wings in 1968–69.

MAPLE LEAF CAREER HIGHLIGHTS

★ Member of four Stanley Cup teams
★ Winner of the Calder Trophy in 1958 with 20 goals
★ Eight seasons of 20 or more goals.
★ Led the team in goal-scoring six straight seasons (1960–61 to 1965–66)

LEAF FACT:

The best game Frank Mahovlich played for the Leafs in the playoffs came against the Montreal Canadiens on April 2, 1964, when he had a five-point (two goals, three assists) night during a 5–3 win by the Leafs.

Frank Mahovlich:
The Big M Made Number 27 Famous

By John Iaboni

Frank Mahovlich, a strapping left-winger from Northern Ontario, grew up at a time when radio was high-tech and low jersey numbers meant regular employment in the National Hockey League. When he made his NHL debut by playing three games for the Toronto Maple Leafs late in 1956–57, Mahovlich wore number 26. Designation of digits like that meant one thing: rookie. "At training camp the following season, I arrived and we had a fellow there by the name of Tim Daly who was our trainer," Mahovlich said. "When he saw me, he said 'Here, Muckle-vitch, here's your number', and that's how I got stuck with number 27." From 1957–58 until he retired from pro hockey in 1978 after four seasons in the World Hockey Association, Frank Mahovlich was the first player to become synonymous with 27.

He became known simply as "The Big M." Players were smaller in his era, so the sight of a six-foot, 205-pounder like Mahovlich in full flight, arms chugging with those long strides down the left boards, made him appear larger than life, especially when he whistled a slap shot. Of the many stories of Mahovlich, two come to my mind. I remember sitting around the radio on a Sunday night in the early 1960s, listening to Foster Hewitt calling a game from old Madison Square Garden in New York. Hewitt's voice reached an incredible crescendo as Mahovlich wired a slap shot that tore the catching mitt off the hand of goalie Lorne "Gump" Worsley. It was theatre of the mind as I lived that play over and over again, particularly trying to envision Worsley shaking and rubbing his hand, as Hewitt described it, feeling the sting of the mighty Big M's slapper. Or how about the time during training camp in 1962 when Mahovlich was embroiled in a contract dispute with the Leafs? On the eve of the NHL All-Star Game — in those days it occurred at the start of the NHL season — an owners' party produced startling headlines when Jim Norris of the Chicago Black Hawks offered one million dollars for Mahovlich. "Norris made the offer with a personal cheque, not a company cheque," Mahovlich said. "At first, it was accepted [by the Leafs], then reneged the next day, so I didn't know where I was. But I got a phone call in the morning to come down to Maple Leaf Gardens and we

signed the new contract [with the Leafs]."

Mahovlich said he was about four years old when he started to play hockey and Hewitt broadcasts of Leafs games influenced him. "I used to listen to Foster on the radio and visualized hockey," Mahovlich said. "Saturday nights, I never missed the game when Syl Apps and Teeder Kennedy were playing for the Toronto Maple Leafs. That's when I started. I couldn't get away from hockey on Saturday nights. I just glued myself to the radio. I got a pair of skates from my godmother and they were size 11s. Those were the skates I first tried on when I went on a little pond just outside my house up in Timmins. Well, they were massive all right. But my dad was a miner and I got these huge woolen socks and I put three or four of them on my feet. My mother made sure to put those socks on me, so that helped quite a bit."

He became a fan of the Detroit Red Wings when he received that club's full outfit one Christmas. He was playing centre at the time. Every NHL team scouted — and made overtures. But his father, Peter, was big on education, so it was off to St. Michael's College in Toronto, where the youngster could play hockey with the Leafs' affiliate while going to a highly regarded school. Needless to say, Mahovlich switched his NHL allegiance from the Wings to the Leafs. And guess what? St. Michael's practised at Maple Leaf Gardens. Before long, Mahovlich was in the NHL, winning the Calder Trophy as NHL Rookie of the Year in 1958 over a hot Chicago left-wing prospect by the name of Bobby Hull. Mahovlich's career as a Leaf began at centre, but he soon moved to the left wing, making Mahovlich and Hull the dominant NHL players at that position through the 1960s and into the early 1970s.

Mahovlich and Bernie "Boom Boom" Geoffrion of the Montreal Canadiens were paramount in 1960–61, embroiled in a scoring duel attempting to match Maurice "Rocket" Richard's record of 50 goals in a season. Geoffrion finished with 50, Mahovlich had 48.

During his time with the Leafs, Mahovlich was never fully appreciated in some quarters even though the club won Stanley Cups in 1962, '63, '64 and '67. Some fans thought him lazy because the big guy looked like

he wasn't giving an effort. General manager/coach Punch Imlach often got under Mahovlich's skin, and it took its toll on the sensitive big guy.

At the end of the day, he was shuffled off in a major trade to Detroit in 1968, where his production continued with a Hall of Fame line consisting of Gordie Howe and Alex Delvecchio. Traded to Montreal in 1971, he had the good fortune of playing some of his finest offensive hockey. With the shackles of the Leafs tight defensive approach removed, The Big M thrived with the fire-wagon hockey of the Canadiens. He and his younger brother, Peter, were teammates — and pivotal scoring factors — when the Canadiens won the Stanley Cup in 1971 and '73. The Mahovlich brothers were also together with Team Canada '72 and its conquest over the Soviet Union in the riveting Summit Series.

These days, The Big M is a senator, though that has nothing to do with the NHL club in Ottawa. In 1998, Prime Minister Jean Chrétien appointed The Big M to the Canadian Senate, with an office on Parliament Hill in Ottawa.

5 | DARRYL SITTLER

BORN: SEPTEMBER 18, 1950 IN KITCHENER, ONTARIO
POSITION: CENTRE
YEARS AS A LEAF: 1970–71 TO 1981–82
SWEATER #: 27
MAPLE LEAF MOMENT: FEBRUARY 7, 1976

WHEN DARRYL SITTLER arrived at his first training camp with the Maple Leafs in the fall of 1970, he was given sweater number 27. Sittler knew that the legendary Frank Mahovlich had previously worn the number for the Leafs, and while he appreciated the gesture, he also realized that the team had great expectations for him. Selected eighth overall by Toronto in 1970, Sittler stepped right into the Leaf lineup on left wing and played in 49 games during the 1970–71 season, scoring 10 goals. He scored 15 the next season, but that total jumped to 29 in his third year when he moved back to his natural position at centre. Sittler soon established himself as one of the top centres in the NHL, and he recorded between 80 and 100 points during most of his years as a Leaf. He set a club record with 100 points in 1975–76, later topping that with 117 in 1977–78. Sittler set a league scoring record with a remarkable night during a game against the Boston Bruins on February 7, 1976.

The Boston club had lost only once in its last 17 games when they arrived for a Saturday night tilt against the Leafs. Toronto owner Harold Ballard had chirped to the newspapers that he was unhappy with Sittler's play to that point in the season. He intimated that the Leafs would be a better team if there were a new centre between wingers Errol Thompson and Lanny McDonald. The bombastic owner would be singing another tune after the game was over.

It all started innocently enough. The Leafs led 2–1 on two first-period goals from McDonald and defenceman Ian Turnbull, with Sittler assisting on both. In the second period, Sittler scored three times and assisted on two others to bring his point total on the night to seven. Sittler's first goal came as he swatted the puck out of mid-air, while his second was a 50-foot drive that beat Boston goalie Dave Reece. His third of the period came after he took a pass from George Ferguson. In the final frame, it was all Sittler, as he scored three more times, setting a new NHL record in the process with 10 points in one game (and raising his season total to 63). His first goal in the last period came on a set-up by Borje Salming, and his second was a beautiful wrist shot from about 40 feet out as he faded away from the net. His final tally came from behind the net as he was trying to set up Thompson in the slot. The puck hit Brad Park's skate and went through the legs of the beleaguered Reece. The crowd at Maple Leaf Gardens reacted more strongly with each point Sittler racked up and gave him a resounding standing ovation when the Leafs finished the game 11–4.

"Undoubtedly, Mr. Ballard will figure his little blast inspired me to set the record, but it just isn't that way," Sittler said. "Maybe now he won't have to hunt quite so hard for that centre he wants."

Boston coach Don Cherry also had praise for Sittler. "You don't like to see something like that happen against your team. But if somebody had to do it, I'm glad it was a player of Sittler's calibre, a guy who works for what he accomplishes."

Teammate Lanny McDonald said that Sittler was full

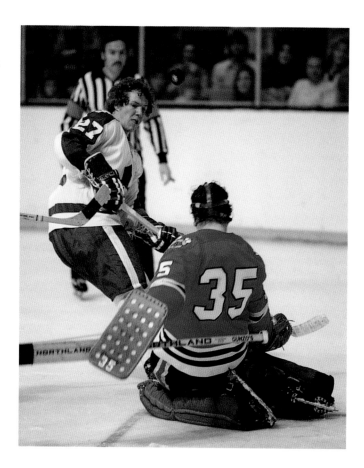

measure for his record. "Nobody can say Darryl picked on a weak team, which makes it all the greater. The guys on this team wouldn't be happier if they had done it themselves. He's such a great team man, and he works so hard."

Sittler had many memorable moments during his Hall of Fame career but none as great as his 10-point night against Boston.

MAPLE LEAF CAREER HIGHLIGHTS

★ Named captain of the Leafs prior to the 1975–76 season
★ Holds club record for most career hat tricks with 18
★ Recorded 65 points (25G, 40A) in 64 playoff games as a Leaf
★ Holds club record for most career points with 916 (389G, 527A) in 844 games

LEAF FACT:

Darryl Sittler tied an NHL record for goals in one playoff game when the Leafs beat the Philadelphia Flyers 8–5 on April 22, 1976. Sittler had not scored a goal during the series but then got five past Bernie Parent at Maple Leaf Gardens as the Leafs avoided elimination.

Darryl Sittler:
Fulfilled Expectations of Greatness

By John Iaboni

Fresh out of the Ontario Hockey Association's London Knights, centre Darryl Sittler was in awe when he checked into his first training camp with the Toronto Maple Leafs in 1970. He was further overwhelmed when jersey number 27 was assigned to him by GM Jim Gregory, knowing what The Big M, Frank Mahovlich, had done wearing that number for the Leafs from 1956 to 1968. "To give me Frank Mahovlich's sweater was certainly a surprise and an honour," Sittler said. "They must have felt there was special meaning to [me] being their first-round pick."

Sittler had been raised in St. Jacobs, Ontario, a small farming community. He loved playing road hockey and grew up a fan of the Canadiens and their classy captain, Jean Béliveau. By the time he left the Maple Leafs in January 1982, Sittler had given the club almost 12 seasons of superb hockey. He left after 844 regular season games in which he had accumulated club records in regular season goals (389) and points (916). In retrospect, of course, Sittler should never have played in the NHL for anyone but the Leafs. However, the union went sour when Punch Imlach arrived for his second tour of duty as Leafs GM. The dismantling began when Imlach traded Sittler's close friend and linemate Lanny McDonald in 1979. The war between Imlach and owner Harold Ballard heightened. And while it was GM Gerry McNamara who invariably had no choice but to trade Sittler to the Flyers, the Leafs lost one of their greatest players in history.

While a Stanley Cup eluded him in his illustrious career, there was no denying his stature as an excellent player. That was verified in 1989 when he was inducted into the Hockey Hall of Fame. Those who got to know Sittler learned of an exceptional leader, as captain of the storied franchise from 1975–76 until 1980–81. In an era dominated by the Flyers, Montreal Canadiens and New York Islanders, Sittler was a cornerstone in the Leafs' renaissance in the wake of a disastrous 1972–73 season when the club was ravaged by player losses to the World Hockey Association.

Of Sittler's 15 professional seasons, the one that most stands out was 1975–76, when he scored a hat trick of mystical proportions. It began at Maple Leaf Gardens on February 7, 1976 when Sittler established the NHL record with 10 points in one game. The irony, of course, is that he had one goal in eight games entering that remarkable night. Other than the fact that Sittler's son, Ryan, fell into some mud earlier that afternoon as he babysat him, Sittler didn't think anything was unusual heading into that Boston game. "It was one of those nights when everything happened," Sittler said that night. "Some nights, you have the puck and nothing happens. It'll be hard to forget something like this."

The brilliance didn't end there, though. On April 22, 1976, Sittler and the Leafs won a brawl-filled sixth game of a playoff series against the two-time Stanley Cup champion Flyers at the Gardens, 8–5. Sittler matched the NHL playoff record for most goals in one game by scoring five times (on Bernie Parent). Led by their inspirational centre, the Leafs forced a seventh game back in Philadelphia that the Flyers eventually won, 7–3. Many who watched that series, including Canadiens' head coach Scotty Bowman, believe the Leafs forcing the Flyers to the limit took its toll on Philadelphia. The Canadiens swept the Flyers in the Stanley Cup final that year.

Sittler, meanwhile, was not done with his heroics. Called to play for his country at the first Canada Cup tournament, Sittler's overtime goal against Vladimir Dzurilla provided Team Canada with the 5–4 overtime win over Czechoslovakia in the deciding game of the championship. That occurred on September 15, 1976, at the Montreal Forum. "The Canada Cup goal was the biggest, satisfying moment in my career in that we won a championship representing Canada in the Montreal Forum, and the goal was scored in overtime," Sittler said. "There's nothing that replaces winning a championship. To me, that was the greatest team I've ever played on and one of the greatest teams ever."

After parting ways with the Leafs, Sittler was brought back to the club in 1991 in one of the first moves by new president/general manager Cliff Fletcher. Sittler serves as a community representative to this day, and he remains one of the most popular and well-known

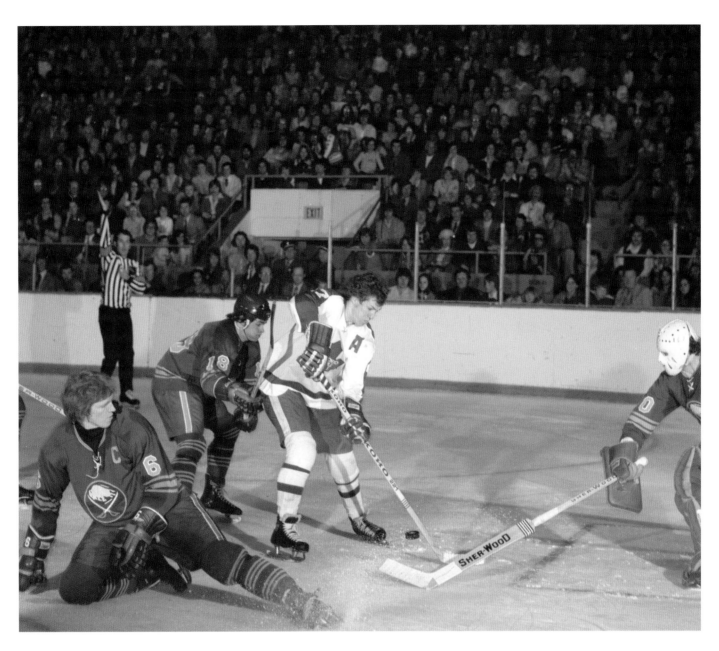

sports personalities right across Canada. Like Mahovlich, Sittler's number 27 has been honoured by the Leafs. The ceremony was to have been for both of them on October 3, 2001. The tribute went on as planned for Mahovlich, but Sittler's was postponed because his wife, Wendy, was dying of colorectal cancer. Sittler's night eventually occurred on February 8, 2003, and in remembrance of Wendy, her name is inscribed on his banner.

WHILE A STANLEY CUP ELUDED HIM IN HIS ILLUSTRIOUS CAREER, THERE WAS NO DENYING HIS STATURE AS AN EXCELLENT PLAYER. THAT WAS VERIFIED IN 1989 WHEN HE WAS INDUCTED INTO THE HOCKEY HALL OF FAME.

6 | CHARLIE CONACHER

BORN: DECEMBER 20, 1909 IN TORONTO, ONTARIO
POSITION: RIGHT WING
YEARS AS A LEAF: 1929–30 TO 1937–38
SWEATER #: 9
MAPLE LEAF MOMENT: JANUARY 19, 1932

CHARLIE CONACHER WANTED to follow his brother Lionel into the world of professional sports, but he was going to pick just one game to excel at, unlike his older sibling who was outstanding at just about anything he tried. Conacher worked long and hard to develop a good shot, but he was not on the ice often enough to develop his skating, so he started out in hockey as a goalie. When it was clear he was not going to be a netminder, the youngster decided he was going to work at his skating, and his efforts soon paid off. At the age of 16 Conacher tried out for the North Toronto Juniors and made the team, scoring nine goals in nine games. He then graduated to the Toronto Marlboros and was named captain of the team when Red Horner moved up to the Maple Leafs. Conacher led the Marlboros to the Memorial Cup and then made Toronto's NHL roster starting in 1929 at only 18 years of age. His shot was feared by all opposition goalies, and Conacher was not afraid to use his size (6'1" and 200 pounds) to his advantage. He was placed on a line with junior teammate Harvey Jackson and centre Joe Primeau, forming the trio known as the "Kid Line," which ran roughshod over the opposition. Conacher would lead the NHL in goal-scoring five times and recorded the most points twice while earning All-Star recognition. It is safe to say he was the Leafs' first superstar player. In 1931–32 he scored 34 goals in 44 regular season games, and his best night of the year came against the New York Americans on January 19, 1932, at Maple Leaf Gardens.

    The Leafs got a big break in this game when Americans' goalie Roy Worters injured his knee in the pre-game warm-up. He was able to start the game but hobbled, and Conacher quickly scored one goal and assisted on another to give the Leafs a 2–0 lead before the game was eight minutes old. At the start of the second period, Conacher scored two more goals, forcing Worters to retire for the night. He was replaced in net by defenceman Allan Shields (no NHL teams carried a backup goaltender in that era), who promptly allowed the Leafs to score three more goals after donning the pads, giving Toronto a 7–0 lead. The Americans then scored a couple, but Conacher scored early in the third to get the Leafs rolling again. By the time the game was over, Toronto had pumped in 11 goals, while the Americans could muster only three pucks past Lorne Chabot in the Leaf net. Every Toronto skater in the game recorded at least one point, except for defenceman Red Horner. Conacher scored the Leafs' final goal of the evening, giving him five tallies on the night — setting a Leaf team record that would be tied by Howie Meeker in 1947 but not broken until 1976 when Darryl Sittler scored six against Boston.

    The Leafs posted a 23–18–7 record in the Canadian Division during the '31–32 season, then knocked off Chicago and the Montreal Maroons to make it to the Stanley Cup finals against the New York Rangers. The Leafs took their first-ever championship by beating the Rangers in three straight games in the best-of-five series. Conacher scored the most goals of any player in the '32 postseason

with six tallies in seven games.

    The 1934–35 season saw Conacher record career highs in goals (36), assists (21) and points (57), but the Leafs could not win the Cup again during his time with the team. Injuries took their toll on the left-winger. He showed tremendous courage just going out to play on some nights. Conacher was dealt to Detroit in 1938 after nine great seasons with the Leafs and played his final two years with the New York Americans. He turned to coaching after retiring and took the Oshawa Generals to the Memorial Cup. He was later coach of the Chicago Black Hawks for three seasons. He was elected to the Hockey Hall of Fame in 1961, and the Leafs honoured his sweater number 9 on February 28, 1998.

MAPLE LEAF CAREER HIGHLIGHTS

★ Member of three Stanley Cup teams with Toronto
★ Named to the First All-Star Team twice (1939 and 1942)
★ Elected to the Hockey Hall of Fame in 1961
★ Recorded 432 points (201G, 231A) in 423 games played

LEAF FACT:

Charlie Conacher is the only Maple Leaf in team history to record a three-goal game (10 times), a four-goal game (three times) and a five-goal game.

7

JOHNNY BOWER

BORN: NOVEMBER 8, 1924 IN PRINCE ALBERT, SASKATCHEWAN
POSITION: GOALTENDER
YEARS AS A LEAF: 1958–59 TO 1969–70
SWEATER #: 1
MAPLE LEAF MOMENT: APRIL 22, 1967

THE LAST GREAT MOMENT in a Toronto uniform for legendary Leaf netminder Johnny Bower came during the 1967 Stanley Cup finals. Bower had joined the Leafs for the start of the 1958–59 season, but he was reluctant to do so. He was firmly entrenched playing minor league hockey with Cleveland in the American Hockey League, and only the security of a two-year contract tempted the 33-year-old back up to the big league. He realized a lifelong ambition by winning the Stanley Cup in 1962, 1963 and 1964 with Toronto. By the 1966–67 season Bower was 43 years old, and most believed his playing career was over. But he would prove he had one more hurrah left in him.

The Leafs surprised the Chicago Black Hawks in the semi-finals with Terry Sawchuk in goal for all their victories in that series. Sawchuk began the finals against Montreal, but a 6–2 shellacking by the Habs forced coach Punch Imlach to turn to Bower for some old-time magic for the second game of the series, played on a Saturday afternoon, April 22, 1967, at the Montreal Forum.

The Leafs came out strong and got a goal from youngster Pete Stemkowski to take a 1–0 lead in the first period. From the opening face-off the Leafs threw everything they had at the Canadiens. Bower faced a total of 31 shots and turned them all back, including great stops on Yvan Cournoyer (two big saves on Montreal power-plays), Jean Béliveau, Claude Larose and Gilles Tremblay, who was foiled when the Leaf netminder slid out to make a stop when he broke in alone. The Leafs' trademark tenacious checking paid off with additional goals from Mike Walton and Tim Horton in the second period to give Toronto an insurmountable 3–0 lead. More than 14,000 fans at the Montreal Forum soon realized that penetrating the Leaf defence was hopeless on this day and started filing out of the building early.

The ever-present Montreal tough guy John Ferguson did his best to disrupt Bower in his crease and twice got a stick in the goalie's face. Imlach was livid, but after the game Bower refused to be critical of Ferguson. "I'm a hockey player and I don't criticize another player. Fergie's a digger, always after the puck, but I don't want to read in the papers that I say he's a dirty player," Bower said. One of Ferguson's forays into the crease area did lead to a cut on the bridge of Bower's nose, but he refused to come out of the net. The shutout was Bower's first in the playoffs since the seventh game of the 1964 finals and also marked the Canadiens' first loss in 15 games going back to the regular season.

Montreal coach Toe Blake said after the second contest that he tried to warn his team about the Leafs' ability to bounce back after a bad game in the playoffs. Still, no one believed the Leafs were going to win this series. But when the Leafs hit their stride in the '67 playoffs there was no stopping them. A win in the third game at Maple Leaf Gardens helped to change the tide in favour of Toronto. Bower played in net that game and faced 62 shots in a game that went into double overtime before the Leafs took it 3–2. Bower was superb throughout the entire game, especially in

overtime, when he used his patented poke check to stop the always-dangerous Cournoyer on a rush toward the Leaf net. The win was Bower's last great moment as a Leaf because a pulled muscle prior to the start of the fourth game ended his season. Sawchuk took over and helped the Leafs win their fourth Stanley Cup of the decade.

MAPLE LEAF CAREER HIGHLIGHTS

★ Member of four Stanley Cup teams
★ Winner of two Vezina Trophies (1961 and 1965, which was shared with Terry Sawchuk)
★ First Team NHL All-Star in 1960–61
★ Sweater number honoured by the Leafs in 1995

LEAF FACT:

Johnny Bower ranks second on the Leafs all-time list for goaltender wins with 220 (behind Turk Broda) and is tied for third for most career shutouts with 33.

Johnny Bower:
A Beloved Ageless Wonder

By John Iaboni

His National Hockey League career did not provide full-time employment until he was in his mid-30s. But from then on Johnny Bower, aptly named "The China Wall" for the impenetrable fashion in which he tended goal, wrote a magical story featuring four Stanley Cups and induction into the Hockey Hall of Fame.

Despite a spectacular, award-filled portfolio in the minors, Bower was a constant victim of the numbers game in the NHL. A six-time AHL All-Star, Bower was the AHL's leading goaltender three times, the Western Hockey League's top goaltender once and winner of the AHL MVP Award twice with the Providence Reds (1956 and 1957) and once with Cleveland (1958). Look, folks, he played in the era of the six-team NHL, and Bower found gaining one of those preciously scarce goaltending jobs an elusive quest for the longest time. Oh, he played a full 70-game season with the New York Rangers in 1953–54, leading the league in minutes played. He was 29–31–10 with a 2.60 goals-against average, sound totals for a fifth-place club. But aside from five games with the Rangers in 1954–55 and two more with them in 1956–57, Bower remained in the minors while the Broadway Blueshirts turned to the younger Lorne "Gump" Worsley as the permanent replacement for Hall of Famer Chuck Rayner.

However, on June 3, 1958, the Toronto Maple Leafs claimed Bower in the Inter-League Draft from the Cleveland Barons of the American Hockey League. Bower and Ed Chadwick shared the Leafs' goaltending duties in 1958–59, but then-club GM/head coach Punch Imlach installed Bower as his club's number one netminder. Imlach knew Bower's capabilities after having coached against him in the AHL, and Bower believed that background knowledge was vital in his acquisition by Toronto.

"Punch coached Springfield when I was in Cleveland, and we had a playoff series against them where I was pretty hot," Bower said. "I guess he remembered that."

Still, when the Leafs drafted Bower, he wasn't sure he wanted to leave the Barons, whom he'd represented over nine seasons beginning in 1945–46. It was only when Barons GM Jim Hendy assured Bower he could return to Cleveland if his attempt with the Leafs failed that the goalie took one final chance at the NHL.

"No, I didn't want to leave Cleveland to be honest with you, particularly at my age of 34," Bower said. "I guess I fooled everybody — plus myself. I went to [the Leafs] training camp in great shape. And, more or less, it became a dream come true because the dream was to have my name engraved on the Stanley Cup. I was able to do that and get a few others after that. So things worked out really well for me, and I'm not sorry I didn't go back to Cleveland, although I did love Cleveland as well. But I'm more than happy and satisfied staying in Toronto, the players I was with and the years that I had. It was just a great career for me."

When Bower retired after playing one game in 1969–70, his NHL service featured 552 games with a 250–195–90 record, 2.52 GAA and 37 shutouts. His Stanley Cup playoff record was 35–34 with a 2.52 GAA and five shutouts. Bower was a First Team NHL All-Star in 1961 when he also captured the Vezina Trophy, an honour he shared with teammate Terry Sawchuk in 1965. On four occasions, Bower played in the NHL All-Star Game.

A stand-up goaltender who played the angles impeccably, Bower was a master of the poke check, a well-timed ploy he constantly practised in order to ensure he confounded shooters more often than not. His proficiency in this art evolved after some tutelage by Rayner in Bower's early days with the Rangers. "I couldn't handle the puck at that time and he told me he was going to teach me the poke check because he said it would be an effective weapon for me," Bower recalled. "I remember one time in the second overtime of a playoff series against Montreal, [Yvan] Cournoyer came off the wing on a breakaway and I poke-checked him. The puck went into the corner. Chief [George Armstrong] got it, threw it up to Bobby Pulford, and he went on to score the winning goal."

Bower was an ageless wonder, a marvellous athlete who displayed superb reflexes and agility against superstars such as Gordie Howe, Rocket Richard, Jean Béliveau, Bobby Hull, Andy Bathgate and Bernie "Boom Boom" Geoffrion. And, don't forget, this was the pre-mask era, so Bower paid the price of many a puck and stick to the face.

Bower idolized Boston's Mr. Zero, Frankie Brimsek, and while his NHL service didn't allow him to play for the Bruins, at least fate was kind enough to eventually see him in the NHL.

Those who covered the Leafs during the 1960s noted how Bower hated to surrender goals, in practices as well as in games — something that pleased Imlach to no end. They also discovered that whenever everything was on the line, Bower rose to the occasion. Hence, he became known as one of hockey's all-time great money goalies.

Bower's dream to play on a Stanley Cup squad occurred for the first time in 1962. He added Stanley Cup honours in 1963 and '64, with the final hurrah of 1967 the stuff of legends. The '67 Leafs averaged over 31 years of age. Bower, at 42, was the Leafs' elder statesman and, in the three games he played in the Cup finals against Montreal, he was 2–0 with a 1.10 goals-against average.

When injury eventually sidelined Bower during that final series against the high-flying Canadiens, his goaltending partner, 37-year-old Sawchuk, stepped in to make sure the mission was completed.

Johnny Bower . . . a beloved hockey legend whose NHL legacy began in his later years. But it was well worth the wait.

BOWER WAS AN AGELESS WONDER, A MARVELLOUS ATHLETE WHO DISPLAYED SUPERB REFLEXES AND AGILITY AGAINST SUPERSTARS SUCH AS GORDIE HOWE, ROCKET RICHARD, JEAN BÉLIVEAU, BOBBY HULL, ANDY BATHGATE AND BERNIE "BOOM BOOM" GEOFFRION.

8 | TIM HORTON

BORN: JANUARY 12, 1930 IN COCHRANE, ONTARIO
POSITION: DEFENCE
YEARS AS A LEAF: 1949–50 TO 1969–70
SWEATER #: 7
MAPLE LEAF MOMENT: JANUARY 15, 1969

TIM HORTON WAS SCOUTED for Toronto by Bob Wilson, who signed the youngster to a C form, which bound him to the Leafs if he turned professional. The robust defenceman came to Toronto to attend St. Michael's College for the 1947–48 season. Leaf manager and owner Conn Smythe thought Horton was the best defensive prospect in all of Canada. In spite of that proclamation, the Leafs assigned Horton to the minors for some experience, and he stayed there for three seasons (he played in a total of five games for the Leafs over this time). The rugged rearguard got a taste of winning with the Pittsburgh Hornets when they won the AHL championship in 1952.

Horton then joined the Leafs for the 1952–53 season. The team hoped that Horton could replace Gus Mortson, a veteran defenceman they had traded away to Chicago. Horton responded with two goals and 14 assists in 70 games as a rookie. The next season saw him score seven goals and total 31 points to earn a spot on the NHL's Second All-Star Team. On March 12, 1955, Horton was hit by Bill Gadsby of the New York Rangers with a devastating bodycheck that nearly ended his career. Horton broke his jaw and leg in the hit, and the Leafs suddenly were not sure about their commitment to the five-foot-ten, 180-pound defender. Luckily for Toronto, Horton recovered and helped lead the Leafs to four Stanley Cups in the sixties. He became a durable player who could clean up his own end with physical play and carry the puck out to get the offence going. He had a low, accurate drive that he used to great effectiveness, and on the night of January 15, 1969, it helped Horton achieve something no other Leaf defenceman had ever done.

The Leafs were struggling to make the postseason during the 1968–69 season, as they battled Detroit and Chicago for the last playoff spot in the East Division, so every point was important. The Bruins, in Toronto for a Saturday night contest against the Leafs, took a 3–2 lead into the third period. Mike Walton tied it for the Toronto, only to see Boston take a two-goal lead on markers by Phil Esposito and Johnny McKenzie. But the Leafs refused to quit. Murray Oliver scored to make it 5–4. Then, with just under three minutes to play, Horton let go a blast from the point that beat Boston netminder Gerry Cheevers to tie the game. The goal was set up by Leaf winger Paul Henderson, who took advantage of Boston defenceman Ted Green getting tangled up with referee John Ashley and got the loose puck over to Horton. It was Horton's 100th career marker, and the crowd at Maple Leaf Gardens gave him an ovation when the milestone was announced. Cheevers was so upset at giving up the late goal that he threw the puck into the crowd, but a fan returned it to the Leafs, who then gave it to Horton as a keepsake. The tie game meant that the Bruins still had not won a game in Toronto since November 27, 1965, when they eked out a 2–1 win. (The Bruins had lost 16 and tied five since that victory.)

Of the goal that tied the game, Horton said, "I couldn't tell you who got the puck over to me or how it went in. I just lowered my head and fired. I'd like to thank the fan who

returned the puck. It will be one of the few mementoes I'll have of this game."

The Leafs made the playoffs in 1969 but were wiped out in four games by, ironically, the Bruins. Horton earned his second-straight First All-Star Team nomination after the season concluded. His defensive partner on the 1968 and 1969 First All-Star Teams was a player who admired Horton as a youngster — none other than Boston's Bobby Orrr.

MAPLE LEAF CAREER HIGHLIGHTS

★ Named to the NHL First All-Star Team three times
★ Recorded 458 points (109G, 349A) in 1,185 games as a Leaf
★ Recorded 41 points (9G, 32A) in 97 playoff games for Toronto
★ Sweater number 7 honoured by the Leafs in 1995

LEAF FACT:

On October 5, 1949, the Leafs played a game against their farm club, the Pittsburgh Hornets, and although they won the game 4–2 they were impressed with Tim Horton, who set up both of the Pittsburgh goals and also tangled with Toronto tough guy Bill Ezinicki on a couple of occasions.

Tim Horton:
Leafs Star before Coffee and Donuts

By John Iaboni

On February 20, 1974, the Maple Leafs silenced GM Punch Imlach and his Buffalo Sabres 4–2 at Maple Leaf Gardens. The pesky Sabres, with former Leafs GM and head coach Imlach running the show since they arrived in the NHL in 1970, had already formed a bitter rivalry with Toronto, only about a 90-minute drive from Buffalo. Spicing up the Buffalo-Toronto showdowns was the presence of veteran Tim Horton on the Sabre defence. A mainstay and six-time NHL All-Star Team selection with the Leafs, Horton was still serviceable, helping the young franchise with his incredible veteran savvy.

On this night, a jaw injury kept Horton on the bench for the entire third period. But yet, he was still selected the third star of the game. After Imlach and Horton chatted outside Maple Leaf Gardens, Imlach boarded the team bus heading back to Buffalo. Horton was given permission to drive back on his own. But in the early morning hours, he lost control of his speeding car and was killed in the single-car crash on the Queen Elizabeth Way near St. Catharines, some 20 minutes away from Buffalo.

News of Horton's death came as a shock. He was one of the most revered defencemen of his time, a superman who seemed invincible on the ice. Throughout his career, Horton was known as the strongest man in the game. He wasn't known for his fighting but rather his sheer strength after quelling many a dispute by simply putting an unbreakable, air-tight bear hug on would-be combatants.

A terrific bodychecker with his frame (5′10″, 180 pounds), the solid-skating Horton also had offensive skill and an excellent shot from the right point. He first played for the Leafs during 1949–50 but was in the NHL to stay from 1952–53 on. When the Leafs obtained Allan Stanley from the Boston Bruins on October 8, 1958, he showed fans and media alike that he was far from done. Stanley not only revived his career, he brought out the best in Horton. Stanley and Horton became one of Imlach's defensive tandems and the duo played its role in Stanley Cup wins for the Leafs in 1962, '63, '64 and '67.

"Tim came into his own when he was 30 and he got paired up with Allan Stanley," said George Armstrong, who captained the Leafs from 1957–58 to 1968–69. Armstrong acknowledged that his role was made easier because Horton was one of many leaders on those great teams. "What really made Tim a great defenceman was his speed — because he was just a premium skater — and his strength. He was born with muscles. We went to high school together in Sudbury, and he never lifted weights or anything. He was born like that. That was hereditary."

Miles Gilbert Horton — those first two names represented those of his grandfathers. It was Horton's mother who took to calling him Tim even before his birth, and that was the way he was always called. After living for a short time in Duparquet, Quebec, where Horton first took to the game of hockey, the Hortons returned to his hometown of Cochrane and then Sudbury before Tim headed to Toronto and the St. Michael's Majors in 1947. The Majors and the Marlies were the prime junior feeders for the Leafs, and eventually Horton followed that trail as well.

He played 1,446 NHL regular season games with the Leafs, Rangers, Penguins and Sabres, scoring 115 goals and 403 assists for 518 points. In 126 career playoff games, Horton scored 11 goals and 39 assists for 50. As a Leaf, Horton played 1,185 regular season games (109 goals, 349 assists) and 97 playoff games (nine goals, 32 assists).

He was chosen to three NHL First All-Star Teams (1964, '68 and '69) and three NHL Second All-Star Teams (1954, '63 and '67). He played in seven NHL All-Star Games and was inducted into the Hockey Hall of Fame in 1977.

While he starred in the NHL, Horton also realized it was essential to prepare for life after hockey. With that in mind, he opened a coffee-and-donut business bearing his name in a 1,500–square-foot location at Hamilton, Ontario, in 1964. By 1967, the franchise had grown to three, and his first franchisee, Ron Joyce, had become a full partner. Unfortunately, Horton's death didn't permit him to see the franchise flourish into one of North America's most successful eateries. In 1995, Tim Hortons (by this time the apostrophe was long gone in the corporate name) merged with Wendy's International.

As of December 13, 2006, Tim Hortons had 2,637 retail outlets in Canada, plus 305 franchises in the United States.

Those old enough and fortunate enough to have witnessed Tim Horton play for the Leafs, New York Rangers, Pittsburgh Penguins and Sabres recall a veritable Rock of Gibraltar. He was one of the game's most identifiable and respected performers. And in the cold of Canadian winter, his name lives on because the Tim Hortons franchises are a magnet for kids and parents for whatever their daily lives involve, usually around a hockey rink. That business is as strong and enduring as the legacy Tim Horton created on the ice.

HE WAS ONE OF THE MOST REVERED DEFENCEMEN OF HIS TIME, A SUPERMAN WHO SEEMED INVINCIBLE ON THE ICE.

9 | TURK BRODA

BORN: MAY 15, 1914 IN BRANDON, MANITOBA
POSITION: GOALTENDER
YEARS AS A LEAF: 1936–37 TO 1951–52
SWEATER #: 1
MAPLE LEAF MOMENT: APRIL 16, 1942

MAPLE LEAF GENERAL MANAGER Conn Smythe could sense that the career of Toronto goaltender George Hainsworth was coming to an end. He began searching for a replacement and knew that the Detroit Red Wings were well stocked at the position with John Ross Roach and Norm Smith occupying the top two spots on their goaltending roster. Detroit manager Jack Adams, who was willing to deal, tried to push a netminder named Earl Robertson on Smythe, but the Leaf manager did his own scouting and liked Walter "Turk" Broda much more. Smythe watched a game featuring both netminders and Broda's team won the contest 8–1, solidifying Smythe's opinion even more. In addition, Broda had taken his team, the Detroit Olympics, to the International Hockey League championship in 1936. Smythe obtained the rights to Broda for $8,000, and it was by far the best investment he made since acquiring defenceman King Clancy from Ottawa.

Broda made the Leaf team in the 1936–37 season (posting a 22–19–4 record in 49 games), forcing Hainsworth into retirement. In the four subsequent seasons, Broda won 24, 19, 25 and 28 games (the NHL regular season schedule was only 48 games long at the time), establishing himself as one of the top goalies in the league. Although Broda was short and chunky at 5´9˝ and 180 pounds, he had great hands and quick feet. Broda had an ability to bounce back from bad goals, and had an air of calm around him that seemed to rub off on his teammates. Despite his great personal numbers, the Leafs were not able to win the Stanley Cup over those seasons (losing three times in the finals), but another opportunity came in the 1942 playoffs when Toronto played Detroit for the Cup. The Red Wings took the first three games of the series, but the Leafs won the next two before the teams returned to the Detroit Olympia on April 16, 1942, for the sixth game of the series.

The Red Wings saw this game as the one they had to win to clinch the Cup. As expected, they stormed out of the gate, peppering the Leafs with a furious attack in the first period. The Toronto club was hemmed in its own end for most of the first 12 minutes of the game, but Broda managed to turn everything aside. The Leaf netminder got help from defencemen Bob Goldham and Wally Stanowski before the Toronto attack got going early in the second period when Don Metz scored just 14 seconds in. The score remained 1–0 into the third period, and the Red Wings kept pressing for the equalizer, but Broda would give them nothing on this night. Goldham and Billy Taylor scored in the third to take away any hope from the Red Wings, and Broda hung on to a 3–0 shutout despite the fact the game was played in debilitating heat inside the arena.

The Leafs' incredible comeback was completed two nights later in Toronto when they beat Detroit 3–1 to win their first Cup since 1931. Over the last four games of the series, Broda gave up only seven goals. It was the first of five times that Broda's name would appear on the Cup as a member of the Maple Leafs, but none would ever match the greatness

of his performance with his team down three games to none.

At the height of his career Broda gave two years to the Canadian army during the Second World War. He returned to the Leaf net during the 1945–46 season, getting into 15 games. He then played every game for the next three seasons and led the league in wins with 32 during the 1947–48 campaign. His last full season with the Leafs was in 1949–50, when he won 30 games in 68 appearances. Broda played in only 31 games the following year but rescued the Leafs one more time in the '51 playoffs, when he filled in for an injured Al Rollins and got Toronto past Boston in the semi-finals. He also won the first game of the finals against Montreal before Rollins resumed the goaltending duties.

MAPLE LEAF CAREER HIGHLIGHTS

★ Member of five Stanley Cup teams with Toronto
★ Holds Leafs' all-time record for most career shutouts (62)
★ Elected to the Hockey Hall of Fame in 1967
★ Posted a 302–244–101 career record in 629 games as a Leaf

LEAF FACT:

Turk Broda was one the greatest clutch goalies in the history of the NHL, appearing in 101 playoff games, winning 60 times while recording 13 shutouts. All those marks are still Leaf team records. He also posted a miniscule 1.98 goals-against average in the postseason.

Walter "Turk" Broda:
Leafs Banked on This "Money" Goalie

By John Iaboni

His records during the regular season for the Toronto Maple Leafs speak volumes about Walter "Turk" Broda's sterling quality. No goalie in Leaf history played as many regular season games (629), won as many games (302) or pitched as many shutouts (62).

But he was even stingier in the playoffs with the Stanley Cup and some much-needed bonus money on the line. Again, no goalie in Leaf history played in as many postseason games (101), won as many games (60), earned as many shutouts (13) or won as many Stanley Cups (five, in 1942, '47, '48, '49 and '51).

Bob Davidson, a solid winger for the Leafs from 1934 to '46 and club captain from 1943 to '45, was once asked if he rated Broda the greatest "money" goalie of all time. "I think that's the right thing to say and I'd go along with it," Davidson said. "He had a lot of confidence in himself and played everything as if he could save it. He wasn't scared or anything. In fact, nothing seemed to bother him. He had a good time and had a good sense of humour. Goaltending didn't bother him. He'd go in the net and be as cool as a cucumber, playing shots like you were supposed to play them. He didn't let in any bad goals that I can remember."

Broda was popular with his teammates and even turned owner Conn Smythe's "Battle of the Bulge" against him in 1949 into some extra publicity on the sports pages for the Leafs. Smythe was on Broda's case to get the goalie's weight down to 189 pounds. The goalie's weight-loss initiatives included running along the streets of downtown Toronto not far from Maple Leaf Gardens, all the while kibitzing with fans.

"He was a lot of fun in the dressing room and always had a couple of stories," Davidson recalled. "What he did kept you loose. He was a heck of a good guy and it was too bad he died so young [on October 17, 1972]."

Like many an aspiring hockey player, Walter Broda was banished to tend goal at a young age because his skating wasn't as polished as that of his peers. The freckles on his face prompted his friends to call him "Turkey Egg," and eventually that became just plain old Turk. He was property of the powerful Red Wings and played with their International Hockey League Detroit Olympics in 1935–36. He caught Smythe's eye and the Leafs purchased Broda on May 6, 1936 from a Detroit organization deep in goaltending. Reports vary, listing the purchase price as either $7,500 or $8,000. Either way, Turk turned out to be a steal for the Leafs.

"You had to say Turk was a good goaltender because Conn Smythe picked him up and put him in there," Davidson said, ever-complimentary to the Major's keen eye for talent.

In the ensuing years the Leafs and Red Wings were bitter rivals, even meeting in the Stanley Cup finals in 1942, '45, '48 and '49, with the Leafs winning each time. Broda was a dominant factor in all of those showdowns except 1945, when he was in combat overseas.

Jack Adams, the Detroit GM who sold Broda, once quipped, "He could play in a tornado and never blink an eye."

Perhaps the finest example of that occurred in the 1942 Stanley Cup finals when the Red Wings won the first three games against the Leafs but then lost the next four. That still stands as the only time in pro sports history that a club has overcome a 3–0 deficit in games to storm back and win that league's ultimate championship trophy. In a *Reader's Digest* article many years later, legendary broadcaster Foster Hewitt (through sportswriter Trent Frayne) recalled game six at Detroit this way: "During the first 12 minutes they could have piled up enough goals for an easy victory but for Turk Broda, who did everything but eat the puck in holding them off. The Detroit fans and players were determined to upset him. Once, a fan even threw a fish at him. It went past my face, missed Turk's cage by inches, and skidded all the way to the blue line. Talk about intimidation! But nothing could distract Turk; he shut them out, the Leafs won 3–0 and tied the series."

The Leafs then won game seven (3–1) before an overflow crowd at Maple Leaf Gardens. Broda had allowed but seven goals in the final four games. After another season with the Leafs, Broda's career was interrupted by his participation in the Second World War. He returned in 1945, whereupon he immediately rejoined the Leafs.

Broda backstopped three consecutive Stanley Cup wins from 1947 through '49, and in 1951 he and Al Rollins combined to seal another Stanley Cup. That '51 final series against the Canadiens saw each of the five games head into overtime. Broda played one game during 1951–52, and the night the Leafs held in his honour on December 22, 1951 served as a tribute for his services. He went on to serve as a coach in the Leafs system, guiding the Marlboros to Memorial Cup championships in 1955 and '56. Bobby Baun and Bobby Pulford were part of both those Broda-coached Marlies, while Billy Harris was there in 1955 and Carl Brewer in 1956.

The astute acquisition by the Leafs proved to have a hand in overwhelming success in various capacities, starting with the reason they obtained him in the first place. Broda made the NHL First All-Star Team in 1941 and '48, the NHL Second All-Star Team in '42 and played in four NHL All-Star Games (1947, '48, '49 and '50). He captured the Vezina Trophy in 1941 and '48 and was inducted into the Hockey Hall of Fame in 1967.

Money-goalie Turk Broda: a great competitor the Leafs could really bank on.

JACK ADAMS, THE DETROIT GM WHO SOLD BRODA, ONCE QUIPPED: "HE COULD PLAY IN A TORNADO AND NEVER BLINK AN EYE."

10 | BORJE SALMING

BORN: APRIL 17, 1951 IN KIRUNA, SWEDEN
POSITION: DEFENCE
YEARS AS A LEAF: 1973–74 TO 1988–89
SWEATER #: 21
MAPLE LEAF MOMENT: APRIL 17, 1976

THE OPENING TWO regular season games he played in North America served to prepare Borje Salming for his NHL career, and he soon became a league All-Star. He played his first game with the Leafs on October 10, 1973, as Toronto beat Buffalo 7–4 at Maple Leaf Gardens. Salming registered his first point (an assist) against Buffalo but was really challenged by the Philadelphia Flyers the next night. Tough guy Dave Schultz tried to engage Salming in a fight (both earned majors and minors for slashing), but it turned out to be more of a wrestling match that did not see the lanky Swede back down at all. The Flyers ran him all over the ice, but Salming was not intimidated by their obvious assaults. It was not the last time Salming would face the Flyers' rough-house tactics, as was evidenced during a 1976 playoff series between Toronto and Philadelphia. On the night of his 25th birthday, Salming showed he was ready to play the game of hockey as it was meant to be.

The Leafs had lost to the Flyers four straight in the 1975 playoffs, and things were not looking much better in 1976 when they lost the first two games of the series in Philly. But the Leafs won the third game at home 5–4 in one of the ugliest games ever played at Maple Leaf Gardens. Salming took one of the worst beatings ever inflicted on a Leaf player when the Flyers' Mel Bridgman beat him up in a fight. Philadelphia took advantage when some of the Leafs' tougher players were not on the ice and cornered Toronto's best player. The Ontario government threatened to intervene if the two teams did not stick to hockey two nights later, but it was Salming who led the way to another Leaf victory to even the series. The defenceman with the rubber body did it all in this game. He set up the opening tally by Errol Thompson, scored a magnificent goal himself and took eight stitches to his chin while conducting his defensive duties.

The highlight of the night was Salming's goal, a play that was started by the defenceman himself. He spotted Darryl Sittler open and hit him with a pass along the boards near centre ice before streaking into the middle to take a return feed. Attacking the Flyer blue line at full speed, Salming split the defence and bore in on goalie Bernie Parent. His high wrist shot beat the Flyer goalie cleanly and sent 16,485 fans into a frenzy. Salming was accorded a two-minute standing ovation, and his marker gave the Leafs a 2–1 lead. The Leafs hung on to the lead for the rest of the contest, with Salming breaking up many of the Flyer offensive efforts, to secure a 4–3 victory.

"I know Parent always stands up as much as he can, so all I did was shoot high. It went in on his glove side, up under the crossbar," Salming said of his beautiful goal. The first star of the game also added, "I don't think I am a hero. But when it [the crowd reaction to a goal] happens in the game, you can't think about anything else. It just feels real nice."

Leaf coach Red Kelly, who had invoked "Pyramid Power" in this series to help motivate his team, said, "If we get another pyramid miracle in Philadelphia and a pyramid

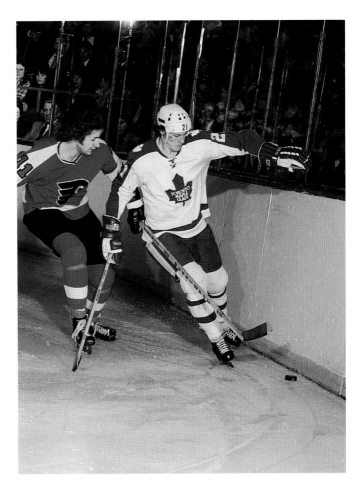

miracle on Thursday here, we can win this series." The Leafs forced the Flyers to a seventh game but lost 7–3. No one, however, would ever forget Salming's great performance during the series.

MAPLE LEAF CAREER HIGHLIGHTS

★ Holds Leaf team record for most career assists with 620
★ Named an NHL All-Star six times
★ Recorded seven straight seasons of 50 or more points for the Leafs
★ Recorded 768 points (148G, 620A) in 1,099 games

LEAF FACT:

When Toronto opened its 1973–74 regular season on October 10 against the Buffalo Sabres, no fewer than five players were making their debuts as Maple Leafs. Borje Salming, Ian Turnbull, Bob Neely, Inge Hammarstrom and Lanny McDonald were all playing in their first NHL contest. Salming and McDonald (two assists) were the only newcomers to record points in the 7–4 Leaf win, and both would go on to Hall of Fame careers.

Borje Salming:
"King" of the European Invasion

By John Iaboni

Borje Salming wasn't the first European-born-and-trained player to perform in the National Hockey League, but he was definitely the first to gain superstar status.

He was born on April 17, 1951 in Kiruna, a small city in northernmost Sweden that is 145 kilometres north of the Arctic Circle. How the Leafs uncovered this rare jewel was an amazing story. Leafs scout Gerry McNamara was in Sweden to scout Inge Hammarstrom with the Brynas club at the Christmas Cup in 1972. But, instead, he placed an excited call that awoke Leaf general manager Jim Gregory in the middle of the night. "Gerry told me he'd just seen an unbelievable defenceman [with Brynas], someone really special," Gregory recalled. "I put him on our negotiation list the next morning."

"I got a misconduct and went to the dressing room when Gerry came in and asked me if I was interested in playing in Toronto," Salming said. "All I said was 'Yes.' I don't think I realized what he was doing there or who he was, but he gave me his card and it said Toronto Maple Leafs on it."

Salming, an enormously gifted defenceman, arrived on North American soil when the Broad Street Bullies — the Philadelphia Flyers — were on the verge of Stanley Cup supremacy, and the Canadian-dominated NHL was in an era of brawling. So, when Salming and countryman Hammarstrom, a talented left-winger, joined the Leafs for the 1973–74 season, their skills and intestinal fortitude were challenged in brutal fashion. They heard taunts of "Chicken Swedes," and they were constant targets.

While Hammarstrom's NHL service consisted of six seasons, it was Salming who proved without a shadow of a doubt that Europeans could thrive in the NHL. In his NHL career, Salming almost lost an eye in a playoff game and had a skate blade go over his face in another season that left him badly scarred. His gaunt but solid frame, often battered, bruised and strapped with ice packs after each contest, withstood the pounding and changed the NHL attitude toward foreign players.

Right from his first training camp with the Leafs, Salming made an impact with remarkable agility and balance. In his fourth game as a Leaf — at the Montreal

Forum, usually Death Valley for Toronto — Salming raised eyebrows by falling into the direct line of a puck from hard-shooting Jacques Lemaire. Then, Salming fell to block another Lemaire blast later in a game the Leafs won 5–3. "The first time he blocked Lemaire's shot, we thought he was crazy," said Leafs defenceman Jim McKenny, a comedian with stand-up wit. "The second time he did it, we knew he was crazy!" Salming's superb performances and willingness to sacrifice his body led to the nickname "King" as in King Salmon. His other nickname was BJ. Why BJ? "Aren't all Swedes named Bjorn?" the quipster McKenny intoned. "So, he's BJ!"

At a time marked by several constant wars between the Leafs and the Flyers, members of the media wrote that the "Philly flu" often afflicted the club when it played in the Philadelphia Spectrum. Once again, Salming rose above that with heart and determination. On one occasion, Dave "The Hammer" Schultz attempted to engage Salming in fisticuffs. When Schultz threw a right, Salming grabbed Schultz's arm with his left hand. When Schultz resorted to tossing a left, Salming used Schultz's right hand to grab that arm. Salming, at 6´1˝, 190 pounds, was far from a 98-pound weakling, his strength a testament to the wonderful conditioning of European players.

Salming's brilliance led to a renaissance for the Leafs. He joined Darryl Sittler and Lanny McDonald as the club's big three. Salming played 16 seasons (1,099 regular season games) with the Leafs and one final campaign in 1989–90 with the Detroit Red Wings before returning to Sweden. From 1975 through '80, nine names accounted for the 24 defensive positions on the NHL First and Second All-Star Teams. Salming led the way with six (a First Team honour in 1977 and Second Team selections in 1975, '76, '78, '79 and '80), followed by Denis Potvin (five), Larry Robinson (four) and Guy Lapointe (three). Unlike Potvin, Robinson and Lapointe, however, Salming's greatness came with a team that failed to win the Stanley Cup over that period and, regrettably, he never did sip from hockey's Holy Grail.

His contributions to the game were rewarded with induction into the Hockey Hall of Fame in 1996. He is a huge celebrity among Maple Leafs Nation and

without question a national hero in Sweden. Did he envision opening the floodgates to the NHL for Europeans? "I don't think I was saying to myself 'I'm going to play good hockey because I'm Swedish,'" Salming said. "I came over and took a chance. Inge and me always said, 'Well, if we don't make it, we always can go back home.' If that happened, playing in the NHL was a good thing to have behind you. It would have been different if I didn't make it in Sweden because then we had nowhere else to go. And, back home, hockey was like a hobby, but all of a sudden you could make money [in the NHL] on your hobby, and that was amazing to us."

Salming was so good that Dave Keon, Leaf captain and Hall of Famer, told Gregory early after the Swede's arrival that he would have starred back in the six-team days of the NHL. The super Swede's entry into the Hockey Hall of Fame in 1996 rubber-stamped Keon's endorsement. "It's amazing that you get inducted into the Hall of Fame," Salming said. "I think you probably don't understand it, until you get there maybe a year after and you see your name up there, that's when you definitely understand what you have done."

All Salming need do to know what he accomplished is to look at every NHL roster these days: Europeans here, there and everywhere. And for that, they should truly hail The King.

SALMING'S BRILLIANCE LED TO A RENAISSANCE FOR THE LEAFS. HE JOINED DARRYL SITTLER AND LANNY MCDONALD AS THE CLUB'S BIG THREE.

11 | RED KELLY

BORN: JULY 9, 1927 IN SIMCOE, ONTARIO
POSITION: CENTRE
YEARS AS A LEAF: 1959–60 TO 1966–67
SWEATER #: 4
MAPLE LEAF MOMENT: APRIL 5, 1962

TORONTO MAPLE LEAF coach and general manager Punch Imlach made many shrewd moves to build his team into a dynasty during the sixties. His best acquisition and one of the best in Leaf history came in February of 1960 when he traded defenceman Marc Reaume to Detroit for Leonard "Red" Kelly. The Red Wings had grown disenchanted with the All-Star defenceman and had tried to move him to the New York Rangers, but Kelly refused to go to the Big Apple. Sensing an opportunity to add a quality veteran player to his young lineup, Imlach first received permission to speak to Kelly and then made the trade with the Red Wings once he came to terms with the player. In an interesting twist, Imlach had no intention of using Kelly on the blue line, putting him at centre instead. The Leaf boss reasoned that he needed someone to go up against Jean Béliveau of the Canadiens, the Leafs' main rival. Kelly took to his new position as if he had played there all his life, and as a bonus his playmaking abilities got the most out of winger Frank Mahovlich.

Kelly also had the ability to score big goals for the Leafs. One of his biggest came on the night of April 5, 1962, when the Leafs beat the New York Rangers 3–2 in overtime to take the fifth game of the semi-finals. The Leafs had won the first two games on home ice, but the pesky Rangers took the next two at Madison Square Garden to even the series. The fifth game thus became a crucial contest. For it, Kelly was teamed with Mahovlich and Ron Stewart on a newly created line. Stewart opened the scoring in the first period on a set-up by Kelly. The Leaf centre took the puck away from Vic Hadfield of New York along the boards in the Ranger end and circled around the New York net before feeding it to Stewart, who rapped it in past Ranger netminder Gump Worsley. Mahovlich made it 2–0 for Toronto when he got a stick on a drive taken by Kelly. The Rangers tied the score in the third period and forced overtime.

The Leafs came out charging in the extra session, but Worsley was outstanding as he turned away one Leaf shot after another. (The Leafs took a total of 50 shots on goal.) Johnny Bower was his equal in the Leaf net, although he did not face as many shots. The game carried on into a second overtime period, when the Kelly line got going again. Mahovlich carried the puck into the Ranger zone and let a shot go that Worsley stopped, but he could not quite cover the puck. "Gump had the puck under his arm above his elbow with about one-third of it showing. He moved a little and it squirted loose. He thought he had smothered," Kelly said after the game. "The puck came loose from under Gump and I shoved it in." Worsley knew he had been beaten by a player with a nose for the net: "Kelly is the type of player who takes advantage of a good opportunity, and when I lifted my head, he poked the puck into the net." The goal sent a crowd of more than 13,000 Toronto fans into raptures, but the New York club felt it got a raw deal on the play.

The Rangers protested to referee Eddie Powers that Worsley had covered the puck and that the whistle should have blown. Powers told Ranger playing coach Doug Harvey

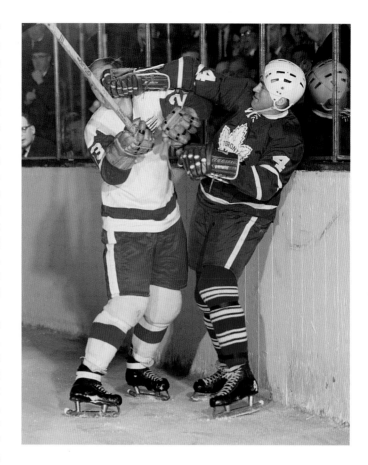

that he could see some of the puck under Worsley, and that the goal would stand. New York was devastated by the loss. The next game at Maple Leaf Gardens was no contest, as the Leafs romped to a 7–1 win, earning a trip to the Stanley Cup finals against Chicago.

MAPLE LEAF CAREER HIGHLIGHTS

★ Member of four Stanley Cup teams
★ Won the Lady Byng Trophy in 1962
★ Led the Leafs in assists (50) in 1961–62
★ Recorded 232 assists and 351 points in 470 games

LEAF FACT:

Leaf trainer Tommy Naylor gave Red Kelly sweater number 4 because other Toronto greats like Hap Day, Harry Watson and Bob Davidson had worn the same numeral. In 2006 the Leafs honoured sweater number 4, recognizing the careers of Kelly and Day.

Red Kelly:
Final Piece of the Puzzle

By John Iaboni

From the start of the 1947–48 NHL season until February 5, 1960, Red Kelly of the Detroit Red Wings ranked as one of the game's finest defencemen. In fact, he was the first-ever recipient of the James Norris Memorial Trophy as the NHL's top defenceman when he was selected in 1954 ahead of Montreal's Doug Harvey, and was twice runner-up in 1955 and '57 (to Harvey). But from the time Kelly joined the Maple Leafs on February 10, 1960, until he played his final NHL game with Toronto's Stanley Cup celebration on May 2, 1967, Kelly rated as one of the game's best two-way centres. Such long-term excellence paved the way for Kelly's induction into the Hockey Hall of Fame in 1969.

An superb skater full of determination, Leonard Patrick "Red" Kelly went right from the 1946–47 Memorial Cup champion Toronto St. Michael's Majors to the Red Wings. Over his 12 and two-thirds seasons in the Motor City, Kelly helped the Red Wings to four Stanley Cup triumphs (1950, 1952, 1954 and 1955). He was an eight-time NHL All-Star Team selection: to the First Team from 1951 through 1955 and again in 1957; and the Second Team in 1950 and 1956. He was a skilled blueliner who played within the confines of the rules as evidenced by the three Lady Byng Trophies as the NHL's most gentlemanly player while with Detroit (1951, 1953 and 1954). For good measure, as a centre with the Leafs he added the Lady Byng Trophy in 1961.

Kelly was the first player to win at least six Stanley Cups without one of them coming as a member of the Montreal Canadiens. By the time Kelly packed it in to become the first head coach in the history of the Los Angeles Kings, he had celebrated eight Stanley Cup championships — thanks to his final four with the Leafs in 1962, '63, '64 and '67.

If Kelly had not balked at his initial trade from Detroit, he might never have become a Leaf. You see, the Wings had shipped him to the lowly Rangers with Billy McNeil for Bill Gadsby and Eddie Shack. Kelly refused to report to Broadway despite the threat of banishment from hockey by NHL president Clarence Campbell. But when a trade was worked out with Toronto, Kelly was more than honoured to become a Leaf.

"Toronto was a tremendous hockey organization," Kelly said. "I'd followed the Leafs [on radio] growing up with Foster Hewitt and played at Maple Leaf Gardens [with St. Michael's]. So Toronto felt like home for me. I was excited and happy to be traded there." When Kelly's number 4 jersey was honoured by the Leafs on opening night of 2006–07, he summed up his feelings this way: "As a kid, I dreamed of making the National Hockey League; I dreamed about playing for the Toronto Maple Leafs, and I dreamed about winning the Stanley Cup. But I never, ever dreamed of them putting my number up at the top of the Gardens, which, of course, now has been replaced by the Air Canada Centre."

Kelly was the quintessential gentlemanly player. In his 20 NHL seasons, Kelly played 1,316 regular season games, scoring 281 goals and adding 542 assists for 823 points. During that time he was assessed only 327 minutes of penalty time. In his 19 trips to the playoffs, he played 164 games, scored 33 goals and 59 assists for 92 points and accumulated only 51 minutes in penalties. He played 470 regular-season games with the Leafs, along with only 74 minutes in penalties. In the playoffs with the Leafs, he generated 55 points (38 assists) in 70 games.

From 1948–49 through 1956–57, Detroit finished first in the NHL eight times — including a stretch of seven straight seasons. Kelly assisted the Leafs, who have seldom been known to lead the NHL standings, to one first-place finish. "When I arrived in Toronto, our first game was against the Canadiens, and Punch said he was thinking of playing me at centre against [Jean] Béliveau," Kelly said. "He said he thought I was the last piece he needed to win the Stanley Cup because he needed somebody to stop Béliveau, and he knew we'd have to beat the Canadiens in order to win the Stanley Cup. He asked me what I thought, and I said it was fine with me."

Not only did Kelly succeed on the ice but, from 1962 to 1965, he combined his hockey career with life as a federal politician. He was twice elected as the Liberal Member of Parliament for the Toronto riding of York West. Somehow, Kelly managed to spend as much time as required in Ottawa while still playing the full regular schedule and playoffs for the Leafs. The dual

role did take a toll on him, and he eventually left the political game in order to concentrate on one more Stanley Cup. In 1967, that goal was realized when Kelly, two months shy of his 40th birthday, was part of the aging Leafs that upset first-place Chicago and then second-place Montreal.

Each of his four Stanley Cups with the Leafs was precious, Kelly said. "The one we won here in '62 was real special after I came over from Detroit and everything so that was great," Kelly said. "The next one, we'd finished first in the league. Then in '64 when I was in Parliament and Harold [Ballard] brought the Cup out to the house with the photographer and the champagne, and took a picture of my family because I was in Ottawa, was something to remember. I didn't get to celebrate here when we'd won it. I had to be in Ottawa because we were in a minority government situation. Well, wouldn't you know it? They sat our infant son, Conn, who was born in January that year, in the Cup and, of course, he did the whole load right in it. Our family always chuckles when we see them drink champagne out of the Cup. The last one in '67, we were the Over-The-Hill Gang. But we won it. I knew I was going to retire that year so it was great to win that one."

The storybook ending capped an incredible career!

BY THE TIME KELLY PACKED IT IN TO BECOME THE FIRST HEAD COACH IN THE HISTORY OF THE LOS ANGELES KINGS, HE CELEBRATED EIGHT STANLEY CUP CHAMPIONSHIPS THANKS TO HIS FINAL FOUR WITH THE LEAFS IN 1962, '63, '64 AND '67.

12 | MATS SUNDIN

BORN: FEBRUARY 13, 1971 IN BROMMA, SWEDEN
POSITION: CENTRE
YEARS AS A LEAF: 1994–95 TO PRESENT
SWEATER #: 13
MAPLE LEAF MOMENT: OCTOBER 14, 2006

THE SMILING FACE on the Sunday sports pages of the Toronto newspapers told the whole story. Leaf captain Mats Sundin and teammate Bryan McCabe were pictured celebrating the game-winning goal scored in overtime by Sundin to defeat the Calgary Flames 5–4 on October 14, 2006. It was no ordinary goal either because the short-handed blast that breezed by Flame netminder Miikka Kiprusoff was the 500th of Sundin's illustrious career. The goal also tied him with Leaf legend Dave Keon for second place on the all-time club list for most career goals at 365.

The game Sundin played against the Flames was one of the best of his time in Toronto and was also seen coast-to-coast on *Hockey Night in Canada*. Sundin's game winner was actually the third goal of the game and gave the Leafs a much-needed win in the early going of the 2006–07 season when many question marks surrounded the team. Sundin started his big night with a goal just as a two-man power-play came to an end. The Leaf centre put himself in great position to accept a pass from McCabe, and he whipped the puck by an outstretched Kiprusoff to make it 2–0 for the Leafs. The young Leaf club soon found itself down 3–2, but another Swede, Alex Steen, tied it up for Toronto.

A minute after Steen's goal, Sundin shot home his second of the night to give the home side the lead again. The Flames tied it in the third to send the game into extra time, and things did not look good for the Leafs when Darcy Tucker took a penalty late in regulation time. But Sundin was not going to be denied on this night. He dug the puck out along the boards in the Leaf end and began a foray up the ice with Toronto defenders Hal Gill and McCabe in hot pursuit. Sundin crossed the Flame blue line before unleashing a howitzer that Kiprusoff just waved at as it went past him. His teammates came off the bench to mob Sundin, and the crowd leaped to its feet and gave the captain the ovation he richly deserved.

"I realized the applause, the people standing up and everybody stayed in the rink for me," Sundin said. "That doesn't happen too often. It was a special moment for me." Indeed it was a true statement as Leaf fans have always held affection back from Sundin since his arrival in Toronto in 1994 after a trade with the Quebec Nordiques. The Leafs had to give up their captain at the time, the very popular Wendel Clark, and defenceman Sylvain Lefebvre in the deal. Leaf fans appreciate Sundin's skill level; he has been one of the best players in the NHL since he joined the league for the 1990–91 season. Perhaps they longed for a Canadian-born leader for their beloved team. Or perhaps they are waiting for Sundin to have a playoff season to remember. But Toronto fans should keep in mind that his final goal against Calgary was the 88th game winner of his career. It was also the 15th overtime winner of his career in the regular season. "I enjoy overtime, the feeling that everything is on the line. I think my game is better when that happens," Sundin commented on his record.

New coach Paul Maurice has been impressed from the moment he took over as the Leafs' mentor. "One of the

pleasures of being here is getting to know him a little bit more and seeing the true personality in the locker room. He is far more involved in the leadership than maybe people think because he does have a quiet persona," Maurice said after the game. Perhaps it would be even better to say that the big Swede has always done his talking on the ice.

MAPLE LEAF CAREER HIGHLIGHTS

★ Holds the Leaf team record for most career game-winning goals with 75 as of May 2007
★ Led the Leafs in points for eight straight seasons (1994–95 to 2002–03)
★ Recorded his 1,000th career point as a Leaf vs. Edmonton, March 10, 2003
★ Recorded his 500th career goal as a Leaf vs. Calgary, October 14, 2006

LEAF FACT:

Mats Sundin's most productive night to date as a Maple Leaf came on April 11, 2006, when he scored four goals and added two assists in a 6–4 win over the Florida Panthers at the Air Canada Centre.

Mats Sundin:
Lucky Number 13 for the Leafs

By John Iaboni

The shockwaves of the trade between the Toronto Maple Leafs and Quebec Nordiques on June 28, 1994, were felt for many years thereafter. It wasn't so much that the Leafs landed a superstar-in-the-making in Mats Sundin but that they actually traded Wendel Clark. It has taken a long time for many die-hard Leaf fans and even some media types to get over that.

Sundin was working at Borje Salming's hockey school in Sweden when he learned of the transaction. While the great former Leaf defenceman waxed poetic to him about how much Sundin would enjoy playing in the hockey Mecca, the youngster also knew how the fans must feel about losing a blood-and-guts icon like Clark. The respectfulness that Sundin employed when asked about it indicated that, in his own right, he was special, too. Sundin said upon his arrival in Toronto, "Wendel Clark and I are different players, so I'm not going to try to do his job or what he did. It's very tough for me to accomplish that. I have a different style and I'm going to play my type of game."

Clark, who returned for two more stints with the Leafs before retiring in 2000, likes to point out that the fact Sundin is still playing should answer those who wonder who got the better of the 1994 Quebec-Toronto deal. And ask any teammate of Sundin's from Clark to Doug Gilmour about the big Swede's talent, leadership qualities and persona and they'll all rave about him.

Although it has taken some time for Leaf fans to warm up to Sundin, all Sundin has done is manufacture points without a big gunner supporting him up front; show sheer joy and emotion more when his teammates score than when he does; humbly accept accolades for any personal achievements; play hurt; wear the captain's 'C' with honour, and always state his undying desire to play for this storied franchise and remain in this city.

When Sundin became the first player to reach the 500-goal plateau while wearing a Leaf jersey with his dramatic short-handed goal in overtime against Calgary on October 14, 2006, he once again showed his class. Introduced as the game's first star, Sundin responded to the cheers of the fans by clapping his support for them.

"We do realize that we have the best fans," Sundin said that night. "The team hasn't won a championship since '67, yet they come to the games and support our team and they don't want anything from us but to do well. Definitely, there are not enough words to say what they mean. They're the reason why we're playing."

At six foot five, 231 pounds, Sundin is a large man with enormous skills. To some, this well-conditioned machine is the best athlete ever to don the blue and white. Setting the NHL scoring standards for goals and points for all Swedish-born players, Sundin is also leaving his place in the Leafs record book. Surpassing Dave Keon in goals and points in 2006–07, Sundin has only Darryl Sittler to eclipse before those marks belong to him.

He started playing hockey on a frozen lake near where he lived. When his older brother, Patrik, played, he followed him to the rink. "He started with the team in a hockey school," he recalls, "and I started, too. That's how I picked it up." Kent Nilsson and Mats Naslund were childhood hockey heroes. Borje Salming was another one. "Those three would have been the guys I looked up to when I was young. I liked the Montreal Canadiens a little bit because of their style of play but mostly because of Mats Naslund."

When the Nordiques selected Sundin in 1989 he became the first European to be picked number one overall in the NHL entry draft. After one more season at home, he was 19 when he joined the Nordiques, scoring 23 goals and 36 assists in his rookie season. Twice in his career (2002 and '04), Sundin has been selected as centre of the NHL Second All-Star Team. He's made eight appearances to date in the NHL All-Star Game, every year from 1996 through 2001 and again in 2004. His numerous appearances for Sweden on the international scene were capped in 2006 at the Torino Olympic Winter Games when he captained his homeland to the gold medal.

Ah, yes, the captaincy. Look around the NHL these days and many players wearing the 'C' are Europeans. Sundin wasn't the first European to get the honour but he was the first do so with the Leafs. It was on September 30, 1997 that Sundin was unveiled as the 16th captain in Leafs history. The announcement took place with the club's ninth (George Armstrong), 11th (Sittler) and 14th (Clark) captains present.

"Mats Sundin, through his great skills and stature, is one of the world's best players, and through

it even better," Sundin said. "Even though I'm from Europe, I know what being captain of the Toronto Maple Leafs means. It's a big honour and there's some responsibility that comes with it, not only on the ice, but off the ice in terms of the community and being a spokesperson for the Toronto Maple Leafs. It's a big day for me and my family, so thank you very much."

Number 13 turned out to be a lucky number for the Maple Leafs.

WHEN SUNDIN BECAME THE FIRST PLAYER TO REACH THE 500-GOAL PLATEAU WHILE WEARING A LEAF JERSEY WITH HIS DRAMATIC SHORT-HANDED GOAL IN OVERTIME AGAINST CALGARY ON OCTOBER 14, 2006, HE ONCE AGAIN SHOWED HIS CLASS.

his desire to lead this team to better times, he earned this honour," said Leaf president Ken Dryden. "With the honour goes a responsibility, because being captain of the Toronto Maple Leafs matters. People such as George Armstrong and Darryl Sittler and Wendel Clark have carried the Leafs' 'C' with great distinction. I am sure that Mats will follow in their footsteps and enhance this tradition."

One of Salming's regrets from his time with the Leafs was turning down the chance to serve as captain. He was proud that Sundin accepted it — and Sundin knew exactly what it meant.

"There's a lot of tradition and a lot of good things follow being captain for the Leafs and, the Toronto Maple Leafs being one of the Original Six teams, makes

13 | GEORGE ARMSTRONG

BORN: JULY 6, 1930 IN SKEAD, ONTARIO
POSITION: RIGHT WING
YEARS AS A LEAF: 1949–50 TO 1970–71
SWEATER #: 10
MAPLE LEAF MOMENT: MARCH 15, 1959

HOCKEY SCOUT BOB WILSON first informed the Maple Leafs about a strapping (6´1˝ and 184 pounds) right-winger named George Armstrong after seeing him play in Copper Cliff and Stratford, Ontario. He was invited to play for the Toronto Marlboros for the 1948–49 season, where he scored 29 goals and totalled 62 points. The Leafs did not think he was quite ready for the big team, so he played senior hockey, scoring 85 times in 75 contests. His performance earned him a spot on the Leafs' farm team in Pittsburgh, where he notched 45 goals over two years. Many considered Armstrong the best prospect in the Leafs organization, and he finally joined the big team in 1951–52. He only played in 52 games in the 1952–53 season but still managed 14 goals.

It soon became clear that Armstrong was not going to be as prolific a goal getter at the NHL level as he was in junior and senior, but he could be counted upon to score between 15 and 20 goals a season. (His best was 23 in 1959–60.) Conn Smythe appreciated his style of game, and in one of his last duties as Leaf owner, he named Armstrong captain. A ferocious checker, Armstrong could handle the puck in tight quarters with the best players in the league and displayed a knack for scoring key goals. He scored 20 goals for the first time in his career in the 1958–59 season, and his most important tallies came on March 15, 1959, in a game at Madison Square Garden in New York.

The Leafs had started '58–59 so badly under coach Billy Reay that unknown assistant general manager George "Punch" Imlach decided he had better take over if the team were to have any chance. It was a season-long struggle, but the Leafs somehow managed to get into the playoff race and were chasing the New York Rangers for the fourth and final spot. The Leafs trailed New York by seven points with only five games to play but had an opportunity in a weekend series against the Rangers to gain some ground. Toronto won the Saturday night game at home by a 5–0 score (with Armstrong getting the first goal of the game), so the next night the New York club was looking to end the Leafs' playoffs dream. The Rangers struck early, with Bill Gadsby scoring after just 3:09 of the first on a power-play while Armstrong was in the penalty box for holding. But Dick Duff tied the score for the Leafs, and Armstrong gave Toronto a 2–1 lead at the end of one period. Andy Bathgate tied it for the Blueshirts, but Frank Mahovlich and Armstrong with his second gave the Leafs a two-goal lead. New York scored twice to tie it, but Armstrong would not let his team surrender and scored his third to give the Leafs the lead again. The Rangers evened the score once more, but Bob Pulford scored on a bouncing shot that got by Gump Worsley in the Ranger goal to give Toronto an improbable 6–5 win in front of 12,280 shocked New York fans. It was a tough game throughout with two fights and plenty of stick work from both teams. The Leafs now trailed the Rangers by three points, but New York had two home games to play, while the Leafs played only one of their final three at Maple Leaf Gardens. Armstrong's hat trick was the first of his career, and his play

was outstanding in both games with the Rangers.

Amazingly, the Leafs won all three of their remaining games, while New York was able to secure just one victory in their final three efforts. The Leafs nailed down the final playoff spot with a 6–4 win over Detroit on the final night of the season, while New York was losing 4–2 to Montreal on home ice.

The Leafs then beat Boston in the semi-finals before losing in five games to Montreal in the finals. In spite of the loss to the Habs, the Leaf dynasty of the sixties may have been born late in the '58–59 season when a captain showed his team the way to win. Armstrong was elected to the Hockey Hall of Fame in 1975, and the Leafs honoured sweater number 10 in 1998.

MAPLE LEAF CAREER HIGHLIGHTS

★ Captain of four Stanley Cup teams with Toronto
★ Second Leaf to play in 1,000 career games
★ Scored 26 goals and 60 points in 110 playoff games
★ Recorded 713 points (296G, 417A) in 1,187 games

LEAF FACT:

George Armstrong recorded the last goal of the Original Six era when he scored into an empty Montreal Canadiens net, as the Maple Leafs won 3–1 to clinch their fourth Stanley Cup of the decade in 1967.

14 | DOUG GILMOUR

BORN: JUNE 25, 1963 IN KINGSTON, ONTARIO
POSITION: CENTRE
YEARS AS A LEAF: 1991–92 TO 1996–97; 2002–03
SWEATER #: 93
MAPLE LEAF MOMENT: FEBRUARY 14, 1993

ALL TORONTO MAPLE LEAF fans were thrilled when Doug Gilmour joined the team midway through the 1991–92 season. Finally, the team had a legitimate playmaker to take over as the Leafs' number one centre. In his first game wearing the blue and white Gilmour scored a goal against the Detroit Red Wings and then led the team to a 20–18–2 record to close out the year. Toronto fans suddenly had a reason to look forward to next season. Gilmour was quickly elevated to the status of former Leaf stars like Dave Keon and Darryl Sittler, and he showed he was worthy of such high praise by recording a team record 127 points (32 goals, 95 assists) in '92–93. The highlight of his great season came on February 14, 1993, when the Minnesota North Stars paid a visit to Maple Leaf Gardens.

By the time the contest against the North Stars was over Gilmour had tied a team record (held by former Leaf defenceman Babe Pratt who set the mark in 1944) with six assists in one game as the Leafs romped to a 6–1 victory. Gilmour set up the recently acquired Dave Andreychuk for two of the goals and also assisted Mike Foligno, Glenn Anderson, John Cullen and Dave Ellett for their markers, all scored against Minnesota's Darcy Wakaluk. On the first goal of the game, Foligno took Gilmour's pass in the face-off dot and blasted a drive over the goalie's shoulder. The slender 165-pound Leaf pivot took a hit to set up Cullen for his goal on a power-play during the first period. In the second period both Andreychuk and Anderson wired home shots from near the face-off circle after taking feeds from Gilmour. In the third period Gilmour sprung Andreychuk past the North Star defence with a pass which the big winger buried, giving Gilmour his fifth helper of the night. Finally, he feathered a pretty pass to Ellett, who came in from his blue line position to slap a 40-footer past a worn-out Wakaluk. The Leafs tried to get Gilmour sole possession of the record but could not score the rest of the way.

More than 15,000 fans at the Gardens let Gilmour know they appreciated his efforts during the game and stayed around to cheer him as the first star of the contest. "It's not like I did anything special. All I did was pass the puck," Gilmour said after the game. "I don't know exactly what this record is all about. But I'll just take it and say thank you. You're going to have certain games where everything goes your way." If Gilmour was being modest his teammates certainly recognized what a great performance they had witnessed. "Gilmour is a great player. He's probably one of the best players I've ever played with. He goes in the corners and he's willing to take a hit. He's got good vision on the ice, too. He sees the play really well. If I keep going to the net for him, things are going to work out," commented linemate Andreychuk.

Minnesota coach Bob Gainey pinned his team's defeat strictly on Gilmour's shoulders. "Gilmour had a great game. He broke the game wide open for them." Leaf coach Pat Burns said of Gilmour, "He's so dedicated. That kind of player makes it so much easier for a coach. I wish our young

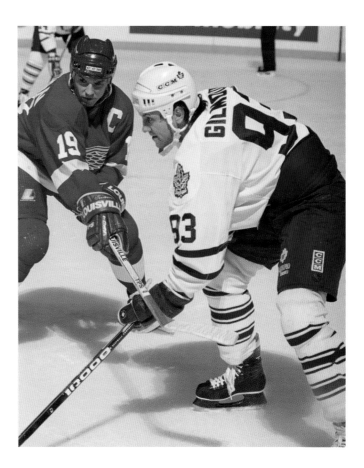

players could watch him and understand better what it takes."

Gilmour kept things light in the Leaf dressing room despite all the accolades thrown his way by suggesting that veteran Foligno had actually played with Pratt! Foligno responded by saying, "I'm happy for Doug, but I don't like the thought that I played with [Pratt]."

Gilmour would later promise that Leaf fans would be rewarded for their loyal patronage. In the 1993 playoffs the team came within one game of the finals, as Gilmour scored 35 points in a remarkable 21-game playoff run.

MAPLE LEAF CAREER HIGHLIGHTS

★ Recorded over 100 points in a season twice (1992–93 and 1993–94)
★ Recorded 77 points in 52 career playoff games for Toronto
★ Winner of the Selke Trophy in 1993
★ Recorded 452 points in 393 games as a Leaf

LEAF FACT:

No Maple Leaf player has won the Hart Trophy as the NHL's most valuable player since Ted Kennedy won it in 1955. Since then only three Leaf players have been the runner-up: Tod Sloan (1956), Johnny Bower (1961) and Doug Gilmour (1993).

Doug Gilmour:
Small Guy... Big Heart

By John Iaboni

The 10-player blockbuster trade that brought Doug Gilmour to the blue and white on January 2, 1992, turned out to be one of the most important acquisitions in Leaf history. Although Gilmour's stay in Toronto — including one final game with the Leafs at Calgary in March 2003 when a knee injury ended his career — spanned only 393 games in the regular season and 52 playoff matches, his fingerprints are all over the club's record books. He scored 131 goals and 321 assists for 452 points to average 1.15 points-per-game during regular season play and added 17 goals and 60 assists for 77 points to average 1.48 points-per-game in the playoffs. Gilmour's 127 points in 1992–93 and 111 points in 1993–94 rank first and third, respectively, on the Leafs all-time list. His 95 assists in 1992–93 and 84 assists in 1993–94 are first and second in Leafs annals. Number 93's playoff totals in assists and points both zoomed to number one on the club; his 25 assists in 1993 and 22 assists in '94 are one-two by a Leaf in the postseason. His six assists during a 6–1 win over Minnesota on February 13, 1993, equalled the Leafs record that defenceman Babe Pratt had set on January 8, 1944.

The Leafs became the third NHL club for Gilmour, whose career had initially spanned five seasons with St. Louis, then three-and-a-half with Calgary, including playing a pivotal role in the 1989 Stanley Cup for the Flames. When he wanted out of Calgary and things stalled, he staged a walkout after New Year's Eve, and his wishes were quickly granted. The fact he was traded to the Leafs was beyond his wildest dreams. "I was never so happy as when I was traded to Toronto," he said at the time. "My family is from Kingston and we grew up following the Maple Leafs."

Gilmour emerged as the central force in restoring pride to the organization. While he always credited the march of the Leafs to the final four in 1993 and '94 as a total team achievement, there's no question those developments would never have happened without Gilmour. At 5′9″ and 177 pounds soaking wet, Gilmour repeatedly sparked the Leafs and proved that, despite the NHL's swing to behemoths, the game still had room for the relentless little guys.

"Players are getting bigger and they're also getting quicker," Gilmour observed during the early phases of his tenure with the Leafs. "But I guess when you put on that equipment you're out there to win. The biggest thing is you don't want to be beaten, and that can be in a corner, anywhere on the ice. Throughout my life, if somebody said I was too small, that just meant I wanted to beat them that much more to prove somebody wrong. I think a lot of smaller guys you see in the league are doing that.

"I've always looked at it that I never thought I was small. I know I am but you never think of it that way when you're in the game. You go out and feel you're the same size as somebody else. Something I read in my first year of junior always sticks in my mind and that's, 'A man shows what he is by what he does with what he has.' I went into camp my first year of junior at 5′9″, 140 pounds and I was a defenceman, but at that point in time, they decided to move me up to centre. Reading that quote really stuck with me because I never really thought I was that small."

While the Flames allowed him to achieve the major prize in the Stanley Cup, his time with the Leafs allowed him to gain individual recognition. In 1993, the same year he won the Frank J. Selke Trophy as the NHL's best defensive forward, he also set the Leafs record for offence in a season! He fulfilled a goal of his by twice playing in the NHL All-Star Game (in 1993 and '94). On August 18, 1994, Gilmour had the 'C' bestowed upon him during a ceremony at the Hockey Hall of Fame. The 15th captain in club history was overwhelmed as former Leaf captains Red Horner (1938–40), Bob Davidson (1943–45), Sid Smith (1955–56), George Armstrong (1957–69), Darryl Sittler (1975–81) and Rob Ramage (1989–91) were on hand to celebrate the event.

"I think Doug Gilmour fits into the mould of traditional Maple Leaf captains," Fletcher said that day. "His competitiveness is second to none in the league. His ability is there because he's one of the better players in the league. And his ability to deal with people in a market like Toronto, where you have such great, intense interest and support, is exceptional. The work he does in the community is exemplary, so, I think not only is he the logical candidate but Doug

Gilmour was born to be captain of the Maple Leafs."

Gilmour's role model in his new capacity came from his time with the St. Louis Blues. "For me, as far as true grit and determination, a captain who I played with — and I was fortunate enough to be his roommate for five years — was Brian Sutter," Gilmour said. "He's a very intense person; a guy who would go out and do anything he could for the team. He was a lunch-bucket guy who worked hard and improved each and every night. He became an elite player through hard work because he was never a guy who was blessed with skills."

Gilmour's never-say-die approach earned him a permanent soft spot and respect from Leafs Nation. Just flashing his image on the scoreboard at Air Canada Centre still draws an overwhelming response. That's why fans were delighted when Gilmour returned to the Leafs on September 15, 2006, as professional development advisor. The little guy with a big heart was back where he belonged.

AT 5´9˝ AND 177 POUNDS SOAKING WET, GILMOUR REPEATEDLY SPARKED THE LEAFS AND PROVED THAT, DESPITE THE NHL'S SWING TO BEHEMOTHS, THE GAME STILL HAD ROOM FOR THE RELENTLESS LITTLE GUYS.

CLARENCE DAY WAS NEVER thrilled about his given first name, but he still had a cheerful disposition and always looked on the bright side. People noticed and took to calling him "Happy," which was often shortened to "Hap," and that worked out well for the hockey player who started playing the game close to his home. The arena where Day started playing his minor hockey was near enough for him to walk to, so Day would hike the distance and developed strong legs as a result. In time he began walking five miles to his games in Midland and then all the way back home. Never heavy at 5′11″ and 175 pounds, he was a very alert player who did not mind the physical aspect of the game.

Day was playing senior hockey in Hamilton while enrolled at the University of Toronto in the Pharmacy program. Charlie Querrie, manager of the Toronto St. Patricks, spotted Day playing for the Hamilton Tigers and thought he had the talent to be a professional player. Before he could get a signature on a contract, Querrie had to assure Day that he could operate a pharmacy while earning a good salary as a pro player. Day joined the St. Pats for the 1924–25 season and scored 10 goals and 22 points in 26 games. Two years later, when Conn Smythe renamed the team the Maple Leafs, Day was one of the very few players he retained from the previous regime. Smythe made one major change to Day's game — he moved him from left wing to defence, even though he had scored 14 goals in the St. Pats' final full season of 1925–26. He scored 11 times in 1926–27 and then had nine the following year, when he recorded the first-ever hat trick in Leaf history. Day recorded his first three-goal game against the New York Rangers on January 14, 1928, in a game played in Toronto.

The Rangers were one of the best teams in the American Division of the National Hockey League going into the contest against the Maple Leafs. It was a wide open game, and both teams focused on the attack, but it was the Toronto players who had the goal-scoring touch on this night. Day's play was exceptional all game long. He scored two goals in the first period to give the Leafs the lead. His first goal came when he rushed in from the blue line to knock home a rebound past New York goalie Lorne Chabot just over seven minutes into the contest. His second goal came when he let go a rocket of a shot as he beat the Ranger defence down the left wing before putting the puck between Chabot's pads. The New York club did not give up by any means, and defenceman Ching Johnson got one back for the Rangers. But in the end it was no contest, as the Leafs took the game 6–1 with Day adding one more goal to give him three on the night. The win evened the Leafs' record to 9–9–3, good enough for third place in the Canadian Division at that point in the season. But the Leafs would finish '27–28 at 18–18–8 and out of the playoffs with a fourth-place finish in their division. (Only the top three teams in each division made the playoffs.)

Day settled in on the Leaf defence and would score six to nine goals a year with about 20 points in each of his 10

years as a Maple Leaf. During the 1929–30 season, Day scored four goals in one game against the Pittsburgh Pirates, making him the first Leaf player to record three or more goals in a road game. He was at his absolute best during the 1932 playoffs when the Leafs won their first Stanley Cup, recording six points (three goals, three assists) in seven playoff games.

The Leafs traded Day to the New York Americans in 1937 in the twilight of his career, but the longtime Toronto captain played only one season with the New York club. Day would go on to be one of the most successful coaches in Leaf history, winning five Stanley Cup titles.

MAPLE LEAF CAREER HIGHLIGHTS

★ Member of Stanley Cup winning team in 1932
★ Recorded six seasons of 15 or more points as a Maple Leaf
★ Elected to the Hockey Hall of Fame in 1961
★ Recorded 161 points (62G, 99A) in 476 games as a Maple Leaf

LEAF FACT:

Of all the former Maple Leaf players to coach the team afterwards, only Pat Quinn won more games (300) than Hap Day (259) while directing the Toronto club. The next best mark belongs to Red Kelly, who won 133 games between 1973 and 1977. The best winning percentage among former players belongs to Quinn, who had a 300–196–52 record as coach of the Leafs for a .591 mark.

16 | HARVEY JACKSON

BORN: JANUARY 19, 1911 IN TORONTO, ONTARIO
POSITION: LEFT WING
YEARS AS A LEAF: 1929–30 TO 1938–39
SWEATER #: 11
MAPLE LEAF MOMENT: APRIL 5, 1932

FRANK SELKE MAY HAVE been Conn Smythe's assistant general manager for many years, but he was a sharp evaluator of hockey talent in his own right. Selke spotted a young man of 16 who would clean and scrape the ice at the Ravina Gardens before practising his hockey skills afterwards. Harvey "Busher" Jackson was a gifted skater with deft moves and a good shot. Selke predicted he would be a Maple Leaf player one day and insisted he sign with the club if he wanted to keep his job at the arena. Jackson was reluctant at first but finally agreed and joined the Toronto Marlboros to play junior hockey. He made the Leaf roster at the tender age of 18 and by 1930–31 was playing regularly on a line with the equally youthful Joe Primeau at centre and Charlie Conacher on the right wing. The "Kid Line" was born, and the Leafs rode the troika to one of the most successful eras in the history of the team. The five-foot-eleven, 195-pound left-winger had the size, speed and skill to become one the best players in the NHL. His graceful stride allowed him to get past defencemen quickly, and he could move with the puck while going full throttle. In just his third year, he led the NHL in points with 53 and would score a career-high 28 times in 1931–32. He saved one of his best performances for the playoffs when the Leafs met the New York Rangers in the first game of the Stanley Cup finals on April 5, 1932, at Madison Square Garden.

The opening game of the finals was played in a manner that suited Jackson perfectly. The contest featured lots of end-to-end action in front of more than 16,000 fans. The two clubs fought hard all game long, but it was a four-goal outburst by the Leafs in the second period that turned the tide in Toronto's favour. The teams exchanged goals in the first period, but Jackson broke up the game in the middle stanza when he scored three times and Conacher scored another to give the Leafs a 5–2 lead. Defencemen Hap Day and Red Horner set up the first two of Jackson's goals, while the third was more of a solo effort when he drilled a shot past Ranger netminder John Ross Roach. The Leafs sat back on their lead to start the third period, and the Rangers made them pay with a couple of goals to cut the score to 5–4. New York was pressing for the equalizer, but the Leafs played strongly in front of goalie Lorne Chabot. Jackson finally corralled the puck, and Horner jumped into the attack after taking a pass from the left-winger. He went in and scored a goal that seemed to take the steam out of the Ranger attack and secured a 6–4 Toronto victory. It was the first-ever victory for the Maple Leafs in the Stanley Cup finals. The Leafs would go on to win the Cup in three straight games. Jackson's performance in the first game of the series certainly went a long way to getting the Leafs off to a good start.

Jackson would score 20 or more goals for the Leafs five times, yet while the team was very successful, the Cup won in 1932 would be the only one of Jackson's career. He was traded away to the New York Americans in a deal that landed the Leafs Dave Schriner in 1939, but Jackson enjoyed more success as a Boston Bruin. In 1942–43 he scored 19

times and was able to play on a line with his brother Art, also a former Leaf. He retired after the 1943–44 season but he was unable to discipline himself away from hockey, struggling with alcohol the rest of his days.

Smythe had tried to help Jackson while he was still with the Leafs but grew disenchanted with his former star player. Jackson was kept out of the Hall of Fame while he was alive but was inducted in 1971, five years after his passing.

MAPLE LEAF CAREER HIGHLIGHTS

★ Member of Stanley Cup team in 1932
★ Named to the NHL's First All-Star Team four times
★ Recorded 25 points (17G, 8A) in 54 playoff games
★ Recorded 351 points (186G, 165A) in 434 games as a Leaf

LEAF FACT:

Harvey Jackson's three-goal effort in the second period of a contest against the New York Rangers made him the first Leaf player to record a hat trick in one period of a playoff game. That mark has never been broken but has been equalled by Darryl Sittler (in the second period on April 22, 1976, in an 8–5 win over the Philadelphia Flyers) and George Ferguson (in the third period on April 11, 1978, in a 7–3 win over the Los Angeles Kings).

17 | KING CLANCY

BORN: FEBRUARY 25, 1903 IN OTTAWA, ONTARIO
POSITION: DEFENCE
YEARS AS A LEAF: 1930–31 TO 1936–37
SWEATER #: 7
MAPLE LEAF MOMENT: OCTOBER 11, 1930

WHEN FRANCIS "KING" CLANCY was a young man living in Ottawa, he wanted to be a football player like his father Tom. However, the youngster was too small (listed at 5′7″ and 155 pounds) for the rigours of football, so he turned to hockey instead. He played hockey while attending high school and then asked Tommy Gorman, manager of the Stanley Cup champion Ottawa Senators of the NHL, if he could try out for the team. Gorman reluctantly agreed and then watched the plucky Clancy battle his way onto the roster. Never afraid to carry the puck, Clancy wanted to be a defenceman so he could get more ice time. He had great courage and good speed and was very well liked by his Senator teammates. He scored four goals and 10 points in his first season with Ottawa in 1921–22 and helped them win another Cup the following year. In 1924–25, Clancy scored 14 times and totalled 21 points in 28 games, and he helped the Ottawa club to another championship in 1927. By the 1929–30 campaign, Clancy had established himself as one of the most colourful players in the league and that year scored 17 goals and 40 points in 44 regular season games. The '29–30 season was his last in Ottawa, which was by this time strapped for cash and players. The Maple Leafs saw an opportunity to take an established star for their club and wanted to make a deal with the Senators for the defenceman's rights. Clancy was acquired by the Leafs just before the 1930–31 season started and began an association with the team that would last the rest of his life.

The Leafs were not the only team pursuing Clancy once it became known that Ottawa was going to trade him away. General manager Conn Smythe, interested in improving his blue line, had sought and signed a free agent defenceman named John Gallagher. However, the NHL board of governors ruled that Gallagher's playing rights would go to the Montreal Maroons and not to the Leafs. The Maroons dropped out of the running for Clancy as a result, and the Leafs pursued him harder while keeping an eye on the New York Rangers, who also coveted Clancy for their team. In the end it was $35,000 in cold, hard cash (an astronomical amount for the times) that won the day for the Maple Leafs. Two players, Art Smith and Eric Pettinger, were also sent to the Senators, but neither of them amounted to much with Ottawa. At the time of the deal, the 29-year-old Clancy was rated almost as good as Boston star Eddie Shore and was an offensive force from the blue line (unusual in that era of hockey) capable of igniting the attack for his team. The Leafs also knew that they would have a new arena soon. (Maple Leaf Gardens would open in November of 1931.) They needed star players to attract crowds to their hockey palace. Speculation also had it that Clancy would put the Leaf team in a position to win the Stanley Cup.

"Everybody seems very enthusiastic about the matter," Smythe said of the impending deal. "I think Clancy is one of the most popular players I've ever known." For his part, Clancy was very well aware of what was going on and fully intended to do everything properly. "I have been tendered a contract by

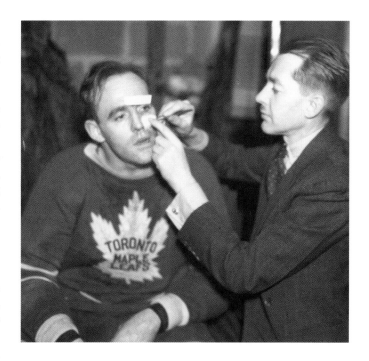

the Ottawa hockey club and will sign it. The contract contains a transfer clause," Clancy reported. "The deal is in the process of completion, and the minute I affix my signature to the contract, it will be turned over to Conn Smythe for the necessary action," he continued. On October 11, 1930, the Leafs' board of directors announced that they had unanimously decided to complete the deal to acquire Clancy. It was one of the best moves the Maple Leafs have ever made.

Clancy was paired with Hap Day on defence, and the Maple Leafs went on to finish their first year playing in the Gardens by winning the Cup in 1932. The star defender was named a league All-Star four times, twice on the First Team (in 1931 and 1934).

MAPLE LEAF CAREER HIGHLIGHTS

★ Member of Stanley Cup team in 1932
★ Recorded 20 or more points four times with the Leafs
★ Elected to the Hockey Hall of Fame in 1958
★ Recorded 130 points (52G, 78A) in 286 games with Toronto

LEAF FACT:

King Clancy has an NHL trophy named in his honour, which has been awarded annually since 1988 to "the player who best exemplifies leadership qualities on and off the ice and has made a noteworthy contribution to his community." Curtis Joseph is the only Leaf player to win the award (in 2000). Other winners who played with the Leafs at some point in their careers are: Lanny McDonald (1988), Joe Nieuwendyk (1995), Kris King (1996) and Ron Francis (2002).

18 | MAX BENTLEY

BORN: MARCH 1, 1920 IN DELISLE, SASKATCHEWAN
POSITION: CENTRE
YEARS AS A LEAF: 1947–48 TO 1952–53
SWEATER #: 7
MAPLE LEAF MOMENT: NOVEMBER 2, 1947

MAX BENTLEY HAD DONE so much for the Chicago Black Hawks that general manager Bill Tobin called him into his office and gave him a chance to decide his future. Bentley had played his entire career in Chicago and had won the NHL scoring title two seasons in a row (1945–46 and 1946–47) as well as one Hart Trophy (1946) and one Lady Byng (1943). Tobin told his star centre that the Black Hawks were in bad shape and needed to get more quality players if they were to turn their fortunes around. The only way the Chicago squad could add the help they needed was to deal Bentley away. When put to him in this manner, Bentley felt he had no choice but to agree to a deal, even if it meant being split up from his brother Doug, another long-time Black Hawk with whom he formed two-thirds of the famed Pony Line. Chicago found a trading partner in the Maple Leafs, who were looking ahead to the day when centre and captain Syl Apps was going to retire. After a few weeks of speculation, Leaf general manager Conn Smythe headed to Chicago to try to complete the deal. On November 2, 1947, one of the biggest deals in NHL history sent shock waves throughout the league.

Acquiring Bentley came at a heavy price for the Leafs, who sent five players to the Black Hawks to complete the transaction. Gone from Toronto were forwards Gaye Stewart, Bud Poile and Gus Bodnar, plus defencemen Bob Goldham and Ernie Dickens. All the players leaving the Leafs had won at least one Stanley Cup with Toronto, but that did not stop Smythe from moving ahead with the deal. "Our purpose in making the deal relates to the centre ice position," Smythe said. "If anything were to happen to Apps, we would be desperate. I feel it's quite a gamble but that it's worth it because were getting the league-leading scorer for centre duties. We've drawn on all our reserves, and we're hoping the trade doesn't weaken either club. It should help Chicago and benefit the whole league." The Leafs also got forward Cy Thomas in the deal, who was seen as a promising young player at the time. Leaf coach Hap Day commented on his new players by saying, "We got the league's top scorer plus a promising rookie. Mr. Smythe made a very smart move."

The former Leaf players tried to put on a happy face when asked about the deal, but Chicago was the worst team in the league at the time. "All I can say about the move is that I will do my best to make the Hawks a better team," said Stewart. Bodnar was happy about getting more ice time with the Black Hawks: "With Chicago I'll get regular play, and I am confident I can prove I belong." Poile was shocked at first: "I was certainly surprised, but I think it's for the best. We'll get Chicago back into the playoffs." Bentley understood that Chicago really had no choice but to make this deal. "There was nothing else Chicago could do. They were desperate for help. They haven't anything coming up. But it's sure tough to say goodbye," he said. Despite sacrificing their star, Chicago still finished dead last that season.

The 1947–48 Leafs may have been the best team in club history, as they finished first with a 32–15–13 record and 77 points. They easily beat Boston in the semi-finals and

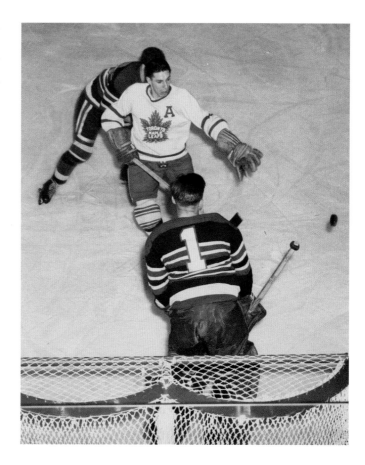

then whipped Detroit in four straight games to take the Stanley Cup, the first of three Bentley would win with Toronto. In the '48 postseason, Bentley had 11 points (four goals, seven assists) in nine games and had a big hand in the Leafs' 4–2 win over Detroit in the second game of the finals on April 10, 1948. He scored the opening goal of the contest in the first period and added another in the second stanza. It was the first of many great playoff performances for Bentley, who recorded 38 points in 40 playoff games for Toronto. The trade for the slick centre had certainly paid off for the Leafs.

MAPLE LEAF CAREER HIGHLIGHTS

★ Acquired in a deal with Chicago on November 2, 1947
★ Member of three Stanley Cup teams with Toronto
★ Elected to the Hockey Hall of Fame in 1966
★ Recorded 256 points (122G, 134A) in 354 games as a Leaf

LEAF FACT:

When the Maple Leafs were considering trading for Max Bentley, general manager Conn Smythe sought advice from an unusual source — Montreal netminder Bill Durnan. The Montreal netminder told Smythe that Bentley was the best centre he had faced. That was all the Leaf manager needed to hear to complete the deal.

19 | JOE PRIMEAU

BORN: JANUARY 29, 1906 IN LINDSAY, ONTARIO
POSITION: CENTRE
YEARS AS A LEAF: 1927–28 TO 1935–36
SWEATER #: 15
MAPLE LEAF MOMENT: APRIL 7, 1932

EVEN THOUGH HE really wanted to be a baseball pitcher, Joe Primeau was steered into hockey by Frank Selke of the Maple Leafs, who had a great eye for athletic talent. Leaf general manager Conn Smythe, when he was still manager of the New York Rangers, had seen Primeau playing hockey and felt sure the young centre would have a career in the pro ranks. He signed Primeau to a personal services contract, so when Smythe was fired by the Rangers he was able to keep the slick pivot away from Broadway. Although Primeau was slight in stature (5′11″ and 153 pounds), he could take the physical punishment dished out by big defencemen. His game was all about getting the puck to his wingers, and he was a very good playmaker his entire career, which was played exclusively with the Leafs.

Primeau had to develop his game with the Toronto Ravinas and the London Panthers before being promoted to the Leafs for the 1929–30 season, where he scored five goals and 21 points in 43 games. He led the NHL with 32 assists the next season, meshing superbly with wingers Charlie Conacher and Harvey Jackson to form the best line in the league. "The Kid Line" featured three All-Star calibre players who took the Toronto club to its first-ever Stanley Cup win in 1932. Primeau was at his best in the finals when the Leafs met the Rangers for the title. The Leafs won the first game in New York, but the first-place Rangers could not play at home on the night of April 7, 1932 (as the circus was booked into Madison Square Garden) and were forced to play the second game of the series in Boston.

Some 13,000 fans came to see the second game of the finals at the Boston Garden even though the Bruins were not involved. The crowd clearly backed the Rangers and cheered to see the New York club take a 2–0 lead by the early part of the second period. But the Leafs suddenly came to life and scored twice on markers by Jackson and Conacher to tie the game by the end of the second. Toronto showed speed and playmaking skills that seemed to dazzle the New York club in the final period. The Leafs had all the momentum and scored four unanswered goals in the third period to win the game 6–2 and earn the respect of the fans in attendance. Primeau and defenceman King Clancy broke away on a rush, and the Toronto blueliner put in a rebound to give the Leafs the lead. Conacher scored another one, and then Primeau assisted on the next two goals by Clancy and Harold Cotton to round out the scoring. His three assists in one period remained a Leaf team playoff record for many years and has been matched only once since then. (Nick Metz had three helpers in the second period against Boston on March 25, 1941, when the Leafs whipped the Bruins 7–2.) With the victory the Leafs were now in a position to win the Cup on home ice on Saturday, April 9. Primeau help set up a goal by Jackson as the Toronto club won its first-ever championship as the "Maple Leafs" (they had won the Cup in 1922 as the St. Patricks) by beating New York 6–4 to sweep the series in three games.

The Leafs were always in contention during the decade of the thirties, but they could not win another Cup as they

faltered in the finals most of the time. Primeau retired by the time he was 30 years old but came back to the game as a coach. He took the Toronto Marlboros to the Memorial Cup title in 1945 and 1947 and then coached the senior Marlies to the Allan Cup championship in 1950.

His success earned him a shot at the Leafs coaching job, and he promptly won a Cup with the team in 1951. He stayed in the position for a couple more years, but business interests took him away from the NHL, though hockey was never far away from his heart. Primeau was elected to the Hockey Hall of Fame in 1963.

MAPLE LEAF CAREER HIGHLIGHTS

★ Member of Stanley Cup team in 1932
★ Winner of the Lady Byng Trophy in 1932
★ Named to the NHL's Second All-Star Team in 1934
★ Recorded 243 points (66G, 177A) in 310 games as a Leaf

LEAF FACT:

Joe Primeau led the Leafs in assists for five consecutive seasons (1929–30 to 1933–34). No other Toronto player accomplished that feat until Mats Sundin, who led the team in assists for seven straight seasons (1995–96 to 2002–03).

20 LANNY McDONALD

BORN: FEBRUARY 16, 1953 IN HANNA, ALBERTA
POSITION: RIGHT WING
YEARS AS A LEAF: 1973–74 TO 1979–80
SWEATER #: 7
MAPLE LEAF MOMENT: APRIL 29, 1978

LANNY McDONALD WAS certainly aware that the Maple Leafs were looking at him very closely as his draft year approached in 1973. The Leafs were going to draft high as a result of their poor showing in 1972–73, and McDonald was considered one of the best junior players available. The hard-shooting and high-scoring right-winger grew up in Alberta idolizing the Maple Leafs as a child. He recalled standing outside a Calgary arena waiting for Frank Mahovlich to sign autographs. After the Leafs selected him fourth overall and gave him a sizable contract to keep him away from the World Hockey Association, he came to Toronto and sat in a dark and empty Maple Leaf Gardens, soaking in the atmosphere.

His first year as a Leaf was not an easy one; he scored just 14 goals, and recorded only 17 the next season. Questions were being asked, and the Leafs nearly dealt him away, but Toronto coach Red Kelly had faith that McDonald would become a star in the NHL. In 1975–76 he scored 37 times playing on a line with Darryl Sittler. He never looked out of place again. He followed that up with 46 goals the next year, and then had 47 in 1977–78, but he saved his most important goal for the playoffs. The Leafs faced the talented New York Islanders in the first round of the playoffs, and the very tough series would be decided in the seventh game played on April 29, 1978, at Nassau Coliseum in Uniondale, New York.

The Leafs were looking to advance to the semi-finals for the first time in 11 years and hoping to win their first best-of-seven series since their last Stanley Cup win in 1967. Toronto won the sixth game of the series against the Islanders by a 5–2 score at home, but had lost two games in Uniondale in overtime previously. They had to go to extra time again to settle the series on this night, only this time the result would be different. The Islanders opened the scoring, but Toronto defenceman Ian Turnbull, playing the best hockey of his career with Borje Salming out of the lineup due to a serious eye injury, slammed home a shot to even the score. Leafs netminder Mike Palmateer made several great stops to keep the game even at 1–1. The tension rose as the overtime period began. Billy Harris nearly scored early for the Islanders, but Palmateer rescued the Leafs once again. The winner came at the 4:13 mark when Turnbull lofted a high pass that McDonald knocked down at the New York blue line — not an easy thing to do when wearing a face mask to protect a variety of facial injuries. The Leaf winger got a good bounce as a couple of Islanders swatted at the puck but missed. Suddenly, McDonald was in alone on Glenn Resch and picked the far side of the net to put home his patented wrist shot. The ecstatic Leafs leaped over the boards and mobbed an exuberant McDonald.

"I remember saying to myself 'Cut into the middle,' then Turnbull put the pass up high — just the way we'd practised. I knocked it down with my glove at the blue line and the puck bounced off both me and [Denis] Potvin, and I was in all alone," McDonald recounted. "I thought about a backhand, but I haven't had much success with it. Then, I saw a spot just over the top of his [Resch's] glove." The New

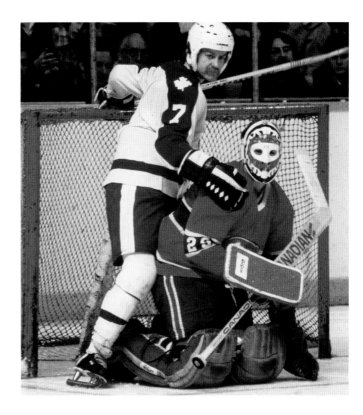

York goalie was thinking the same way. "I thought McDonald was going to his backhand, but I wasn't completely set for his shot," Resch said.

First-year Toronto coach Roger Neilson said, "The nucleus of this club is a gang of guys who have been together about five seasons. Maybe our time has come because we've reached a maturity as players." Turnbull echoed his coach's comments. "In the five years I've been here, we worked hard but couldn't get past the quarter-finals, and it was getting frustrating."

The frustration was over for a little while as McDonald's goal turned the clock back to a time when the Leafs were winning important playoff games.

MAPLE LEAF CAREER HIGHLIGHTS

★ Selected to the NHL's Second All-Star Team in 1977
★ Scored over 40 goals three times as a Leaf
★ Recorded 459 points (219G, 240A) in 477 games
★ Elected to the Hockey Hall of Fame in 1992

LEAF FACT:

Lanny McDonald set a club record for the fastest three goals by one player when he notched a hat trick against Philadelphia in 2:54 during a 5–5 tie at Maple Leaf Gardens on October 16, 1976. McDonald also had a four-goal game that season against the Flyers during the playoffs, but the Leafs lost that game 6–5 in overtime on April 17, 1977.

21 | WENDEL CLARK

BORN: OCTOBER 25, 1966 IN KELVINGTON, SASKATCHEWAN
POSITION: LEFT WING
YEARS AS A LEAF: 1985–86 TO 1993–94; 1995–95 TO 1997–98; 1999–2000
SWEATER #: 17
MAPLE LEAF MOMENT: MAY 27, 1993

THE MAPLE LEAFS WERE very pleased when they were able to draft Wendel Clark first overall at the 1985 entry draft. Leaf management was hoping to find a youngster who could inject some life into the moribund club. The 18-year-old rookie did not disappoint, becoming the talk of Toronto on the way to scoring 34 goals in his first season. He followed that up with a 37-goal effort the following year, but then injuries took over. Clark was frequently in and out of the lineup over the next seven seasons, often missing large chunks of time as he dealt with various ailments (the worst of which was a chronic back injury). When he did play, the five-foot-eleven, 194-pound Clark was always a force to be reckoned with for the opposition. He possessed a wicked wrist shot and an inclination to drop the gloves with devastating consequences for most of those who chose to challenge him to a fight. By the 1992–93 season the Leafs had rebuilt their team under general manager Cliff Fletcher and finally had a coach in Pat Burns who could get the team to play as a cohesive unit. The Leafs had a 44-win season in '92–93 and beat Detroit and St. Louis to start the playoffs. They were leading the Los Angeles Kings 3–2 in the conference final when they made another trip to the west coast, hoping to wrap up the series on May 27, 1993.

Any Leaf fan who watched the sixth game of the series from Los Angeles that evening will never forget it. Clark scored three times in the hotly contested game, only to see his team lose 5–4 in overtime. The game started well for the Leafs when Glenn Anderson scored after just 57 seconds of play. But the Kings tied it before the first period ended, when Tony Granato was allowed to plow into Leaf netminder Felix Potvin and have a goal stand despite his obvious presence in the crease. Clark scored his first goal of the night in the second period when he broke in alone and put a gorgeous backhand drive over the glove of Kelly Hrudey. But by the time the middle frame was over, the Leafs were down 4–2 as the Kings took advantage of numerous power-play opportunities (going four for five on the night) afforded them by referee Kerry Fraser.

The Leafs refused to die. Clark brought them closer with a goal at 11:08 of the third when he took a pass from Bob Rouse and then snapped a shot past Hrudey from near the Kings' blue line. The game was winding down when Potvin made a great save and then sent his team up the ice on a rush by moving the puck ahead. Clark jumped over the boards and skated into the Kings' zone to take a pass from Doug Gilmour. Clark whipped in a wrist shot for his third goal of the night at 18:39 of the third. It looked like the Leafs had all the momentum, but a terrible call on Anderson put the Leafs down a man to end the period and for the start of overtime. The Leafs nearly had the penalty killed off, but Wayne Gretzky was set up right in front of the Leaf net. He made no mistake, ending the game 5–4 for the Kings. The Leafs were furious Gretzky was even on the ice since he had cut Gilmour with his stick (for eight stitches), but there was no penalty called as Fraser let the Kings' superstar get away with it.

Clark's effort was called "Herculean" and "spectacular," but as usual he was modest. "I just got the bounces, that's all," the Leaf captain told reporters after the game. The Leaf leader could have lashed out at reporters who had ridiculed his efforts earlier in the '93 postseason, but Clark was very classy. He scored two more goals in the final game, played at Maple Leaf Gardens, but Gretzky scored three. The Leafs lost 5–4, once again missing a chance to play their ancient rivals Montreal Canadiens in the Stanley Cup final.

MAPLE LEAF CAREER HIGHLIGHTS

★ Drafted first overall by the Maple Leafs in 1985
★ Named captain of the Leafs on August 8, 1991
★ Scored a career-best 46 goals for the Leafs in 1993–94
★ Scored 260 goals and 441 points in 608 career games as a Leaf

LEAF FACT:

The *Sporting News* has been handing out awards to hockey players since the 1967–68 season. The only Leaf ever to win a *Sporting News* award was Wendel Clark, who was named rookie of the year in 1985–86. Clark had 34 goals that year, more than fellow rookies Kjell Dahlin (32), Petr Klima (32), Joel Otto (25) and Mike Ridley (22).

SID SMITH WAS not even aware the Maple Leafs were interested in him, but the team was keeping an eye on the local boy. Smith was blessed with great speed, a good shot and a nose for the net. The five-foot-ten, 173-pound left-winger played high school hockey for De La Salle College in Toronto, even though he was actually attending Central Commerce. He then went to the Oshawa Generals of the OHL to complete his junior hockey in 1944–45. The Leafs signed him in 1946, and he got into 14 games with Toronto in 1946–47 (scoring two goals) but also played for the Quebec Aces (QSHL) and the Pittsburgh Hornets (AHL) that season. He played 31 games for the Leafs (seven goals, 17 points) the next season and 30 games for Pittsburgh, accumulating 40 points. He was called up to the Leafs for the 1948 playoffs but was injured after only two games and had to heal his knee before the Leafs would consider him for their lineup. He went to back to Pittsburgh for the 1948–49 season and recorded a league-best 112 points (55 goals, 57 assists) in 68 games. He only got into one game with the Leafs that year but was called up for the '49 playoffs. Smith had a night to remember when the Leafs played the second game of the Stanley Cup finals on April 10, 1949, in Detroit.

The Leafs had opened the finals on the road and beat the Red Wings 3–2 in overtime. Smith was the hero of the second contest as the Leafs won the game 3–1 and he got all the Toronto tallies. He scored his first of the night at 8:50 of the first period when he put home a rebound by defenceman Garth Boesch and the next one by deflecting home a drive by Leaf rearguard Bill Barilko to give Toronto a 2–0 lead. Smith completed the hat trick late in the second period when he went to the front of the net and took a pass from captain Ted Kennedy that he backhanded past Detroit netminder Harry Lumley. The Red Wings got one goal back in the third period and pulled their goalie late in the game, but the Leafs were able to hold them off without any further scoring. The three goals gave Smith a total of five in the playoffs (he scored two against Boston in the semi-finals) and more importantly, sent the Leafs home with a 2–0 lead in the finals. The Leafs wrapped up their third straight Cup with two wins (both games were 3–1 victories) on home ice.

Smith became a very consistent player for the Leafs, scoring between 22 and 33 goals over the next six seasons. He missed only two games over that same period but then only played in 55 contests in 1955–56. He was back to playing in all 70 games in 1956–57, his last full year as a Maple Leaf. He recorded his third and final regular season hat trick in '56–57 when the Leafs bombed the New York Rangers 14–1 on March 16, 1957, in a game at Maple Leaf Gardens. The 14-goal total established a team record for most goals in one single contest by a Leaf team. Smith scored a goal in each period of the game and also added two assists. Ranger netminder Gump Worsley was so exasperated after the game that he said to his teammates, "It's a good thing you guys didn't go to a dance last night. You wouldn't know enough to check your hats!"

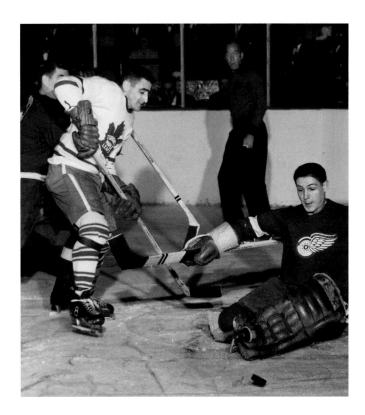

The three goals gave Smith 16 on the year, and he then added another as he scored the game-winning goal in New York the next night. The Leafs missed the playoffs in 1957, and Smith's 17-goal total was the lowest total he had in any full season with Toronto. After he got off to a slow start in 1957–58 (two goals in 12 games) the Leafs offered to trade him to Detroit, but the 32 year old decided to return to senior hockey.

MAPLE LEAF CAREER HIGHLIGHTS

★ Member of three Stanley Cup teams (1948, 1949 and 1951)
★ Two-time winner of the Lady Byng Trophy (1952, 1955)
★ Named to the NHL First All-Star Team once (1955) and the Second Team twice
★ Recorded 369 points (186G, 183A) in 608 games as a Leaf

LEAF FACT:

Playoff hat tricks are rare, and scoring three goals on the road is even more rare. Harvey Jackson recorded the first Leaf playoff hat trick away from home, and Sid Smith had the second when he pulled off the feat against Detroit, 17 years after Jackson's big night. Other Leafs to score three on the road in the postseason include Dave Keon, Lanny McDonald, Ed Olczyk, Wendel Clark and Alex Mogilny.

23 | ALLAN STANLEY

BORN: MARCH 1, 1926 IN TIMMINS, ONTARIO
POSITION: DEFENCE
YEARS AS A LEAF: 1958–59 TO 1967–68
SWEATER #: 26
MAPLE LEAF MOMENT: APRIL 2, 1960

WHEN PUNCH IMLACH took on the role of assistant general manager of the Maple Leafs in August of 1958, he immediately wanted to shore up a poor Toronto defence. Since he was familiar with those in the Boston organization (from where the Leafs had hired him), Imlach sought to acquire a veteran blueliner. It was thought that the Leaf manager was looking at Bob Armstrong, but the Bruins were not interested in parting with him. However, they considered Allan Stanley expendable. Toronto sent defenceman Jim Morrison (a seven-year Leaf) to the Bruins to complete the deal just before the start of the 1958–59 season. Many believed that the Leafs had acquired a 32-year-old veteran who had nothing left, but Stanley would prove them wrong by giving the Leafs a great 10 years of service before his career was over.

Stanley had previously disappointed the fans in New York, Chicago and Boston in his career, mostly due to unrealistic expectations. But Toronto fans came to appreciate "Snowshoes," as Stanley was known (due to his laborious skating style) because he could play solid defence. He was especially good at angling the opposition off to the corners. He could also help out with the attack when needed. The six-foot-two, 195-pound Stanley was at his absolute best in 1960 when the Leafs were trying to make it to the Stanley Cup finals for the second year in a row. Toronto was facing Detroit in the semi-finals, and the series was tied at two games each when the Red Wings came into town on the night of April 2, 1960, to face the Leafs.

Both teams had won games on the road, and each had won games in overtime in this very tight series, but the Leafs were determined to get back home-ice advantage during this Saturday night contest before 14,003 fans. Stanley opened the scoring at the 5:11 mark of the first when he slammed home a pass from Red Kelly right in front of the Detroit net occupied by Terry Sawchuk. He then helped set up a goal by Bert Olmstead that gave the Leafs a 2–0 lead before the end of the first. Detroit tied the game in the second period with a couple of goals before the 12-minute mark, but Stanley scored his second of the night, with assists going to Olmstead and Bob Pulford on the play, to give the Leafs a 3–2 lead. The teams exchanged goals in the first half of the third period to keep it close, but Stanley and George Armstrong set up Larry Regan for a fifth Leaf goal. A late goal by Detroit's Alex Delvecchio made the final score 5–4 for Toronto.

The very next night in Detroit, the Leafs were able to knock out the Red Wings with a 4–2 victory. Pulford paced the Leaf attack with two goals, while Frank Mahovlich and Dick Duff got the others for a Toronto team that scored three times in the third to pull away. Stanley was very much involved in the attack and had one assist on Pulford's second goal of the night. He was also very strong in his own end and did not let any of the Red Wings loose around goaltender Johnny Bower. After the game Stanley said this of his performance in the last two contests: "I was really weary in the first four games [of this series], but I felt good on the weekend."

The victory over Detroit sent the Leafs into the finals for the second consecutive year against the Montreal Canadiens. Stanley offered this opinion: "Our only chance against Montreal is to work our hardest every minute of every game." However, the Habs dispensed with the Leafs in four straight. Veterans like Stanley, who played in 82 playoff games for Toronto, were soon rewarded with three straight Cups in 1962, 1963 and 1964. Stanley and longtime defensive partner Tim Horton were still together in 1967 when the Leafs won their fourth Cup of the decade. Stanley was 42 years of age when he played his final season with the Leafs, the 1967–68 campaign that saw him record 14 points in 64 games.

MAPLE LEAF CAREER HIGHLIGHTS

★ Member of four Stanley Cup teams with Toronto
★ Named to the NHL's Second All-Star Team three times (1960, 1961, 1965)
★ Matched a career-high 10 goals and recorded 33 points in 1959–60
★ Recorded 233 points (47G, 186A) in 633 games

LEAF FACT:

Allan Stanley made it into the Hockey Hall of Fame primarily for his defensive play, but as a Leaf defenceman he also had to take face-offs in his own end. His most famous draw came against Jean Béliveau of the Montreal Canadiens in the last minute of play in the 1967 finals. Stanley tied up Béliveau and the Leafs scored into an open net to clinch the Cup.

24 | RICK VAIVE

BORN: MAY 14, 1959 IN OTTAWA, ONTARIO
POSITION: RIGHT WING
YEARS AS A LEAF: 1979–80 TO 1986–87
SWEATER #: 20 AND 22
MAPLE LEAF MOMENT: MARCH 24, 1982

RICK VAIVE JOINED the Maple Leafs for his first game on February 19, 1980, just one day after he and Bill Derlago were acquired in a deal with Vancouver. Vaive potted two goals in the Leafs' 6–4 win over the Islanders, and he basically never stopped scoring until he was dealt away by the club in 1987. A gifted junior with Sherbrooke in the QMJHL (127 goals over his last two seasons), Vaive turned professional with the Birmingham Bulls of the World Hockey Association for the 1978–79 season (scoring 26 times) but was selected fifth overall by Vancouver in the '79 entry draft after the WHA merged with the NHL. After only 47 games in a Canucks uniform, the rangy six-foot-one, 200-pound right-winger was dealt to the Leafs.

Vaive quickly showed why the Leafs moved quickly to snap him up by displaying his explosive shot and a willingness to take punishment to score goals. He was never afraid to go into the corners and showed a knack for drilling the puck on net as he came down the wing, often netting him a goal. He scored 33 times in his first full season as a Leaf and was named captain at the age of 22 when Darryl Sittler was traded away during the 1981–82 season. Vaive was not mature enough to handle the scrutiny of the media in Toronto at such a young age, but he proved he could lead the team on the ice with a great performance in '81–82, scoring 54 times and totalling 89 points in 77 games. His most memorable goal came on the night of March 24, 1982, when the Leafs hosted the St. Louis Blues.

Vaive had scored four goals in the previous game, when the Leafs beat Chicago 8–5 on home ice, to give him 49 goals on the season. The Toronto club had more on its mind than Vaive's goal-scoring total, as the St. Louis squad was ahead of them in the playoff hunt. The Leafs had to win this game or be eliminated from contention for postseason play. Vaive went to work early and set up Derlago for the opening goal, but the Blues tied the score. The Leafs then went on a power-play. Defenceman Jim Benning got the puck to Derlago, who spotted an open Vaive on his wrong wing. Derlago teed up a backhand pass over the stick of Blues defenceman Guy Lapointe. Vaive did not hesitate as he shot home the puck before goalie Mike Liut could even move, for his 50th of the year at 14:57 of the first period. The Gardens crowd gave Vaive an ovation, as he had just become the first-ever Leaf player to score 50 goals in one season. The Blues went ahead 3–2 in the third period, but Toronto tied it on a goal by Walt Poddubny and then won it with 12 seconds to play when Vaive set up Miroslav Frycer for the winner to keep the Leafs' dim playoff hopes alive. (With only 20 wins and 56 points they did not make it to the postseason.) It was an all-round great night for the 22-year-old Vaive.

"After the other night I thought I might never get this close to 50 again, so make the best of it. Even with the kind of year it's been for the team, it's still a big thrill. It's awfully nice to do it, but it would also be nice to trade in a few goals for points [in the team standings]," Vaive said afterwards.

"My 50th wouldn't have been half as sweet if we didn't win the game."

Toronto coach Mike Nykoluk was enthused about what Vaive was bringing to the Leaf team. "Ricky has helped a great deal in injecting a good attitude in our team, especially since he was named acting captain."

Vaive went on to score 51 goals in 1982–83 and 52 in 1983–84, but the Leafs still did not make the playoffs in either season. Vaive then became a consistent 30-goal scorer the rest of his time as a Leaf, finally getting some playoff action in 1986 and 1987.

MAPLE LEAF CAREER HIGHLIGHTS

★ Holds Leaf team record for most goals in one season with 54
★ Scored 50 or more goals three times as a Leaf
★ Scored 30 or more goals four times with Toronto
★ Recorded 537 points (299G, 238A) in 534 career games with Toronto

LEAF FACT:

Since 1974, the Molson Cup has been awarded to the Maple Leaf player that accumulates the most points by being named one of the three stars of the games during the regular season. Rick Vaive won the award three times, joining two other Leaf captains who also won the award on more than one occasion: Darryl Sittler (four times) and Mats Sundin (three times).

25 | BOB PULFORD

BORN: MARCH 31, 1936 IN NEWTON ROBINSON, ONTARIO
POSITION: CENTRE/LEFT WING
YEARS AS A LEAF: 1956–57 TO 1969–70
SWEATER #: 20
MAPLE LEAF MOMENT: APRIL 25, 1967

WHEN THE MAPLE LEAFS recruited youngster Bob Pulford, they started him out with the Weston Dukes for the 1953–54 season, but he also got into 17 games with the Toronto Marlboros (recording 14 points) during that same year. He was with the Marlboros for the next two seasons (producing 24- and 30-goal campaigns) that both ended with Memorial Cup championships. The sturdy five-foot-eleven, 188-pound centre never played a single game in the minors, joining the Leafs for 65 games during the 1956–57 season, scoring 11 goals and adding 11 assists. Two seasons later he scored 23 for the Leafs and followed that up with 24 the next year. When Red Kelly and Dave Keon joined the team the Leafs boasted the best group of centres in the NHL. The trio helped the Leafs win three consecutive Stanley Cups, and Pulford's contributions to those championships were considerable. Other teams often asked about Pulford's availability for a trade, but coach and general manager Punch Imlach always considered Pulford a solid two-way player who was indispensable to his team. He scored a career-high 28 for the Leafs in 1965–66 but slumped a little the following year when he scored only 17 times. The Leafs barely scraped into the playoffs after the 1966–67 season, but Pulford was ready for the postseason with his new linemates, Peter Stemkowski and Jim Pappin. They were especially good in the finals against Montreal, and on the night of April 25, 1967, they combined to score perhaps the most important goal of the series.

Pulford was playing left wing on his new line, which had been thrown together by King Clancy, who had replaced an ailing Imlach as coach for part of the '66–67 season. The threesome had played very well against the Chicago Black Hawks in the semi-finals but saved their greatest efforts for the Canadiens. Montreal won the first game 6–2, but Stemkowski was instrumental in the Leafs' 3–0 win to even the series. The pivotal third game was scheduled for Maple Leaf Gardens, and fans witnessed a classic that went into double overtime before it was settled. The Canadiens opened the scoring on a power-play with just 2:27 gone in the contest. The Leafs scored on a power-play of their own when Stemkowski put one home. Pappin put Toronto ahead 2–1 in the second before John Ferguson tied it for Montreal. There was no scoring in the third or in the first overtime, as Toronto goalie Johnny Bower held the Leafs in the game. Bower would face 62 shots, while Rogie Vachon took 54 Toronto shots before the fateful drive was delivered.

With a face-off in the Montreal end, the Leafs got possession of the puck. Pappin swept the disk toward the Habs' net. Pulford shook himself free and got in front of the crease. The puck went right to his stick, and he redirected it past a startled Vachon.

"That's probably the most thrilling goal I've scored. It's the first overtime one I've ever had," Pulford said later. "Pappin is the one who got it over to me. If I'd missed that one, it was game over. Just as I turned around, the puck came over and all I had to do was steer it in."

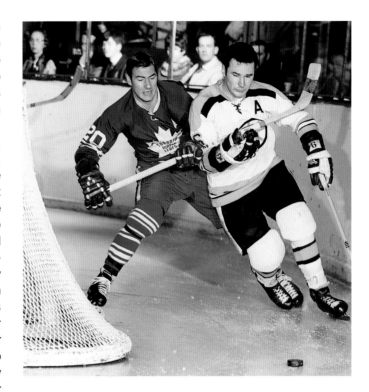

Vachon said he did not see Pulford open. "I'm protecting against Pappin, and I don't even see Pulford on the far side. I couldn't cover all three of them," he said in reference to Pulford and his two linemates. Detroit Red Wing star Gordie Howe was at the game and observed, "They have size, muscle, speed, good moves and are great defenders. When they're not knocking you off the puck, they're driving in for the big goals." Imlach said of his best playoff line, "They're playing big hockey for us. They're giving us the balance that we need."

Pulford finished the '67 playoffs with 11 points in 12 games, while Stemkowski scored five times and Pappin had seven tallies, including the Stanley Cup winner for the Leafs.

MAPLE LEAF CAREER HIGHLIGHTS

★ Member of four Stanley Cup teams with Toronto
★ Recorded four 20-or-more-goal seasons as a Leaf
★ Scored 25 goals and 26 assists in 89 playoff games with the Leafs
★ Recorded 563 points (251G, 312A) in 947 games

LEAF FACT:

When the Leafs won their first Stanley Cup of the sixties, it was Bob Pulford who scored a hat trick in the key fifth game to help give the Leafs a 3–2 series lead. The Leafs won the fifth contest 8–4 on home ice when Pulford scored just 17 seconds into the match, and he had another before the first period was over. He also scored the final goal of the game.

26

RED HORNER

BORN: MAY 28, 1909 IN LYNDEN, ONTARIO
POSITION: DEFENCE
YEARS AS A LEAF: 1928–29 TO 1939–40
SWEATER #: 2, 11 AND 15
MAPLE LEAF MOMENT: DECEMBER 12, 1933

RED HORNER'S FAMILY moved around a little bit when he was a youngster, but by the time he was ten years old they had settled in the Toronto area. At the age of 16 Horner already weighed 160 pounds and was interested in playing hockey. After failing during one tryout he was told he must improve his skating. Frank Selke of the Maple Leafs developed a rapport with the red-haired Horner, and eventually the youngster was good enough to play junior hockey with the Marlboros. He carved out his niche by taking on all comers, playing a physical brand of hockey. Horner was also a leader on the team and was named as captain of the Marlies in 1928. Leaf manager Conn Smythe liked what he saw of the young blueliner, and after watching him play a game on a Saturday afternoon, he told Horner he would be playing with the Leafs that night! The Leafs lost the game 3–2 to Pittsburgh but Horner managed to deck Frank Fredrickson of the Pirates. Even though Horner was penalized on the play, Smythe was delighted with his efforts and knew he had a new NHL player on his team.

Horner got into 22 games for the Leafs in 1928–29 and registered 30 penalty minutes, a total that would rise to 96 the next season. From 1931–32 to the end of his career, Horner never registered less than 82 penalty minutes in any one season. He led the NHL in penalty minutes a remarkable eight straight seasons, and his presence made the Leafs one of the toughest (and most successful) teams in the thirties. On the night of December 12, 1933, Horner came to the aid of a fallen teammate and let the hockey world know that he would not stand idle and watch his team get pushed around.

The game against the Boston Bruins was a rough contest right from the start. Horner got called for tripping, and then he and King Clancy both took runs at Bruin star defenceman Eddie Shore. The first period ended in a 1–1 tie, but trouble seemed to be lurking around the corner. Horner was involved in a scuffle early in the second that featured two players from each team, but cooler heads prevailed. After Horner nailed Shore with a hard smack into the boards, the Bruin was determined to exact some revenge, even though he was woozy from the hit. Shore hit the first Leaf in his way, who happened to be forward Ace Bailey, striking the Toronto player from behind. Bailey's head hit the ice with an ugly thud, and it was obvious he was badly hurt. Shore skated back to his defensive position, but Horner immediately confronted Shore. After a few words were exchanged, the hulking Leaf defenceman punched the Bruin player in the face with such force that Shore hit the ice as well. Both Bailey and Shore were taken off on stretchers, while Horner and Shore each received match penalties. Shore was cut for seven stitches. Bailey, more seriously injured, was taken to hospital for medical attention. Conn Smythe, who was in attendance at the Boston Garden, fought with a fan who suggested Bailey was faking his injury. The fan was struck by a punch thrown by Smythe, suffering a cut near his eye, and his glasses were shattered as well.

After play resumed Toronto scored three times (two goals by Hec Kilrea and one by Joe Primeau) to take home a 4–1 victory, but they had to leave Bailey behind while Boston-area doctors tried to determine the extent of his head injuries. Dr. Ralph Crotty said that Bailey suffered terrific head pains through the night in hospital, but he also added, "His condition is serious but not dangerous." Luckily Dr. Crotty was correct, and Bailey did not die as many in the Leaf organization feared, but he never played hockey again.

Horner was suspended for a short time as a result of his hit on Shore, but it did not change his style one bit — he recorded over 100 minutes in penalties six straight years — but he also contributed offensively, tallying a career-high 24 points in 1937–38.

MAPLE LEAF CAREER HIGHLIGHTS

★ Member of Stanley Cup team in 1932
★ Recorded 17 points (7G, 10A) in 71 playoff games with the Leafs
★ Elected to the Hockey Hall of Fame in 1965
★ Recorded 152 points (42G, 110A) in 490 career games with Toronto

LEAF FACT:

George Reginald "Red" Horner played in the Stanley Cup finals a total of seven times (1932, 1933, 1935, 1936, 1938, 1939 and 1940) as a member of the Maple Leafs but came away a winner only once, in 1932. He also played on five Leaf teams (1932–33, 1933–34, 1934–35 and 1937–38) that had the best regular season record in the NHL.

27

CARL BREWER

BORN: OCTOBER 21, 1938 IN TORONTO, ONTARIO
POSITION: DEFENCE
YEARS AS A LEAF: 1957–58 TO 1964–65; 1979–80
SWEATER #: 2, 18, 25 AND 28
MAPLE LEAF MOMENT: OCTOBER 18, 1958

DEFENCEMAN CARL BREWER was one of the most talented players to ever put on a Maple Leaf uniform, but he was a little different from your average NHL player. A thoughtful and educated man, Brewer did not always mix well with his teammates who liked to unwind with a drink or two. The skilled blueliner did not like to drink, and he also had trouble flying, often meeting up with the team in another city by taking a different method of transportation. On the ice there was no doubting Brewer's value to the team. A fast skater who could move with the puck, Brewer did not put up great offensive numbers, but his effective play was recognized with All-Star selections. The five-foot-ten, 180-pound Brewer was also very aggressive (often around the 100-penalty-minute total), although he did not fight very often despite an ability to get under the skin of the opposition. He was teamed with Bobby Baun on the Leaf defence. The pair of Toronto Marlboro graduates complemented each other perfectly for seven seasons and grew together as young players on a developing team. Brewer joined the team on a full-time basis in 1958–59 (when he still had junior eligibility) and scored his first goal on October 18, 1958, when the Boston Bruins, Stanley Cup finalists the previous spring, came into Toronto for a Saturday night game.

The game against the Bruins was typical of the way Brewer played his entire time with the Maple Leafs. He showed skill, toughness and a little bit of a nasty edge that upset the Boston club. The Bruins opened the scoring in the first period, but Brewer and Dick Duff set up Ron Stewart for a goal in the second to even the score. The Leafs kept pressing in the second period, and the puck went back to Brewer at the Boston blue line after a scramble in front of the net. He trapped the puck from leaving the offensive zone and weaved his way toward the Bruin net, directing a shot that appeared to hit a leg and bounced in for his first-ever NHL goal. But Brewer was not finished causing havoc as he nailed Boston's Bronco Horvath with a solid check that the Bruins claimed was an elbow. (The hit broke Horvath's jaw.) Horvath returned to the game and took a healthy run at Brewer, but he only got a penalty for his efforts. The Bruins tied the contest when Jerry Toppazzini scored his second of the night, but Stewart got his second of the game in the third to give Toronto a 3–2 win. Stewart's winner came on power-play with Horvath in the penalty box for his charge on Brewer. It was the first win of the young season for the Leafs, who had dropped their first three contests.

Boston coach Milt Schmidt was furious after the game, since two of his players had to undergo surgery to fix broken jaws. (Doug Mohns was the other injured Bruin player.) "I can take a defeat," he said, "but not the loss of two players because of elbow checks. And, the Leafs are still using the type of elbow pad that has been outlawed by the league." Brewer insisted that his hit was clean and not an elbow at all, but rather it was his head and shoulder that struck Horvath in the face. There was no penalty on the play to Brewer, whose night featured one goal, one assist and the

wrath of the opposition — a taste of what was to come from the brash Brewer.

Brewer finished second to Montreal's Ralph Backstrom for the rookie of the year award in 1959 and went on to play on three straight Stanley Cup teams for the Leafs before he decided he had had enough of coach Punch Imlach. The All-Star defenceman decided to leave the Leafs during their 1965 training camp, quitting hockey temporarily, and despite efforts to lure him back, Brewer stayed away from the Leafs until he went back to work for Imlach again in 1979–80 at 42 years of age!

MAPLE LEAF CAREER HIGHLIGHTS

★ Member of three Stanley Cup teams
★ Led the NHL in penalty minutes in 1959–60 with 150
★ Named to the NHL's First All-Star Team once (1963) and Second Team twice (1962 and 1965)
★ Recorded 155 points (19G, 136A) in 473 games as a Leaf

LEAF FACT:

Carl Brewer was such a good athlete that he was offered a professional baseball contract by the Cleveland Indians, but his dream was to be a Maple Leaf. His first contract negotiation with Punch Imlach was not easy, but he did get a $16,500 deal over two years plus another $4,000 in bonuses.

28 | NORM ULLMAN

BORN: DECEMBER 26, 1935 IN PROVOST, ALBERTA
POSITION: CENTRE
YEARS AS A LEAF: 1967–68 TO 1974–75
SWEATER #: 9
MAPLE LEAF MOMENT: MARCH 9, 1968

NORM ULLMAN HAD BEEN a Detroit Red Wing for many years, yet during the 1967–68 season he sensed that his days in Motown were numbered. He did not know where he would be dealt, but when he found out it was to the Maple Leafs, Ullman was very pleased to be donning a blue and white sweater. The deal that happened on March 3, 1968, was one of the biggest in hockey history, though both teams were struggling at the time and out of the playoff picture. A bulldog of a forechecker, Ullman's game was built around his determined skating. He always kept his legs in great shape, and he was always focused on succeeding. He could score a goal (16 seasons of 20 or more goals) or make a nice pass to set one up with equal ability, and he was often in the top 10 of NHL scoring. He did all of this with little fanfare, yet he was liked by his teammates for making younger players feel welcome. Ullman came to Toronto along with Paul Henderson (who would be his linemate for many years with the Leafs) and veteran Floyd Smith. The trio got to face their old club just six days after the deal was done when the Red Wings came to Toronto on March 9, 1968, for a Saturday night coast-to-coast broadcast on *Hockey Night in Canada*.

Much of the pre-game talk centred on the return of Frank Mahovlich to Maple Leaf Gardens, where he had starred for many years before being sent to Detroit in the big deal. Leaf coach and general manager Punch Imlach, who engineered the trade with Sid Abel of Detroit, felt like crawling under the bench when Mahovlich opened the scoring at 7:41 of the first by beating Bruce Gamble in the Toronto net. The Big M got a standing ovation from the Toronto crowd. Gary Unger, another ex-Leaf involved in the trade, scored early in the second stanza (assisted by Mahovlich) to give the visitors a commanding 4–0 lead, and the Toronto crowd was not in a good mood. But then Ullman went to work, scoring the Leafs' first goal of the night and setting up Smith (stealing the puck from Mahovlich) for another before the second was over. The revived Leafs stormed out in the third and got goals from Dave Keon and Ron Ellis to tie the game before the period was five minutes old. At the 6:05 mark, Ullman scored his second of the night to give the Leafs their first lead of the game with his 32nd goal of the season. Detroit tied it, but Keon and Mike Walton (on a penalty shot) scored to give Toronto a wild 7–5 victory.

The game in March of '68 was not the only time Ullman got some revenge against his old club. The Leafs had another wild game against Detroit on January 2, 1971, when the Leafs obliterated a very disinterested Red Wing team by a 13–0 score (setting a club record for the highest-scoring shutout victory). Ullman opened the scoring in this game with less than three minutes gone, and the floodgates opened. Ullman also scored the Leafs' 11th goal of the evening in the third period and assisted on both of Henderson's goals. In total the Leafs recorded 35 scoring points — 13 goals and 22 assists — and the game marked the Leafs' seventh straight win at home. Mahovlich, a 49-goal scorer for Detroit in 1969–70, was still with the Red Wings and left the game

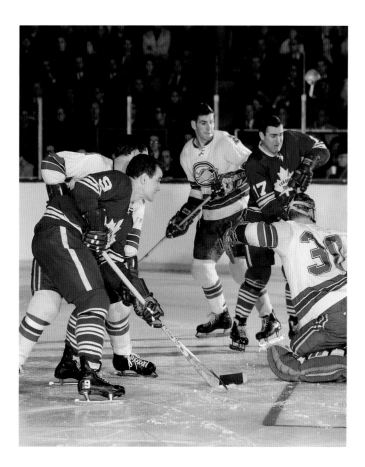

early. Eight days later, Mahovlich was dealt to the Montreal, and he would go on to star in the 1971 playoffs for the Stanley Cup winning Canadiens.

Early in the 1971–72 season during a game against the New York Rangers, Ullman became the first player to record his 1,000th career point (an assist) in a Maple Leaf uniform. Ullman continued to perform well for the Leafs until he left the team after the 1974–75 season.

MAPLE LEAF CAREER HIGHLIGHTS

★ Led the Leafs in goals (35), assists (42) and points (77) in 1968–69
★ Led the Leafs in points in 1970–71 (with 85) and 1971–72 (with 73)
★ Recorded three career hat tricks with the Leafs
★ Recorded 471 points (166G, 305A) in 535 career games with Toronto

LEAF FACT:

Norm Ullman led the Leafs in assists for four consecutive seasons between 1968–69 and 1971–72, and then again in 1973–74 when he had 47 helpers (and 69 points) in 78 games. He was elected to the Hockey Hall of Fame in 1982.

29 | **DICK DUFF**

BORN: FEBRUARY 18, 1936 IN KIRKLAND LAKE, ONTARIO
POSITION: LEFT WING
YEARS AS A LEAF: 1954–55 TO 1963–64
SWEATER #: 9
MAPLE LEAF MOMENT: APRIL 22, 1962

DICK DUFF COULD ALWAYS score goals, and the Maple Leafs were so desperate for some offence in the mid-fifties that the scrappy left-winger (5′9″, 166 pounds) got no time in the minor leagues to hone his game. The St. Michael's graduate proved that he did not really need any seasoning by scoring 18 times as a rookie in 68 games for the 1955–56 edition of the Leafs. Duff then scored 26 goals in each of his next two years and got his points total up to 49 in the 1957–58 season. The Leafs were still very much a floundering club early in the 1958–59 season, but Duff managed to score 29 goals and was instrumental in the Toronto drive to the playoffs in '59. He scored the winning goal against Detroit on the final night of the season to secure for the Leafs the final spot in postseason, and scored an overtime winner in the finals against Montreal. Duff's goal scoring then started to decline somewhat (not scoring more than 19 in subsequent seasons as a Leaf), but he still saved his best performances for those times when everything was on the line. One of his many clutch goals came on April 22, 1962, at Chicago Stadium, with the Stanley Cup hanging in the balance.

The defending Cup champion Black Hawks trailed the Leafs 3–2 in the '62 finals but were very confident they would return to Toronto for a seventh game. Chicago Stadium was a tough building to win in, and the Leafs still had not proven they could win the big game. It was an intense contest throughout, deadlocked 0–0 at the start of the third period. Glenn Hall in the Black Hawk net (27 saves to that point in the game) and Don Simmons (12 shots) in the Leaf goal had turned back every drive directed their way. The Leafs were hungry to end their long Cup drought, but a giveaway by Duff in the Leaf end went right to superstar Bobby Hull, who made no mistake to give Chicago a 1–0 lead. The Stadium crowd went wild with delight and delayed the game for about 10 minutes.

The stoppage gave the Leafs a chance to regroup, and they resumed their attack on the Black Hawk net. Bob Nevin scored almost immediately to tie the game for the Leafs, and then a penalty to Chicago's Eric Nesterenko gave the Leafs a chance to take the lead. Tim Horton set up Duff on a couple of chances, and the second attempt proved to be successful, as he beat Hall with a drive to make it 2–1. Horton took a late penalty, but the Leafs would not be denied on this night and held Chicago off the board until time ran out. The celebration was on, as Simmons raced from his net and jumped on the first teammate he saw.

In the dressing room after the Cup had been presented to the Leafs, Duff spoke about his winning goal. "I really drove that winning goal home," he said. "I saw a little net as Hall came rushing out and I just put everything I had in the shot. This team has come a long way, and we've got a lot of guys around that other people didn't think were good enough to win a Stanley Cup."

One of those players Duff spoke about was defensive stalwart Allan Stanley, who commented, "I've been waiting 14 years for this night. I guess we choked that homer tag

down people's throat. We did it right in [the Black Hawks'] own backyard, hit them where it hurt most, and it feels wonderful. I'll be back next season to help defend the Cup." Leaf goalie Johnny Bower chimed in, "I've got one more good season left, and Don Simmons will be around to spell me off. He did a great job for us tonight." Toronto captain George Armstrong added, "Tim Horton and I have been waiting 10 years for this. What a night! I even took a sip of champagne, my first drink in over five seasons and last until we win the Cup again next season."

The Leafs, with Dick Duff playing a key role, did defend their championship successfully in 1963.

MAPLE LEAF CAREER HIGHLIGHTS

★ Member of two Stanley Cup teams with Toronto
★ Recorded 37 points (14G, 23A) in 54 playoff games
★ Recorded 339 points (174G, 165A) in 582 games
★ Elected to the Hockey Hall of Fame in 2006

LEAF FACT:

Dick Duff scored his 100th career goal on October 17, 1959, when the Leafs defeated Boston 3–0 at Maple Leaf Gardens. (Ted Hampson assisted on the play.) Duff hit the milestone in his 280th game as a Maple Leaf.

30 | RON ELLIS

BORN: JANUARY 8, 1945 IN LINDSAY, ONTARIO
POSITION: RIGHT WING
YEARS AS A LEAF: 1963–64 TO 1974–75; 1977–78 TO 1980–81
SWEATER #: 11, 8 AND 6
MAPLE LEAF MOMENT: MARCH 4, 1978

RON ELLIS TURNED professional when he joined the Maple Leafs at the age of 19 for the 1964–65 season, despite the fact that he had one more year of junior eligibility left. He had played in his first NHL game with Toronto in 1963–64 (against the Montreal Canadiens) but really made his mark with the junior Marlboros (who won the Memorial Cup that season) by scoring 46 goals in the regular season and then adding 28 points in 18 postseason games. The Leafs wanted to add some youth to their veteran-laden team that had just won three straight Stanley Cups, and Ellis was the best prospect in the system. He did not disappoint, scoring 23 goals as a rookie, the first of 11 seasons of 20 or more goals. Ellis was a major contributor to the Leafs' surprise Cup win in 1967 and was year in and year out one of the most reliable players on the Toronto roster. He quit hockey after a 32-goal season in 1974–75 but returned to the Leafs for the 1977–78 season. On March 4, 1978, in a home game against the Vancouver Canucks, Ellis reached a major milestone, the last of a solid NHL career.

The Canucks checked the Leafs closely all night long and got off to a good start when rookie Jere Gillis opened the scoring in the first period. The Leafs came out much stronger in the second period and scored three consecutive goals to take a 3–1 lead. Darryl Sittler got the first for Toronto, while rookie Ron Wilson scored his first-ever NHL goal to give the Leafs the lead. Ellis got his 300th career goal when he took a drop pass from centre Stan Weir and drilled a shot from about 35 feet out that beat Curt Ridley in the Canuck net. (Leaf defenceman Brian Glennie also earned an assist on the goal.) The Leafs came off the bench to congratulate the veteran Leaf right-winger, but the Canucks were not going to go quietly. Hilliard Graves and former Leaf Mike Walton tied the score for Vancouver, but a late goal by Lanny McDonald secured a 4–3 win for the Leafs. It was a special night for Ellis, and 16,485 fans went home happy.

The goal marked only the second time to that date that a Leaf had scored 300 or more goals for the team (the other was Dave Keon, who had 365 when he left Toronto). Ellis spoke of his goal after the contest: "Possibly a third of my goals were scored from that area. I remember my first one was against Boston [on October 17, 1964, at Maple Leaf Gardens] with Eddie Johnston in goal. Frank Mahovlich sent the pass to me and I shot it from right there [the right wing about 30 feet out]," Ellis recounted. A photo of Ellis holding the puck from his first goal against the Bruins hung in the lobby of the Gardens for many years. The tally against Vancouver was the 24th of the season for Ellis, and getting his 300th career marker was a goal he had set for his comeback year. "Now the main thing is to finish as high as we can [in the standings]. If a few more goals come my way after this, it's all gravy."

Under coach Roger Neilson the Leafs had one of their best seasons in '77–78, finishing with 92 points and 41 victories. Ellis tallied 26 goals and 50 points in 80 games during the season and added three goals in the playoffs, which saw the Leafs upset the New York Islanders in a tough seven-game series. Ellis played with the Leafs until midway through the 1980–81 season. He is the last Leaf player to retire having played his entire career in Toronto.

91

MAPLE LEAF CAREER HIGHLIGHTS

★ Led the Leafs in goals scored in 1966–67 with 22
★ Scored one goal when Leafs won the Stanley Cup on May 2, 1967
★ Scored a career-high 35 goals in 1969–70
★ Scored 332 goals and 640 points in 1,034 career games

LEAF FACT:

The Leafs have only retired two sweater numbers in their history — 5 and 6. Ace Bailey, who wore number 6 prior to a career-ending injury, asked that his number be given to Ron Ellis prior to the start of the 1968–69 season because he respected the way Ellis played the game. The number was put out of circulation once again when Ellis retired.

31 | BOB BAUN

BORN: SEPTEMBER 9, 1936 IN LANIGAN, SASKATCHEWAN
POSITION: DEFENCE
YEARS AS A LEAF: 1956–57 TO 1966–67; 1970–71 TO 1972–73
SWEATER #: 21 AND 26
MAPLE LEAF MOMENT: APRIL 23, 1964

BOB BAUN PLAYED his first game as a Maple Leaf on November 29, 1956, and immediately made an impression by going after Henri Richard and Jean Béliveau of the hometown Montreal Canadiens. Baun ended up playing 20 games for the Leafs in '56–57 (recording five assists and 37 penalty minutes) and served notice he was going to be a big part of Toronto's new-look club in the late fifties. Teamed with Al MacNeil on the blue line of the Toronto Marlboros, the sturdy five-foot-nine, 182-pound Baun was part of a Memorial Cup win in 1956. The hard-rock defender used a low centre of gravity to deliver devastating bodychecks that kept the opposition on alert at all times. Early in his career Baun would go out of his way to line up a hit, but as he gained more experience, Baun would not take himself out of the play to deliver a crushing blow. He developed his shot from the point by shooting as many pucks as he could during practice. Being paired with the talented Carl Brewer seemed to get the best out of the youngster. Baun was also known for having an incredible pain threshold, and that was never more evident than on the night of April 23, 1964, when the Leafs played in Detroit during the Stanley Cup finals.

The Red Wings sensed that their long Cup drought (since 1955) was going to come to an end at the Detroit Olympia as they led the Leafs 3–2 in games, but it was Bob Pulford who opened the scoring for Toronto. However, Detroit scored two in the second to take the lead before Pulford scored once again to tie it. Gordie Howe scored on Toronto's Johnny Bower to give the Red Wings the lead one more time, but Billy Harris got that one back for the Leafs to even the score by the end of the second period. There was plenty of tension, but no one could score by the end of the third, sending the game into overtime. There was one significant play before the third period came to a close that would affect the game in the extra session. With less than seven minutes to play Baun went down to the ice after he blocked a Detroit drive right on the ankle. He was lifted off the ice on a stretcher, unable to put any weight on his leg. Somehow he came back to finish the third period, but now he had to figure out a way to play in the overtime.

The doctors attending Baun taped his ankle tightly and then administered a shot of painkiller, allowing the defenceman to join his teammates for the start of the extra period. On his first shift out on the ice, Baun had the puck come to him at the point on a Detroit clearing attempt. He quickly let go a shot that hit the stick of Red Wing defenceman Bill Gadsby and deflected over the shoulder of Detroit goaltender Terry Sawchuk just 1:43 into overtime. The Leafs rushed out to mob the hero of the night, and Baun leapt in the air in celebration.

Baun explained how he got hurt and that there was no way he was going to stay out of the game: "There was this face-off in our end and I took it with Howe. Then I wheeled and my leg just turned into cream cheese. I collapsed and the next thing I knew they were carrying me off. I want it known that it was my decision to get back to the game after being hurt."

"Nothing could have stopped Baun," Leaf coach Punch Imlach said after the game. "He had a charge in him that would have blown up the rink." As for the winning goal, Sawchuk provided the best summation. "It's simple. Baun's shot hit Gadsby's stick and went past me. I couldn't move on it. That's all. You saw the game."

Baun made himself scarce during the off-day but showed up on Saturday night to play his regular shift as the Leafs took their third straight Cup with a 4–0 win on home ice. Later it was revealed that he had played the balance of the sixth game and all of game seven with a small broken bone in his foot, an effort made possible by heavy taping, shots of painkiller and heroic determination.

MAPLE LEAF CAREER HIGHLIGHTS

★ Member of four Stanley Cup teams
★ Compiled 1,155 career penalty minutes as a Leaf
★ Played in 92 playoff games for the Leafs (recording 15 points)
★ Recorded 169 points in 739 career games with Toronto

LEAF FACT:

Bob Baun was on two Memorial Cup-winning teams during his junior career with the Toronto Marlboros (1955 and 1956). Other prominent Leafs on those teams who went on to help Toronto to Stanley Cup wins were Billy Harris ('55), Carl Brewer ('56), Bob Nevin ('56) and Bob Pulford ('55 and '56).

32 | ACE BAILEY

BORN: JULY 3, 1903 IN BRACEBRIDGE, ONTARIO
POSITION: RIGHT WING
YEARS AS A LEAF: 1926–27 TO 1933–34
SWEATER #: 6, 12 AND 8
MAPLE LEAF MOMENT: MARCH 21, 1931

COACHES ARE VERY important in developing players, and in the case of Irvine "Ace" Bailey his mentor was Mike Rodden. Bailey had started out playing hockey as a goaltender, and when that did not go well he switched to defence. Rodden told Bailey his future in hockey was as a forward, so the five-foot-ten, 160-pound player moved over to right wing, staying there until his premature retirement in 1933. Bailey was determined to succeed, and soon his good two-way play was noticed by hockey scouts. He played junior hockey in Toronto and senior hockey in Peterborough. When Rodden was hired as coach of the Toronto St. Patricks he brought Bailey with him, and the youngster scored 15 goals and totalled 28 points in 42 games in 1926–27. He was one of the few players to survive the new management when Conn Smythe purchased the franchise and renamed the team the Maple Leafs. Beginning in 1928–29, Bailey put together three consecutive seasons of 20 or more goals, including a league-leading 22 in '28–29. The 1930–31 campaign saw Bailey score a career-high 23 markers, and one of the best nights of his career occurred on March 21, 1931, against the Ottawa Senators.

The Saturday night contest at the Mutual Street Arena saw the Leafs outlast the Senators by a score of 9–6, the many goals making it an entertaining game for the 4,000 fans in attendance. The Senators came out strong and built up a 3–1 lead. Bailey got the Leafs' only goal of the first, but the Ottawa side responded with three tallies to take control of the game. Bailey led the Leafs back with two markers in the second period to even the score, but Ottawa regained the lead before the period ended. The third period witnessed a scoring explosion with the Leafs scoring six times (including another by Bailey and three by Charlie Conacher), while the Senators could only respond with two tallies of their own. The Leafs scored all their goals on netminder Alex Connell, while taking 45 shots during the game. The four-goal effort by Bailey was the only time he recorded that many goals in a game.

The Leafs were disappointed when the Chicago Black Hawks knocked them out of the '31 playoffs in two games, outscoring Toronto 4–3. The following season saw the Leafs move into Maple Leaf Gardens and win their first Stanley Cup in the new building. Toronto knocked out the Black Hawks and the Montreal Maroons (both in a total-goals format) to reach the final against the New York Rangers. The Leafs won the first two games of the best-of-five series and came home in position to wrap up the championship on Gardens ice on April 9, 1932. Toronto got two goals from Andy Blair to open the game and then added another in the second period to go up 3–0. The Rangers finally got one back before the second was over, but Frank Finnigan and Bailey scored early in the third to give the Leafs some breathing room. New York scored three more times to get close, but another Leaf goal from Bob Gracie ended any hope of a comeback and gave Toronto a 6–4 victory. Bailey's third-period goal ended up being the winning tally, as he combined with Hap Day and Conacher to score the decisive marker.

Bailey's career was cut short when he was brutally attacked by the Bruins' Eddie Shore in a 1933 contest played in Boston. A fractured skull, at first feared to be life-threatening, brought an end to the career of one of the best players in the early days of Toronto Maple Leaf history. His sweater number 6 was retired by the Leafs as a result of his injury. Bailey tried his hand at coaching (at the University of Toronto) but really became a fixture around the Gardens as a penalty box operator during Leaf games. The Leafs finally raised a banner in his honour in 1992, but unfortunately the Hall of Fame player had already passed away.

MAPLE LEAF CAREER HIGHLIGHTS

★ Member of Stanley Cup team in 1932
★ Led the NHL in points in 1928–29 with 32
★ Scored Stanley Cup-winning goal in 1932
★ Recorded 193 points (111G, 82A) in 313 games

LEAF FACT:

When the Maple Leafs won the 1931 Stanley Cup they did not skate around the arena with the trophy. Instead a microphone was brought out near the penalty box and the Toronto players skated over there to speak to the Gardens crowd. Coach Dick Irvin spoke first, next manager Conn Smythe, and then captain Hap Day, followed by the rest of the Leaf players. Most of the crowd remained to cheer each of their heroes after he said a few words. Fans listening at home on the radio could hear the comments as well.

33 | GORD DRILLON

BORN: OCTOBER 23, 1914 IN MONCTON, NEW BRUNSWICK
POSITION: RIGHT WING
YEARS AS A LEAF: 1936–37 TO 1941–42
SWEATER #: 12 AND 21
MAPLE LEAF MOMENT: MARCH 19, 1938

BY THE 1936–37 SEASON, Toronto left-winger Charlie Conacher was beginning to show signs of wear and tear. Replacing the Big Bomber was no easy task, but it was a task that fell to Gord Drillon. The six-foot-two, 178-pound right-winger was called up from Syracuse of the American Hockey League and was placed on a line with Syl Apps and Buzz Boll. Drillon quickly showed that he was a more than adequate replacement by scoring 16 goals and 33 points in 41 games. For the next six seasons Drillon would make his mark on Maple Leaf history. It was true that Drillon was not the best checker in the NHL, but he could score from just about anywhere on the ice. Drillon had a deft touch around the net, and playing alongside Apps certainly helped him produce great numbers. The 1937–38 season was memorable for Drillon, who led the NHL in scoring with 52 points (26 goals, 26 assists), while linemate Apps finished second with 50 points. The scoring title was not settled until the last weekend of the season when the Leafs played two games against the New York Americans, the first to be played in Toronto on March 19, 1938.

Going into the final two contests of the '37–38 season, Drillon had a three-point lead on Apps for the scoring title (50 to 47). The Leafs wanted to tighten up on defence, but that did not work out so well in the first game, even though they won the contest 8–5 before 9,434 fans at Maple Leaf Gardens. The Leafs were up 3–1 going into the third period, and then the teams combined to score nine times in the final stanza. Drillon picked up an assist in the third when Bob Davidson scored, nudging in a Drillon rebound past Americans' goalie Earl Robertson. Apps also assisted on the play, giving him two helpers on the night and bringing him to within two points of the leader. Drillon actually scored a goal in this contest on a penalty shot in the second period, but the Americans were able to convince the referee they were not ready and forced the shot to be taken again. Drillon missed on the second attempt and suffered a leg injury late in the game. He made the trip to New York for the rematch on Sunday night and scored a goal in the first period to give Toronto a 2–0 lead. Apps set up the goal by splitting the American defence and slipping a pass over to Drillon on the right wing. It was the last goal of the night for the Leafs, who lost the game 4–2, but Drillon hung on to his league-high point total, edging out Apps by two points.

The first-place Leafs easily dispatched the Bruins in the playoffs but were shockingly upset by Chicago in the finals. Drillon did have a great postseason, with seven goals and eight points in seven games. The next season saw Drillon play in only 40 games, scoring 18 times. The Leafs once again made it to the finals, but they lost to Boston. Drillon was outstanding in the postseason with 13 points in 10 games. In 1939–40, Drillon scored 21 goals and totalled 40 points, but another loss in the finals made the Stanley Cup seem an elusive dream.

The 1940–41 season saw Drillon lead his team in goals (23) and points (44), but a quick elimination from the playoffs put another damper on the season. Drillon played his last season in Toronto in 1941–42, and he once again netted 23

for the second year in a row and totalled 41 points (good for eighth overall). He was also named to the Second All-Star Team. However, the playoffs were a personal disaster for Drillon, who could not get going, and a benching in the finals against Detroit ended his days in Toronto. The Leafs finally did get going after they were down three games to none. Drillon was finally a part of a Cup-winning team, but ironically the team won it all with its top scorer not playing.

MAPLE LEAF CAREER HIGHLIGHTS

★ Led the Leafs in goals scored four times
★ Named an NHL First Team All-Star twice (1938, 1939)
★ Elected to the Hockey Hall of Fame in 1975
★ Recorded 244 points (127G, 117A) in 262 games with Toronto

LEAF FACT:

Gord Drillon was one of the league's best point producers during his time with the Maple Leafs. He finished in the NHL's top 10 scorers four times. In addition to his first place finish in 1937–38, he was fourth in 1939–40 and third in 1940–41.

34 | TERRY SAWCHUK

BORN: DECEMBER 28, 1929 IN WINNIPEG, MANITOBA
POSITION: GOALTENDER
YEARS AS A LEAF: 1964–65 TO 1966–67
SWEATER #: 24 AND 30
MAPLE LEAF MOMENT: APRIL 15, 1967

GOALTENDER TERRY SAWCHUK was 35 years old when the Maple Leafs selected him from the Detroit roster during the 1964 intra-league draft, even though Toronto had defeated him and the Wings in a seven-game Stanley Cup final the previous spring. Leaf coach and general manager Punch Imlach had great faith in Sawchuk's abilities, and knew he needed someone to share the goaltending duties with 40-year-old Johnny Bower. In his first year with the Leafs, Sawchuk played in 36 games and, together with Bower, allowed the fewest goals in the NHL (173 in 70 games). Injuries held Sawchuk back for the next two seasons, though he posted a record of 15-5-4 in 28 games during 1966-67. However, Sawchuk's time in Toronto will be best remembered for his performance in the '67 postseason, especially for one Saturday afternoon game at the Chicago Stadium on April 15, 1967.

The Leafs finished the '66-67 campaign with some good play after staggering through most of the regular season. They were expected to be no match for the first-place Chicago Black Hawks, who finished 17 points ahead of third-place Toronto. Chicago had no trouble in the opening game, taking the Leafs 5-2. Sawchuk did not have a good game and even knocked one puck into his own net. The second game was a different story, as the Leafs tied the series with a 3-1 victory. The heat in the building was getting to Sawchuk, and he felt he lost 10 pounds during the game. Nothing seemed to bother the Leafs when they got back home, as they won the third game 3-1 to take the lead in the series. But Chicago dug deep, rallying for a 4-3 win to even the series once again. Although Sawchuk played well, especially in the second period, the Leaf goalie was bruised pretty badly, forcing Imlach to turn to Bower for the all-important fifth game.

Bower was extremely shaky in the first period and gave up two goals. Imlach called him over to the bench, and Bower agreed this was not going to be his day. Sawchuk asked if he could start the second period rather than go in cold, so Bower hung on to finish the period with the score tied 2-2. Sawchuk was greeted by a Bobby Hull howitzer early in the second that sent the Leaf goalie down to the ice. The shot appeared to hit Sawchuk in the shoulder and knocked him flat, as Hull had the opportunity to wind up for one of his lethal blasts. Leaf trainer Bobby Haggert came on to the ice to check the Leaf netminder and asked Sawchuk if he could continue. "I stopped the shot, didn't I," he was reported as saying. He stayed in the game, even though the snickering Black Hawk players thought he was all done. The Chicago taunts only served to motivate Sawchuk, who put on a brilliant display while the Leafs got a couple of goals to take the game 4-2.

After the game the Chicago players were using words like "brilliant," "fantastic" and "great" to describe Sawchuk's performance. Hull said he was worried he might have hit Sawchuk in the throat, and the Leaf netminder was asked if he saw the shot. "Are you kidding? All you do is hope it hits you. There's no skill in that," he replied modestly. He was still

feeling the sting of the game. "I feel 57 not 37 [years of age]. Sometimes you get lucky. I move out to cut down the angle and the puck hits me. Lucky." Before he hit the showers he added, "I'd like to leave hockey like that. In good style."

Sawchuk did not have to be as great in the next game, which Toronto took 3-1, putting them into the finals against Montreal. He was superlative again during both his wins in the finals, giving the Leafs their fourth Cup of the decade. It was the last great moment of a truly stellar career.

MAPLE LEAF CAREER HIGHLIGHTS

★ Shared Vezina Trophy with Johnny Bower in 1964-65
★ Member of Stanley Cup team in 1966-67
★ Won Stanley Cup-clinching game 3-1 on May 2, 1967
★ Posted a 42-29-14 career record with the Leafs with four shutouts

LEAF FACT:

Terry Sawchuk recorded 103 career shutouts, securing his 100th while he was with the Leafs. It came against Chicago on March 3, 1967, when the Leafs beat the Black Hawks 3-0. "This is my Centennial project and I was beginning to think I'd never make it," he said of the milestone.

35

HARRY LUMLEY

BORN: NOVEMBER 11, 1926 IN OWEN SOUND, ONTARIO
POSITION: GOALTENDER
YEARS AS A LEAF: 1952–53 TO 1955–56
SWEATER #: 1
MAPLE LEAF MOMENT: MARCH 11, 1954

KNOWN AS "APPLE CHEEKS" for his boyish looks, Harry Lumley won a Stanley Cup with the Red Wings in 1950 (knocking off the Maple Leafs in the semi-finals), and his six full seasons in Detroit proved he was a very capable big league goalie. The Red Wings first signed him when he was 16 years old to fill in for players gone to fight in the Second World War. He twice led the league in wins and once in shutouts but was dealt to the Chicago Black Hawks because a goalie named Terry Sawchuk was primed to take over the Detroit netminding duties. Chicago was not a great place to play hockey in the early fifties, and Lumley's win totals plummeted to 12 and 17 in his two seasons as a Black Hawk. At about the same time, the Toronto Maple Leafs were no longer content with the goaltending of Al Rollins and had an interest in acquiring Lumley. The Maple Leafs liked the fact that the burly (six-foot, 195-pound) Lumley was a tough competitor who was not above chewing out a teammate if he made a mistake that led to a goal. They also liked Lumley's talent for stopping the puck and sent Rollins along with Cal Gardner, Ray Hannigan and Gus Mortson to Chicago for his playing rights in September of 1952. It was quite a lot to give up for the slumping goalie, but with the defensive-minded Maple Leafs playing in front of him, Lumley regained his old form quickly.

The Leafs built their team around defensive play in the mid-fifties. This produced some dull, low-scoring playoff teams that never got any farther than the semi-finals. Some nights all the Leafs had was a terrific Lumley in goal. He lost none of his feisty nature and was still chopping down any opposing forwards who dared to venture into his crease. Leaf general manager Hap Day would fine him for penalties, but coaches like King Clancy would pay the fines for Lumley since he was the Leafs' best player. On the night of March 11, 1954, Lumley made Leaf history when he shut out the Canadiens in the Forum.

The Leafs had tied Montreal 0–0 the last time the two teams played at the Forum in late February, with Lumley in goal for the shutout. The Leaf netminder played in all 70 regular season games in 1953–54, so he would face the Habs once again on this evening. He was peppered with 30 shots in the first two periods, but the Canadiens still could not score a goal. Lumley was especially sharp in the second frame when he stopped Dickie Moore, Ken Mosdell, Lorne Davis and Tom Johnson in rapid-fire fashion. He might have made his best save against Jean Béliveau when he was able to get a skate on a drive that skittered off the goal post and into the corner of the rink. As the shots were bouncing off Lumley, the Leafs got goals from Ted Kennedy, Jim Thomson (his first tally in 208 games) and Tod Sloan to seal a 3–0 victory. The Leafs checked tightly in the third, giving Montreal only four shots on goal, but a couple were difficult drives from Maurice Richard. Lumley also took a penalty during the game when Doug Harvey of the Canadiens ran into his crease and the Leaf netminder grabbed Harvey's stick for a holding call. It was the 13th shutout of the season for Lumley, breaking the

club record held by the legendary Lorne Chabot.

In each of 1952–53 and 1953–54, Lumley led the NHL in shutouts (with 10 and 13 respectively), and he won a Vezina Trophy with a miniscule 1.86 goals-against average as a Leaf in 1954. By the 1955–56 season the Leafs were back to being a fourth-place team, and Lumley's play slipped a little (21–28–10 in 69 games played) from previous years. He was sold to Chicago along with the disappointing Eric Nesterenko in May of 1956 for $40,000. He played with the Buffalo Bisons of the AHL for a couple of years before the Boston Bruins acquired him in 1958.

MAPLE LEAF CAREER HIGHLIGHTS

★ Led the NHL in shutouts twice as a Leaf
★ Named to the NHL's First All-Star Team twice (1954 and 1955)
★ Elected to the Hockey Hall of Fame in 1980
★ Recorded 104 wins and 34 shutouts in 267 games with Toronto

LEAF FACT:

Goaltender Harry Lumley won the Vezina Trophy on the last night of the season (March 21, 1954), even though the Leafs lost the contest 6–1 to Detroit. The Toronto tally, scored by Jim Thomson against Terry Sawchuk of the Red Wings, gave Lumley the trophy by a single goal.

36

HARRY WATSON

BORN: MAY 6, 1923 IN SASKATOON, SASKATCHEWAN
POSITION: LEFT WING
YEARS AS A LEAF: 1946–47 TO 1954–55
SWEATER #: 4
MAPLE LEAF MOMENT: APRIL 19, 1951

WHEN THE MAPLE LEAFS acquired Harry Watson from the Detroit Red Wings they were not quite sure where he would fit in on the team. There was talk that the six-foot, 203-pound Watson would be tried on defence, but the Leafs quickly put an end to that experiment and instead slotted him on a line with Syl Apps and Bill Ezinicki, creating a formidable trio. Watson could shoot the puck hard and skated well for a man of his size. He was also a gentle sort who did not use his body to intimidate the opposition, but all were wary about getting him upset. For instance, the normally mild-mannered left-winger went after Boston defenceman Murray Henderson during a playoff game, and the results were devastating for the Bruin rearguard, who had to leave the game with a smashed nose. Another time he tangled with some of the Montreal Canadiens, and when he cornered Maurice Richard of the Habs, the Rocket quickly let it be known he did not want to fight the Leaf winger.

With some room to operate on the ice, Watson strung together consistent seasons as a Maple Leaf by scoring 19, 21, 26, 19 and 18 goals during his first five years with Toronto. He helped the Leafs to four Stanley Cups, the last of which came in 1951 when the Leafs and the Canadiens met in the finals. Every game in the series had gone into overtime, as, on the night of April 19, 1951, the two teams squared off in the fourth game at the Montreal Forum.

The Leafs were up 2–1 in games and were looking to put a stranglehold on the series. Toronto's Sid Smith opened the scoring after just 38 seconds of play when Ted Kennedy sent him a pass from the corner and Smith knocked it past Gerry McNeil in the Canadien net. Montreal tied it up on a goal by Maurice Richard at 14:41 of the first, but Howie Meeker, assisted by Watson, got that one back for Toronto, who took a 2–1 lead into the third period. The Leafs tried to nurse the lead all the way behind the superlative netminding of Al Rollins. But Elmer Lach tied it for Montreal with just over six minutes to play, and the Habs pressed hard for a game winner before 14,452 screaming fans. Rollins turned back all the drives, and for the fourth straight contest, the game went into overtime (setting an NHL record for most consecutive overtime games in one playoff series).

Watson had struggled in the playoffs after coming back from a shoulder injury, but he was ready for the extra session. He jumped over the boards, taking a pass from Max Bentley as he hit the ice, and got past Montreal defenceman Doug Harvey. Watson fired a shot past McNeil from 20 feet out, giving the Leafs a 3–2 victory, one win away from their fourth Cup in five years. Watson had played his best game of the playoffs so far, and it was obvious he enjoyed being back with his regular linemates for most of the 1950–51 season: Meeker on right wing and Cal Gardner at centre. Watson's goal in this contest was the only goal he scored in the '51 playoffs, but it had crushed the Canadiens' spirit.

Watson played a significant role in the next game at Maple Leaf Gardens. He was on the ice when the Leafs had Rollins out of the net late in the game with the score 2–1 for

the Habs. Watson skated down a loose puck as it was heading for the empty net and got it back up the ice where the Leafs forced a face-off. The Leafs managed to tie the score and send the game into overtime for the fifth straight time. Watson (who earned an assist on the winning goal) and his linemates were out on the ice when Bill Barilko scored early in the extra session to clinch the Cup for the Leafs.

MAPLE LEAF CAREER HIGHLIGHTS

★ Member of four Stanley Cup teams with the Leafs
★ Scored 20 or more goals four times with Toronto
★ Elected to the Hockey Hall of Fame in 1994
★ Recorded 285 points (163G, 122A) in 500 games

LEAF FACT:

It is never easy to trade away a skilled and popular player, but the Maple Leafs did just that when they sent the smooth skating Billy Taylor to Detroit in exchange for Harry Watson. Taylor played one year in Detroit (leading the NHL in assists) before he was sent to Boston (and later New York), playing in just 39 games the next year. Taylor's career was over after a gambling suspension, but Watson thrived in Toronto and scored a Stanley Cup-winning goal in 1948 versus Detroit.

37 | SWEENEY SCHRINER

BORN: NOVEMBER 30, 1911 IN SARATOV, RUSSIA
POSITION: LEFT WING
YEARS AS A LEAF: 1939–40 TO 1945–46
SWEATER #: 11
MAPLE LEAF MOMENT: APRIL 18, 1942

MAPLE LEAF GENERAL MANAGER Conn Smythe was one of the more astute traders during his time in the NHL, and his trade to acquire Dave "Sweeney" Schriner was no exception to his well-earned reputation. A big left-winger for the era at six feet and 185 pounds, Schriner broke into the league with the New York Americans in 1934–35 and became the NHL's leading point producer for two straight seasons beginning in 1935–36. He also put together consecutive 21-goal seasons but then dropped off to 13 in 1938–39. Smythe seized the opportunity to make the deal with the Americans. The Leafs sent five players to New York in exchange for Schriner and never regretted the move. Schriner moved well for a player of his size, had good hands in close and rarely took a penalty (only 148 minutes in penalties over his entire career). He had a little trouble getting going with the Leafs (only 11 goals in his first year) but came back to score 24 and 20 in his next two seasons. The 1941–42 season saw Schriner get his first chance at a Stanley Cup, and when everything was on the line he came through for the Maple Leafs in dramatic fashion. Every Leafs fan will remember the night of April 18, 1942, when their team played the Detroit Red Wings in the seventh game of the finals after the Toronto club had battled back from being down three games to none.

A total of 16,218 fans packed Maple Leaf Gardens on this Saturday night during one of the bleakest times of the Second World War. The Leafs had captured the imagination of the entire country with their improbable comeback, and it was now down to one contest for the championship. The game was still tied at 0–0 when Syd Howe scored for the Red Wings in the second period to give his team a lead it took into the final stanza. Schriner then went to work and evened the score with a goal on a Leaf power-play at 6:45 of the third period. The play developed when defenceman Bingo Kampman kept the puck in at the Detroit blue line. The puck went to Billy Taylor, who sent it to Lorne Carr and then to Schriner, who backhanded a drive past Detroit goalie Johnny Mowers. The Gardens crowd went wild, having held in their hopes for the home team for more than two periods. "It was a blind shot," Schriner would say after the game. "I didn't know I had scored until I heard the crowd shouting and then saw the light go on. It was the biggest light I ever saw in my life."

The Leafs then moved in for the winner when Bob Davidson did the work to get the puck out to defenceman Bob Goldham, who then relayed the disk to John McCreedy. A shot on goal was stopped, but the rebound went right out to Pete Langelle, who slammed it home before Mowers could get back into position. Toronto was not out of trouble yet, as they were called for a penalty to Nick Metz, but they managed to kill it off. Then Taylor and Carr got the puck into the Detroit end, where Schriner picked up a loose puck and came in from the wing to beat Mowers with a drive for his second of the night to seal the victory at the 16:13 mark of the third period.

When the game ended Toronto coach Hap Day jumped on the ice, and one of the first players he congratulated was

Schriner. "Hello champ!" Day said to his clutch shooter. "Champ yourself," Schriner said back. The Stanley Cup was then presented to the Leafs by NHL president Frank Calder. Smythe, taking a break from his wartime duties, was in attendance. Captain Syl Apps said to the Leaf manager, "Come on out, Conn, you waited long enough for this Cup. Come and get it." It was the Leafs' first championship since 1931.

Schriner played three more years with the Leafs, winning one more Cup in 1945, before going out to play senior hockey in western Canada.

MAPLE LEAF CAREER HIGHLIGHTS

★ Member of two Stanley Cup teams with Toronto
★ Scored 20 or more goals three times as a Leaf
★ Elected to the Hockey Hall of Fame in 1962
★ Recorded 192 points (109G, 83A) in 244 games as a Leaf

LEAF FACT:

When Dave Schriner made the NHL's First All-Star Team in 1940–41, he became only one of five Maple Leaf left-wingers to make the prestigious squad. The other First-Team left-wingers were Harvey Jackson, Gaye Stewart, Sid Smith and Frank Mahovlich.

38 | BOB DAVIDSON

BORN: FEBRUARY 10, 1912 IN TORONTO, ONTARIO
POSITION: LEFT WING
YEARS AS A LEAF: 1934–35 TO 1945–46
SWEATER #: 4, 5, 17 AND 18
MAPLE LEAF MOMENT: APRIL 12, 1942

BORN AND RAISED in Toronto, left-winger Bob Davidson was a Maple Leaf his entire life. He grew up in the east end of the city and played his junior hockey for the Toronto Canoe Club and the Marlboros. He also played senior hockey with the Marlboros in 1933–34 and played professionally the next season when he got into five games with the Leafs and played 28 games for the Syracuse Stars of the IHL. He attended the Leafs' training camp in the fall of 1935 and made the team when Buzz Boll suffered a knee injury. Davidson then stayed around for the next 11 years. The sturdily built Davidson (5′11″ and 185 pounds) was never going to be a goal scorer at the NHL level, so he adjusted to being a reliable checker and defensive forward for the Leafs. Between 1935 and 1941, Davidson never scored more than eight goals in a season and never recorded more than 26 points (a mark he hit twice during those years). He forged a solid career as a reliable digger who showed good judgement by not taking bad penalties. In 1942 the Leafs made the finals against the Red Wings but lost the first three games of the series and were on the verge of being swept on the night of April 12, 1942, at the Detroit Olympia.

There was no scoring in the first period, but the large crowd of 13,604 fans at the Olympia were very excited to see the Red Wings score twice in the second period to give them a 2–0 lead on goals by Mud Bruneteau and Sid Abel. It looked like the Leafs were done, but then Davidson, assisted by linemates Pete Langelle and John McCreedy, slapped the puck past Johnny Mowers in the Detroit net. The Leafs tied it soon after when Lorne Carr put one in, and the second stanza ended in a 2–2 draw. Detroit took a 3–2 lead in a controversial third period, but goals by Syl Apps and Nick Metz secured a 4–3 victory for the Maple Leafs. The win breathed some life back into what had been a moribund Leafs club. The Red Wings were furious with referee Mel Harwood, and their coach Jack Adams would be suspended for the rest of the series when he got into a fight with the official after the game was over. One Detroit fan tried to attack Davidson, who had been a standout performer all night long, but he defended himself with his stick and the fan was removed at the request of the referee.

Toronto coach Hap Day was naturally relieved that his team was still alive and said, "The boys worked hard. That's the whole thing in a nutshell. We play them [the games] one at a time." He then singled out Davidson and defenceman Wally Stanowski for their good efforts: "They worked a little bit harder than most."

Billy Taylor summed up the Leafs' thoughts best when he said, "We win tomorrow night and we're only one down. And I'm pretty sure we can do it. We might take that old Cup in four straight after all." It was a prophetic statement as the Leafs did exactly what Taylor predicted.

Davidson had his best two offensive years in 1943–44 (19 goals and 47 points) and 1944–45 (17 goals and 35 points) and was with the Leafs for another championship in 1945. He played his last season with Toronto in 1945–46 and

then tried his hand at coaching in the American Hockey League with the St. Louis Flyers in 1946–47. He joined the Leafs organization as a scout and would go on to recruit some of the greatest Leafs (including the likes of Frank Mahovlich and Dave Keon) that formed the nucleus of the Leaf dynasty of the 1960s.

MAPLE LEAF CAREER HIGHLIGHTS

★ Member of two Stanley Cup teams with Toronto
★ Recorded 22 points (5G, 17A) in 79 playoff games
★ Named winner of the Bickell Trophy in 1995 for longtime service
★ Recorded 254 points (94G, 160A) in 491 games with the Leafs

LEAF FACT:

Bob Davidson attending the opening of Maple Leaf Gardens with his father on November 12, 1931, and would go on to be the only local-born captain of the Maple Leafs to lead the team to the Stanley Cup, when they won it in 1945. Davidson was named captain of the team while Syl Apps was in the army for two seasons.

39 | BILL BARILKO

BORN: MARCH 25, 1927 IN TIMMINS, ONTARIO
POSITION: DEFENCE
YEARS AS A LEAF: 1946–47 TO 1950–51
SWEATER #: 5
MAPLE LEAF MOMENT: APRIL 21, 1951

WHEN THE MAPLE LEAFS were looking for defensive help during the 1946–47 season they went to an unlikely source for an answer. Bill Barilko was playing for the Hollywood Wolves of the Pacific Coast Hockey League when he was recommended to Smythe by Tommy Anderson, a former NHL player with the New York Americans. Smythe had a particular affinity for players born in Northern Ontario, and Barilko did not lack for confidence when he got the call. Barilko had an easy smile and an infectious manner that quickly endeared him to his teammates. On the ice the five-foot-eleven, 180-pound defender was a devastating body-checker, and he hit to make the opposition feel it. He played his first game as a Leaf on February 6, 1947, and even though the Leafs lost 8–2 to the Montreal Canadiens, Barilko did make an impression by dishing out some hard bodychecks.

Soon he had a new nickname, "Bashin Bill," and he gave the Leafs a strong physical presence on the blue line. His style of play had many on the opposing teams taking runs at him, but Barilko was never afraid to hold his ground. He was not a big goal scorer (seven goals and 17 points in 1949–50 was his single-season high in both categories), but he knew when he could jump in to help the Leafs' attack. His sense of timing was never greater than when he came in from his defensive position on the night of April 21, 1951, with the Leafs and Canadiens battling for the Stanley Cup in overtime.

The Leafs were hoping to finish off the Canadiens during the Saturday night contest at Maple Leaf Gardens, but the Montreal club was not going to give up without a fight even though they were down 3–1 in games. Maurice Richard opened the scoring in the second period for Montreal, but Tod Sloan evened the score for the Leafs before the middle stanza was over. Paul Meger gave the Habs a 2–1 lead early in the third, and the Leafs looked like they were running out of time when they pulled goalie Al Rollins for an extra attacker. Off a face-off in the Montreal end, the Leafs managed to even the score as they stormed the net, and Sloan scored his second of the night. The Gardens crowd of 14,577 fans went wild with only 32 seconds to play.

The Leafs came out hard when the overtime began, anxious to end the game quickly. Howie Meeker started the play for the winning goal when he carried the puck into the Montreal end. Montreal defenceman Tom Johnson stopped Meeker's attack behind the Montreal goal, but the puck came out to Harry Watson and the Leaf winger took a swipe at the puck. It bounced out to the face-off circle and lay there tantalizingly. Barilko noticed the loose disc and defied orders from coach Joe Primeau by charging in and taking a sweeping backhand shot that beat Montreal goaltender Gerry McNeil for the winning goal at 2:53 of overtime. Pandemonium broke out as the Leafs swarmed Barilko to congratulate him on his winning tally, and even Primeau found his way out to the defenceman he had told to stay back. Barilko had scored the goal while sporting a broken nose courtesy of a check he took earlier in the game from Montreal's Bert Olmstead, but he was determined to tough it

out with the Cup at stake and even blocked a Richard drive to keep the Leafs alive.

After the game, Smythe entered the Leaf dressing room and shook hands with the hero of the night. They exchanged a laugh and Smythe commented on Barilko's gutsy effort. "We wouldn't be feeling so good right now if it hadn't been for Barilko," Smythe said. "That was really the old college try." Barilko spoke about his winning goal and simply said, "It is something I've dreamed about doing all my life."

Sadly, it was also the last goal of his life, as he was killed in a plane crash in August of 1951. Barilko will never be forgotten as one of the great Leafs of all time.

MAPLE LEAF CAREER HIGHLIGHTS

★ Member of four Stanley Cup teams with Toronto
★ Led the NHL in penalty minutes in 1947–48 with 147
★ Recorded five points (3G, 2A) in 11 games in 1951 playoffs
★ Recorded 57 points (26G, 36A) in 252 games

LEAF FACT:

Each member of the 1951 Maple Leafs received $2,500 in bonus money for winning the Stanley Cup. They got $1,000 for winning two playoff series and $500 for finishing second in the league standings during the regular season.

When the plane Bill Barilko was on could not be found late in the summer of 1951, Leaf owner Conn Smythe offered a $10,000 reward for information leading to the recovery of the missing defenceman. Barilko's remains were not found until 1962, shortly after the Leafs had won their first Cup since '51.

40 PAUL HENDERSON

BORN: JANUARY 28, 1943 IN KINCARDINE, ONTARIO
POSITION: LEFT WING
YEARS AS A LEAF: 1967–68 TO 1973–74
SWEATER #: 19
MAPLE LEAF MOMENT: MARCH 6, 1968

TORONTO COACH and general manager Punch Imlach always liked the way Detroit Red Wing Paul Henderson played the game. Perhaps the Leaf manager remembered Henderson for a goal he scored with just one second left in a 1966 contest at Maple Leaf Gardens that snatched away a Leaf victory. Or maybe he was impressed with Henderson scoring 77 NHL goals in less than five seasons. Imlach told the speedy left-winger that he would one day get him in a deal. Henderson was flattered by Imlach's comments but never thought it would happen. However, on March 3, 1968, one of the greatest trades in NHL history was completed between the Leafs and the Red Wings with Henderson being one of the prominent names coming to Toronto. Norm Ullman and Floyd Smith also came in the deal that saw Leafs superstar Frank Mahovlich head to Detroit along with three others. Toronto fans were shocked and upset at the trade, and many wondered how everyone would react when the new Leafs made their debut just three days later at home.

On March 6, 1968, the Leafs faced the expansion Philadelphia Flyers. The upstart club had knocked off the established Toronto club 2–1 at the Gardens in January. Throughout that first year of the NHL's great expansion the Leafs had plenty of trouble with the new teams. But on this night the defending Stanley Cup champions were ready to flex their muscles.

After a scoreless first period, the crowd was impatient with the Leafs' play. But starting in the second period they responded warmly to the barrage on Flyer netminder Doug Favell, as the Leafs ripped in five goals in the middle stanza to take a 5–1 lead. Ever the showman, Imlach put the newly acquired players on one line. All three missed good chances to score before they clicked. Both Smith and Ullman scored in the second period onslaught, while Henderson added one in the third period as the Leafs pasted the Flyers 7–2. Henderson's goal came as he hung around the Philadelphia net and redirected a drive through Favell's legs for the Leafs' sixth goal of the game. Fans were pleased by the end of the evening to see seven Toronto goals — a rare treat in the '67–68 season.

"I don't know when I've been so tight before a game. My dinner tasted like paste, and I couldn't relax," a relieved Henderson said after the game. "Whew, I'm glad this one is over. I've lost four pounds since the trade. All of us have lost weight. The crowd really made us feel welcome. At least they didn't boo us out of the place."

Imlach felt the new players could have done even better if not for Favell. "They could have had four or five goals. But that Favell was robbing them blind in that first period," the coach said after the game. Assistant general manager King Clancy was even more enthusiastic, saying, "Did you see them driving in on the net all night? None of that lollygagging behind the goal."

In spite of the win, the Leafs were still 12 points out of a playoff spot with less than a month to go before the end of the regular season. The Leafs went 8–4–1 after the deal was

made (Henderson would record 11 points in those 13 games including five goals) but still missed the playoffs by four points. Imlach would lament that he should have made the trade sooner.

MAPLE LEAF CAREER HIGHLIGHTS

★ Scored 38 goals in 1971–72
★ Selected to Team Canada in 1972
★ Had five seasons of 20 or more goals with Toronto
★ Scored 162 goals and 318 points in 408 games as a Leaf

LEAF FACT:

After Paul Henderson scored three game-winning goals in Moscow to win the 1972 Summit Series for Canada, phone callers to the Leaf offices at the Gardens were greeted with "Maple Leaf Gardens, home of Paul Henderson."

41

CURTIS JOSEPH

BORN: APRIL 29, 1967 IN KESWICK, ONTARIO
POSITION: GOALTENDER
YEARS AS A LEAF: 1998–99 TO 2001–02
SWEATER #: 31
MAPLE LEAF MOMENT: MAY 25, 2002

WHEN THE MAPLE LEAFS decided to bring in Pat Quinn as coach to start the 1998–99 season, it was assumed by most that Felix Potvin would be the number one goalie. However, a chance meeting between Leaf president Ken Dryden and the agent for goaltender Curtis Joseph got the Toronto club to consider making a change. It's unlikely that the struggling Leafs (an awful 30–43–9 the previous season) were the first choice for a free agent like Joseph, who was looking at contenders such as Philadelphia, but Toronto came up with a four-year deal at $6 million per season to sign the acrobatic netminder. Potvin was eventually traded away, and Joseph took over the number one duties in goal. He won 35 games in '98–99 for the upstart Leafs, who earned 97 points during the season and went all the way to the Eastern Conference final before losing to Buffalo in five games.

The man known as "Cujo" became an instant fan favourite in Toronto and gave the offensively minded team superb netminding when they needed a save at a crucial moment. The next two years saw Joseph win 36 and 33 games respectively, but the Leafs did not get past the second round of the playoffs. He was well on his way to winning more than 30 games again in the 2001–02 season when he broke his hand late in February, missing most of the remainder of the year and finishing with 29 victories. Joseph was fresher for the playoffs in 2002 and got the Leafs past the New York Islanders and the Ottawa Senators before facing the Carolina Hurricanes in the conference final. A badly limping Toronto club was expected to beat the Hurricanes, but the Leafs found themselves down 3–1 in games when they journeyed back to Carolina on May 25, 2002, facing elimination.

Injuries had ravaged the Toronto lineup for most of the '02 postseason, and Joseph was having a difficult time getting back into form after his hand problems. He was improving steadily as the playoffs progressed, and in front of 19,016 mostly hostile fans, Joseph played perhaps his best game as the Leafs eked out a 1–0 victory to send the series back to Toronto for a sixth contest. He made 28 saves during the game, and the Leafs rode a first period goal by Darcy Tucker (who was playing with a broken shoulder blade) to keep Toronto's dream of a Stanley Cup alive. Joseph was at his best in the second period when the Leafs were short-handed for eight minutes (including a two-man disadvantage), and his work in that stretch was highlighted by a save off a drive by Carolina defenceman Brett Hedican. In the third period the Leafs were outshot by a 16–2 margin, but Joseph was stellar once again. The shutout was the third for Joseph in these playoffs (and the 15th of his career), and he was named the first star of the game.

Afterwards, he spoke of what the Leafs were capable of doing. "I see this team believing in ourselves in this dressing room. When push comes to shove, we can come up with a big game and we have a lot of confidence in the room [because] of our veteran guys. I think that's the attitude you need to be able to come back." Joseph then spoke about this particular game. "I think for our team, playing with a lead

is very important," he said. "The Hurricanes play such a suffocating style where they try not to make any mistakes and just play great defence. If we get a lead we force them to open up a little bit."

The next game turned out to be Joseph's last performance as a Maple Leaf. Carolina's Jeff O'Neill scored a goal in the third period to give his team a 1–0 lead, and only a last minute goal by Mats Sundin forced overtime. The Leafs' luck ran out when Martin Gelinas scored to put the Hurricanes into the finals for the very first time. Joseph surprisingly decided to leave the Leafs for Detroit before the start of the next season, a move that was regretted by all those involved.

MAPLE LEAF CAREER HIGHLIGHTS

★ Signed as a free agent on July 15, 1998
★ Won 33 or more games three times as a Leaf
★ Recorded 17 shutouts with Toronto
★ Posted a 133–88–27 win-loss record as a Maple Leaf

LEAF FACT:

Curtis Joseph played in 60 playoff games during his career with the Leafs and posted a 32–28 record. His win total is third highest on the Leafs all-time list behind Turk Broda and Johnny Bower. His postseason shutout total of eight ranks him second to Broda's 13.

42 LORNE CHABOT

BORN: OCTOBER 5, 1900 IN MONTREAL, QUEBEC
POSITION: GOALTENDER
YEARS AS A LEAF: 1928–29 TO 1932–33
SWEATER #: 1
MAPLE LEAF MOMENT: APRIL 3, 1933

WHEN CONN SMYTHE was putting together the New York Rangers he remembered how goaltender Lorne Chabot had played senior hockey with the Port Arthur Ports for five seasons, winning two championships. Smythe signed Chabot for the Rangers in 1926 and the netminder immediately paid dividends by posting a 22–9–5 record to go along with 10 shutouts and a 1.46 goals-against average in the 1926–27 season. Chabot was a big goalie for this era of hockey (6´1˝ and 185 pounds) and was known for his quick movement and nerves of steel. The Rangers won their first-ever Stanley Cup the following season, but Chabot suffered a serious eye injury during the playoffs. The Rangers were unsure Chabot would be able to recover, so they were happy to deal him to Toronto where Smythe was now in charge. The Leafs gave up goalie John Ross Roach and forward Butch Keeling to make the deal.

Chabot rewarded the Leafs' faith in acquiring him by winning 20 or more games four times with Toronto and taking the team to its first championship in 1932 (defeating the Rangers in the finals). The 1932–33 season saw Chabot win 24 games for Toronto and get the Leafs back into the finals, against the Rangers once more. Prior to meeting the Rangers, the Leafs had to get by Boston in a tough five-game semifinal that was not decided until the Leafs scored an overtime winner on the night of April 3, 1933, at Maple Leaf Gardens.

Boston opened the series with a 2–1 overtime victory, but the Leafs took the next game 1–0, also in extra time. The next three games were to be played at the Gardens. The Bruins took the first one 2–1 in overtime, but the Leafs bounced right back and won the fourth game 5–2 on April 1. That meant the series would be decided two nights later, and more than 14,000 fans packed the arena to see what turned out to be an epic battle. The two teams were scoreless after 60 minutes of regulation play (the game began at 8:30 p.m.) and then played over 104 minutes of overtime before the issue was settled (at 1:50 a.m.). Both teams took five penalties in regulation time, but the power-plays were not working this evening as Chabot and Boston's Tiny Thompson stopped all the shots directed their way. The Bruins thought they had scored late in the third period, but the play was called offside. Boston took six of the 10 penalties handed out during the course of the overtime, but the Leafs were denied the only goal by another offside call, which negated a King Clancy marker.

At one point the teams considered flipping a coin to decide the issue, but the Leafs were firmly against that notion, while someone else suggested that the goalies be taken out. This, too, was rejected, so the game continued into the sixth overtime stanza. Then, little Ken Doraty of the Leafs took a pass from teammate Andy Blair. Somehow Doraty found the energy to get around the Bruin defence before depositing a shot past Thompson for the winning goal, ending the longest game in Leaf history.

The 1–0 shutout was well earned by Chabot, who had to make several outstanding saves in the Leaf net. He

stopped a close-in drive by Joe Lamb of the Bruins, turned back drives by Eddie Shore and Dit Clapper and was brilliant in defending a shot by Nels Stewart early in the third overtime period. He later stopped Art Chapman by coming out to take away the angle as the Bruin player flew down the wing in an attempt to score. In all, Chabot stopped 93 shots while the Leafs pelted 114 at Thompson.

The battered and bruised Leafs had to leave immediately after the game for New York to start the Stanley Cup finals and predictably lost the first game 5–1. The Leafs were able to win only one game as the Rangers took the Cup on Gardens ice with a 1–0 win in overtime in the fourth game of the series. It was the last game Chabot played for the Leafs.

MAPLE LEAF CAREER HIGHLIGHTS

★ Acquired in a trade with New York Rangers on October 18, 1928
★ Member of Stanley Cup team in 1932
★ Recorded 33 shutouts with Toronto
★ Posted a 103–80–31 record in 214 games as a Leaf

LEAF FACT:

Not many Maple Leaf netminders have won a playoff game 1–0 in overtime, but Lorne Chabot did it twice in the same series (vs. Boston in 1933). Other goalies to accomplish the same feat are: Turk Broda (vs. Boston in 1938), Felix Potvin (vs. Chicago in 1994) and Curtis Joseph (vs. Ottawa in 2001).

43 | FELIX POTVIN

BORN: JUNE 23, 1971 IN ANJOU, QUEBEC
POSITION: GOALTENDER
YEARS AS A LEAF: 1991–92 TO 1998–99
SWEATER #: 29
MAPLE LEAF MOMENT: OCTOBER 23, 1993

FELIX POTVIN'S DEVELOPMENT as the Maple Leafs' number one goalie was a neat and orderly process. The Leafs drafted the netminder 31st overall in 1990, and he returned to Chicoutimi in the Quebec Major Junior Hockey League (QMJHL) for one more season. He posted a 33–15–4 regular season record and then took his team to the Memorial Cup finals. Potvin won many accolades over his final year of junior, but he started his professional career with St. John's of the American Hockey League for the 1991–92 season. He was 18–10–6 during the season, then won another seven playoff games as the St. John's club lost the league final in seven games. Potvin also played in four games for Toronto (earning one tie) and showed he could handle the big-league duties during his brief stay. Potvin started the following season back in the minors, but an injury to Toronto starter Grant Fuhr gave him the chance he needed to play for the Leafs. He won 25 games while recording a 2.50 goals-against average, and the Leafs soon realized they no longer needed Fuhr (who was traded to Buffalo). Potvin took the Leafs all the way to the seventh game of the Western Conference final before losing to the Los Angeles Kings. The Leafs were riding high as the 1993–94 season began, and Potvin picked up right where he had left off the previous year. In fact, the Leafs had a chance to set an NHL record when they went to Tampa Bay on the night of October 23, 1993.

The Leafs began the '93–94 campaign with an eight-game winning streak, which tied an NHL record held by the 1934–35 Maple Leafs and the 1975–76 Buffalo Sabres. Toronto was winning close games (such as 2–1 victories over Detroit and Chicago) and blowing out the opposition in other contests (such as 7–1 over Washington and 7–2 against Hartford). The Leafs won their eighth in a row when they beat Florida 4–3 in overtime on Rob Pearson's winner two nights before their game against the Lightning. The Leafs relied on Potvin again on this evening, but they also got some timely goals (both scored by Mark Osborne) and kept the game simple as they took a 2–0 victory. The Leaf netminder made 25 saves to earn his first shutout of the season before a huge gathering of 22,880 fans in the Thunderdome. Tampa Bay was strong in the first period when they outshot the Leafs 9–6 and forced Potvin to make some fine stops. The win was even more impressive when you consider that Pearson and Todd Gill were nursing injuries, star Doug Gilmour was tossed in the third for fighting, and defenceman Bob Rouse was out due to a suspension. The game was lost in the Toronto newspapers the next day since the Toronto Blue Jays were clinching their second consecutive World Series in a dramatic fashion (on a Joe Carter home run) while the Leafs were defeating the Lightning.

"It feels good to do something that hasn't been done in the whole history of hockey," Potvin said after the game. The Leaf starter had eight of the nine wins, while Damian Rhodes recorded the other victory. Toronto coach Pat Burns was very impressed with Potvin's work. "Felix has been a big part of this start. He's really played well throughout and came up big

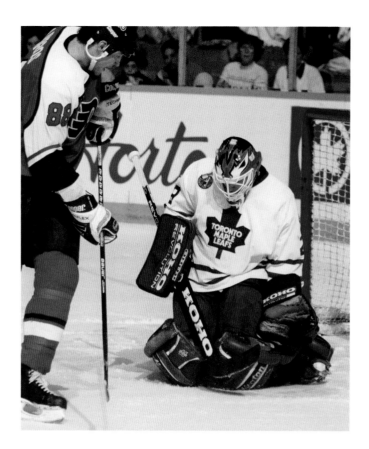

for us again," he said. "We didn't talk much about the record, but it was in the back of our heads."

Leaf captain Wendel Clark said he was surprised at how well the team was doing. "We were hoping for a great start, but nobody predicted this would happen," he said. The Leafs beat Chicago 4–2 to make it a record 10 games but lost to the Montreal Canadiens 5–2 to bring an end to the streak. The Leafs went on to play in the Conference final for the second straight year, but this time they lost to Vancouver in five games. The Leafs came agonizingly close to winning a Stanley Cup, and there was no way they would have been that close without the stellar work of Potvin in net.

MAPLE LEAF CAREER HIGHLIGHTS

★ Drafted 31st overall by the Leafs in 1990
★ Posted a 2.87 goals-against average with 12 shutouts for Toronto
★ Won 160 games in 369 regular season appearances with the Leafs
★ Won 25 games in the playoffs with five shutouts

LEAF FACT:

Felix Potvin recorded his first career shutout when the Leafs beat the Montreal Canadiens 4–0 on February 25, 1993, at Maple Leaf Gardens. Potvin made 29 saves in the game that was played against his childhood hero, Patrick Roy, in the Montreal net.

44 | DAVE WILLIAMS

BORN: FEBRUARY 3, 1954 IN WEYBURN, SASKATCHEWAN
POSITION: LEFT WING
YEARS AS A LEAF: 1974–75 TO 1979–80
SWEATER #: 22
MAPLE LEAF MOMENT: JANUARY 18, 1975

TORONTO MAPLE LEAF scout Torchy Schell strongly recommended that the team select Dave "Tiger" Williams during the 1974 entry draft. Schell believed Williams had the spirit, the drive and the will to do anything to be successful. When Williams was in high school he had written the letters "NHL" across a guidance form that asked what he wanted to do in life. His junior career in Swift Current showed that he could score (52 goals in his final year) despite his laborious skating style, and his toughness (even though he was only 5′11″ and 190 pounds) was legendary. The Leafs selected Williams 31st overall but were not quite sure what they had in the feisty left-winger. He scrapped with defenceman Ian Turnbull at his first Leaf camp but was sent down to Oklahoma City for some pro seasoning. He took the demotion without a great deal of complaint and scored well in the minors with 16 goals and 27 points in 39 games. Meanwhile, the Leafs were getting pushed around, and the call was made to bring Williams up to the big club on January 7, 1975. The Leafs lost the first game Williams played with the team, but they won three of their next four, then went into Montreal on the night of January 18.

The Montreal Canadiens were undefeated in 21 games going into the contest, but the Leafs were ready for this encounter and played one of their best games of the year, much to the chagrin of the Habs and their fans. The Leafs matched the Canadiens' vigour and style and walked out of the Forum with a 5–3 win. Toronto opened the scoring on a goal by Norm Ullman late in the first period, but Steve Shutt quickly tied it up for Montreal. The teams traded goals in the second, but Montreal took a 3–2 lead halfway through the third period on a goal by Pete Mahovlich. Then the game seemed to turn. Set up by Darryl Sittler and Gary Sabourin, Williams scored his first NHL goal to even the score. Sittler fed Williams the puck right in the slot, and the 20-year-old snapped a shot into the top corner of the net past Montreal netminder Michel "Bunny" Larocque. Williams did a little dance after the goal, and it sparked the Leafs, who scored another less than a minute later, when Bob Neely beat Larocque to give the Leafs a 4–3 lead. The Leafs hung on behind the superlative netminding of Doug Favell until the Habs pulled their goalie while the Leafs were short-handed for the final 55 seconds. Dave Keon won an important face-off in the Toronto end, and winger Bill Flett scored his second goal of the night into the empty net to secure a remarkable win for a struggling team.

Williams was able to keep up with the swift Canadiens and showed poise beyond his years. He got into a dust up with Montreal veteran Jimmy Roberts and more than held his own. (Both players were given double minors.) Montreal defenceman Larry Robinson was very impressed with the Leaf rookie. "[Williams] has a great shot [and] he played very well," Robinson commented. For his part Williams was nonchalant about his first NHL goal. "It was no big deal. Lanny McDonald got his first goal at the Forum. I wanted to match him. I'm glad it was a good clean goal, not a tip-

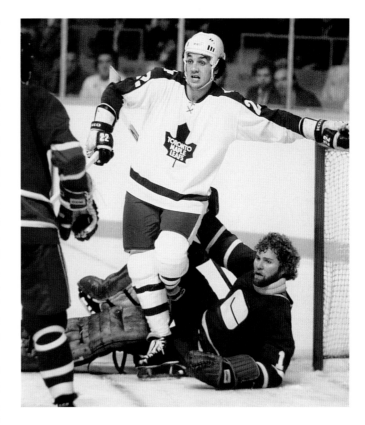

in or deflection. I saw the upper shelf open and put a wrist shot right there."

Williams finished his rookie year with 10 goals and 29 points in 42 games. He also became the Leafs' undisputed enforcer, but he was also a talented player who could score, just as he showed the night he notched his first big-league goal.

MAPLE LEAF CAREER HIGHLIGHTS

★ Drafted 31st overall by the Leafs in 1974
★ Ranks second on all-time Leafs list with 1,670 penalty minutes
★ Led the Leafs in penalty minutes five consecutive seasons (1974–75 to 1979–80)
★ Scored 109 goals and 241 points in 407 games as a Leaf

LEAF FACT:

When he played in Toronto, Dave Williams took his wife and children to visit with Maple Leaf founder and long-time owner Conn Smythe at his home in the country. The unexpected Williams was welcomed into the Smythe residence, and the one-time Leaf manager said Williams was "a natural man who was filled with spirit." Smythe would also admonish Leaf general manager Punch Imlach when he dealt Williams to Vancouver, saying such loyal players should not be traded away.

45

HOWIE MEEKER

BORN: NOVEMBER 4, 1924 IN KITCHENER, ONTARIO
POSITION: RIGHT WING
YEARS AS A LEAF: 1946–47 TO 1953–54
SWEATER #: 11 AND 15
MAPLE LEAF MOMENT: JANUARY 8, 1946

RIGHT-WINGER HOWIE MEEKER had enjoyed some success in junior hockey when he played the 1941–42 season with Stratford (29 goals in 13 games played), but he joined the military in 1943 and missed two entire seasons of hockey. He suffered serious leg injuries while in the army and thought his hockey career was over. But he played senior hockey when he returned home and scored eight times in just seven games. The Maple Leafs were looking for young players and signed the feisty five-foot-nine, 165-pound Meeker as a free agent. He made the Leafs for the 1946–47 season and surprised everyone with a 27-goal season, the best total of his eight-year career, which was played entirely as a Leaf. His first NHL goal came on October 19, 1946, in a 6–3 Leaf victory over Detroit at Maple Leaf Gardens, when he knocked home a pass from Ted Kennedy. As memorable as that game was for Meeker, his performance on January 8, 1946, during a home game against Chicago is still talked about whenever rookie records are mentioned.

The Black Hawks opened the scoring when Max Bentley got one past Leaf netminder Turk Broda, but Meeker got his first goal of the night when he tipped home a Wally Stanowski drive to knot the game up at 1–1. The teams exchanged goals in the second period before Meeker once again had a Stanowski drive hit him for his second of the night. (Stanowski was actually credited with both goals originally, but Leaf coach Hap Day happened to hear Meeker saying that he had touched the puck on each shot before it went past Paul Bibeault in the Chicago net. Day brought this information to the official scorer and the change was made.) Meeker then finished off a passing play with Ted Kennedy and Joe Klukay for his third of the evening to give Toronto a 4–2 lead going into the third period.

The final stanza was a wild one, as a total of six goals were scored. Nick Metz scored one for the Leafs just 1:51 into the final frame. Meeker followed that up with another tally, his fourth of the night, 21 seconds later. Bill Mosienko got one back for the Black Hawks before Metz and Meeker both scored once again. For Meeker it was his fifth of the night (setting a new NHL mark for most goals in one game by a player in his first year, a record that has been equalled only once, by Don Murdoch of the New York Rangers in 1976), with Kennedy and Klukay getting the assists on the last goal. The Leaf rookie with the distinctive crewcut now had 16 goals on the season. Bud Poile added one more for the Leafs before Chicago got two to make it a 10–4 final for Toronto. The victory put the Leafs into first place by five points over the Montreal Canadiens.

The Leafs ended up finishing the '46–47 season in second place but then defeated Boston and Montreal in the playoffs to win the Stanley Cup. Meeker totaled 45 points in 58 regular season games and scored three goals and added three assists in 11 playoff games in the postseason to put a great finishing touch on his first NHL campaign. He scored 14 times in his second season, then his goal total fell to seven in 1948–49 when he played in only 30 games due to a broken collarbone.

Meeker was on four Stanley Cup teams in his time with the Leafs, but injuries took their toll on him. He was forced to retire after playing in just five games in 1953–54 and was named coach of the team for the 1956–57 season (only 21 wins in 70 games). He was going to take on the role of general manager, but a severe disagreement with Stafford Smythe led to his dismissal before a game was even played in 1957–58. Meeker found his post-career niche when he became a game analyst for *Hockey Night in Canada*, where he brought a distinctive energy to the program for many years.

MAPLE LEAF CAREER HIGHLIGHTS

★ Signed as a free agent by the Leafs on April 13, 1946
★ Member of four Stanley Cup teams with Toronto
★ Won the Calder Trophy for the 1946–47 season
★ Recorded 185 points (83G, 102A) in 346 games with Toronto

LEAF FACT:

On February 9, 1952, Howie Meeker set a team record by scoring two power-play goals in six seconds during a 3–2 win over the Montreal Canadiens. Meeker scored at 10:14 of the second period and then got another at 10:20. George Armstrong scored another goal on the power-play at 11:30 of the period, helping to set another team mark — fastest three power-play goals (1:16).

46 | BILL EZINICKI

BORN: MARCH 11, 1924 IN WINNIPEG, MANITOBA
POSITION: RIGHT WING
YEARS AS A LEAF: 1944–45 TO 1949–50
SWEATER #: 12, 16 AND 17
MAPLE LEAF MOMENT: APRIL 10, 1947

WHEN A PLAYER is known as "Wild Bill" you have to know he is making an impression with just about everybody. Left-winger Bill Ezinicki was the player with the nickname, and he was alternatively loved (in Toronto) and hated (everywhere else in the league) during his NHL career. Ezinicki was not a large man at 5′10″ and 170 pounds, but he had long, strong arms and a chiselled body developed from lifting weights. He turned bodychecking into an art form, and he made sure his stick was on the ice when he delivered a rollicking hit.

Although he hailed from Manitoba, Ezinicki played junior hockey for the Oshawa Generals. His rights were owned by Buffalo of the AHL, from whom the Maple Leafs acquired Ezinicki in exchange for two players. He got into eight games with Toronto in 1944–45 (one goal, four assists), but he also had to finish a stint in the army. He split 1945–46 between Toronto (four goals in 24 games) and Pittsburgh of the AHL. From then on, for the next four years, he was a full-time Leaf. He scored 17 goals and added 20 assists in his first full year, but his greatest contribution came in the playoffs, though he did not score a goal in 11 postseason games. The Leafs played the Montreal Canadiens in the Stanley Cup finals in 1947, and Ezinicki was given the task of checking Maurice Richard in the series. A predictable flare-up between two fiery competitors happened on the night of April 19, 1947.

The Leafs were awful in the first game of the series at the Montreal Forum and were thoroughly beaten 6–0. They were much better prepared for the second contest. Richard had scored a goal in the opener, and the Leafs were determined to shut down the Rocket on this night. Ted Kennedy scored the first goal of the game just a little over a minute into the first period, and Vic Lynn added another shortly after to give Toronto an early 2–0 lead. Both goals came on the power-play with Butch Bouchard of the Canadiens in the penalty box. The Leafs got another goal with the extra man when Gaye Stewart scored at 6:37 of the second period, this time with Richard sitting out a high-sticking penalty.

Late in the second stanza, Richard lost his temper when checked by Ezinicki, and he clubbed the Leaf forward over the head with his stick. The skirmish between the two began as they exchanged high sticks, but then Richard decided that was not enough punishment for the Leaf tough guy. Ezinicki's blood was on the Forum ice when referee Bill Chadwick ruled that Richard would be given a five-minute major that was upgraded to a match penalty when the official believed Ezinicki was gone for the night. Ezinicki returned for the third period and saw Harry Watson make it 4–0 for Toronto when he beat Bill Durnan in the Montreal net. Ezinicki received six stitches to the head from Richard's stick assault, and the Canadien star would have to face NHL president Clarence Campbell before he would be allowed to play again.

Montreal coach Dick Irvin was furious with the call and insisted that Chadwick was guilty of a misinterpretation. The rule at the time stated that the referee had to be certain that an injured player was not coming back before a match penalty could be applied. The coach (Hap Day) of the team

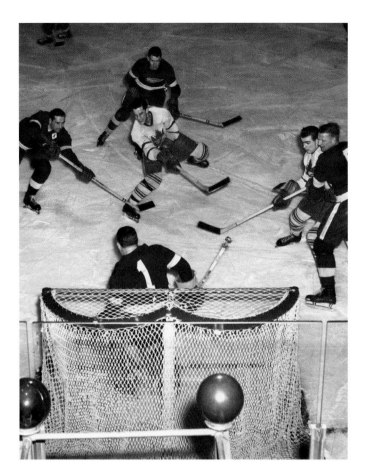

with the injured player (Ezinicki) was not consulted as the rule stated he must be, and Irvin insisted that he had pointed this out. "I told Chadwick about this, but he paid no attention. That is all I could do," Irvin said. Richard was suspended for the next game (a 4–2 Leaf win), and Toronto took the series and the Cup in six games. Riling up Richard and keeping him out of one game in the finals may have been Ezinicki's greatest contribution to the Toronto cause in '47.

MAPLE LEAF CAREER HIGHLIGHTS

★ Member of three Stanley Cup teams with Toronto
★ Scored three goals in nine playoff games in 1948
★ Led the NHL in penalty minutes two times
★ Recorded 135 points (56G, 79A) in 271 games as a Leaf

LEAF FACT:

The Maple Leafs were the toughest team in the NHL during the late forties behind the likes of Bill Ezinicki, Jim Thompson, Bill Barilko and Gus Mortson. Each of these players recorded at least 90 minutes in penalties in a season (three of the four had 100 or more minutes at least once), and all had a significant hand in helping the Leafs to the Stanley Cup in 1947, 1948 and 1949.

47 | BRYAN McCABE

BORN: JUNE 8, 1975 IN ST. CATHARINES, ONTARIO
POSITION: DEFENCE
YEARS AS A LEAF: 2000–01 TO PRESENT
SWEATER #: 24
MAPLE LEAF MOMENT: NOVEMBER 15, 2005

PAT QUINN'S TENURE as the Leafs' general manager had many good and bad moments, but everyone would agree that he made a great trade when he picked up defenceman Bryan McCabe in a deal with the Chicago Blackhawks. The Leafs were having trouble re-signing blueliner Alexander Karpovtsev to a new deal and were fortunate former Leaf general manager Mike Smith was now in charge of the Chicago club. Smith was always impressed with Russian-born players and gladly took Karpovtsev off the Leafs' hands, along with a fourth-round draft choice, in exchange for McCabe. It's a deal the Leafs would never regret as the hard-shooting McCabe blossomed into one of the best defenders in the NHL.

Selected 40th overall in 1993 by the New York Islanders after an All-Star junior career with Spokane and Brandon in the WHL, McCabe was traded to Vancouver after three years with the Isles. The Islanders had named McCabe team captain prior to the start of the 1997–98 season but wanted to land Trevor Linden in the deal with the Canucks. After only one full year in Vancouver (21 points in 79 games), McCabe was on the move again, as he was dealt to Chicago in a trade involving premium draft choices. He was a Blackhawk for just one season before the Leafs rescued him and gave him a home on their blue line brigade. Since that time McCabe has improved his offensive numbers steadily, going from 29 points in 2000–01 to 68 in 2005–06. His defensive play has not always been as high as his attacking skills, but when he is focused McCabe moves the puck well and takes charge of the point on the power-play. The 2005–06 season was a breakout year for McCabe, and he had many good outings like the one on November 15, 2005, during a home game against the New York Rangers.

Both the Leafs and Rangers were playing better than all the pundits had suggested they would prior to the start of the season coming off the lockout year. Many teams had made changes to their rosters in the new salary cap system, and some clubs adjusted better than others. The power-play was now one of the most important units on any team, and the Leafs were getting wins largely based on their play with the extra man. On this night, as he did much of the entire '05–06 season, McCabe was strong on the power-play, scoring twice as the Leafs beat the Rangers 2–1. McCabe's first goal opened the scoring when Leaf centre Jason Allison and fellow defenceman Tomas Kaberle set up the Leaf blueliner on a two-man advantage. McCabe's one-timer beat Kevin Weekes in the New York net for the only marker of the first period. The Rangers tied it on a goal by Jaromir Jagr, but McCabe scored at 3:37 of the third period as he put another drive through the legs of the Ranger netminder to give the Leafs the lead once again. (Kaberle and winger Jeff O'Neill assisted on the goal.) Backed by the goaltending of Ed Belfour (who stopped 26 of 27 shots), the Leafs hung on for the victory to give them a 10–7–0 mark on the season.

"Tommy [Kaberle] made a couple of great passes which let me get the puck on the net," McCabe said. "We are

playing better defensively. Keeping out of the box made the difference tonight. We now have a couple of wins under our belt, but we need to get a roll going."

Captain Mats Sundin commented on how well McCabe was playing. "It's like he's scoring at will right now. He's the best defenceman in the league right now." Ranger netminder Weekes was also impressed. "They executed two good plays. Their power-play is certainly humming, and Bryan McCabe is outstanding."

McCabe went on to record a total of 68 points (including 19 goals) during the season, and the Leafs missed him dearly when he was out with an injury. A losing skid in January and February meant no postseason action for Toronto in 2006, but McCabe earned himself a lucrative new five-year contract based on his fine season.

MAPLE LEAF CAREER HIGHLIGHTS

★ Acquired in a trade with Chicago on October 2, 2000
★ Has scored 16 or more goals three times as a Leaf
★ Led all NHL players in average ice time in 2005–06 (28:17)
★ Recorded 274 points (78G, 196A) in 469 games as a Leaf (as of 2006–07)

LEAF FACT:

Bryan McCabe played in his 800th career game with the Leafs on November 11, 2006, at the Air Canada Centre as Toronto whipped Montreal 5–1 in the annual Hall of Fame Game. McCabe was named the player of the game for Toronto with a two-goal performance.

WHEN THE 1976–77 SEASON began the Toronto Maple Leafs figured their goaltending needs were in good hands with incumbent Wayne Thomas. After all, Thomas had led a resurgent Leaf team to the playoffs in 1975–76 and had played exceptionally well in front of a young squad. However, Thomas faltered in the early going of the '76–77 campaign and the Leafs (who were 1–5–3 at the time) could not afford to wait for him to regain his form. General manager Jim Gregory put out a call to a young netminder who was with the Leafs' farm club in Dallas. Goaltender Mike Palmateer cheerfully said to the Leaf manager, "Your troubles are over, Mr. Gregory. When do you want me?" Palmateer, who was no stranger to Toronto as he had played all his junior hockey in the Marlie chain, started and won his first game on October 28 as the Leafs beat Detroit 3–1. He recorded his first shutout on November 13 when the Leafs knocked off Vancouver 3–0. Four days later, on November 17, 1976, the defending Stanley Cup champion Montreal Canadiens were in Toronto for a game.

The cherubic, cocky netminder was not expected to shut down the mighty Habs, but the Leafs were hopeful their newest goalie could keep them in the game. The Leafs got a goal from winger Lanny McDonald at 8:26 of the first period (assisted by Darryl Sittler and Ian Turnbull) and then matched the Montreal club for the first two-thirds of the game. Palmateer seemed to gain confidence by making early saves on Steve Shutt and Rejean Houle. In the third period, the Canadiens, who had not been shut out in 168 games dating back to November 2, 1974, fired a barrage of shots at the Leaf youngster, who did not flinch once as he turned back 16 shots over the final 20 minutes. The Leafs were able to withstand long periods bottled up in their own end. Palmateer had to stop a total of 39 shots to secure the win. Montreal's offensive surge left them open to counter-attacks, but Ken Dryden was equal to the task in the Habs net, stopping 29 Leaf drives. As the game came to a close, 16,485 spectators gave the Leafs and their 22-year-old rookie goalie loud support and stayed in their seats for the three stars: Palmateer, Dryden and Leaf defenceman Borje Salming.

After the game, all the talk centred on the performance of Palmateer. "We had the chances. There were some bad breaks around their net, but you can't take anything away from Palmateer's performance. He played exceptionally well," commented Montreal coach Scotty Bowman. Dryden added, "It's the first time I've seen him, but on that basis I'd say he has a lot of confidence. He's small but quick and so fast on his skates." Leaf coach Red Kelly was equally effusive in his praise of Palmateer. "His confidence is good, and he doesn't get rattled. Even in the third period when they came bearing down on him he stood his ground."

One person who was not tossing laurels Palmateer's way was Montreal superstar Guy Lafleur, who snorted, "[I] wasn't all that impressed. He played well, but we missed too many chances and made him look good."

For his part, Palmateer admitted to being very nervous before the game and even during the contest. "Yeah, I was really nervous through the game and really, really nervous in the last ten minutes. The way they shoot I was hoping to get through with only three or four goals on me."

The big win against Montreal gave the Leafs a record of 7–7–4, and they would finish 33–32–15 for the season (good for third place in the Adams Division) to earn a playoff spot. They defeated Pittsburgh in the opening round best of three but once again were eliminated by Philadelphia in the next round.

MAPLE LEAF CAREER HIGHLIGHTS

★ Selected 85th overall by the Leafs in the 1974 entry draft
★ Recorded 15 career shutouts
★ Posted a 34–19–9 season in 1978–79
★ Won 129 games in 296 appearances

LEAF FACT:

Mike Palmateer holds the Leafs' team record for most career assists by a goaltender with 16. His highest one-season total was five in 1978–79.

49 | GAYE STEWART

BORN: JUNE 28, 1923 IN FORT WILLIAM, ONTARIO
POSITION: LEFT WING
YEARS AS A LEAF: 1942–43 TO 1947–48
SWEATER #: 15 AND 16
MAPLE LEAF MOMENT: MARCH 16, 1946

GAYE STEWART HAD a most unusual start to his career as a Maple Leaf. He had just finished his second set of playoffs in the spring of 1942 when the Leafs called upon him to play another series of postseason games, this time with the Stanley Cup on the line. Stewart had started the 1941–42 season as a junior with the Toronto Marlboros (for whom he was a top goal scorer), and when they were knocked out of the playoffs he was sent to the Leafs' farm team in the American Hockey League, the Hershey Bears. When the Bears lost in the finals, Stewart thought his season was finally over, but this was not the case. The Leafs had lost three straight games to the Detroit Red Wings in the finals and were looking to add some new bodies in a last-ditch attempt to salvage their season. They called upon Stewart to be added to the forward ranks, and he played so well that coach Hap Day kept the 18-year-old left-winger in the lineup. Although he did not score a goal or record a point, he was on the Cup-winning team after only three NHL games!

The 1942–43 season was actually Stewart's rookie year, and he won the Calder Trophy with a 24-goal, 47-point performance in 48 games. The six-foot, 175-pound Stewart played his rookie year on a line with Bud Poile and Jack McLean. He did not rack up many penalty minutes, but he had an aggressive approach that made him popular with the fans. Stewart spent the next two years in the army, but he returned to the Leafs for the 1945–46 campaign and promptly set a team record for most goals in a season with 37, the best total in the NHL that year. Stewart secured that lofty status with his performance on the last weekend of the season, when Detroit was the opposition for the final two games, beginning on March 16, 1946.

The Leafs did not have much to play for in the last two contests of the '45–46 campaign, since they were not going to make the playoffs. Stewart was leading the league with 33 goals and added another when the Leafs romped to a 7–3 win during the first game between Toronto and Detroit. The two teams were tied 3–3 going into the final period, but after Detroit took the lead the Leafs responded with four straight goals, including one from Stewart, to seal the victory. Stewart also earned some penalty minutes for one of the few times in the season (only eight minutes on the year) for his part in a large scuffle late in the third period. Leaf forward Billy Taylor contributed three goals for the winners as well.

The next night in Detroit saw Stewart score a hat trick as the Leafs won a wild one by a score of 11–7. Linemates Gus Bodnar and Bud Poile were prominent in assisting Stewart on all his goals over the two games. Stewart also added two assists in the season finale to give him 52 points on the season, second only to Max Bentley of the Chicago Black Hawks, who had 61. Stewart scored a goal in each period during the Leafs' road victory, giving him 37 on the year and six up on Bentley, who had 31. Other top goal scorers included Toe Blake of Montreal with 29 and Maurice Richard, who had 27 for the Canadiens. The win gave the Leafs a 19–24–7 record to close the year five points out of a playoff spot.

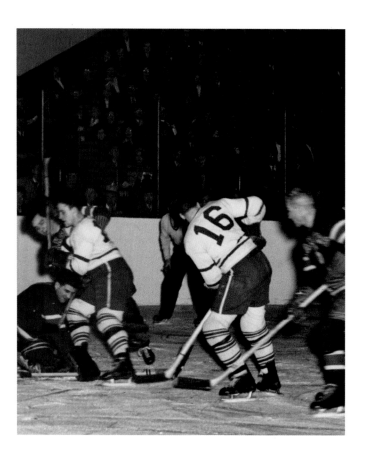

Stewart did not have as great a season in 1946–47, but he put up respectable numbers with 19 goals and 33 points in 60 games. He played in 11 playoff games and helped the Leafs recapture the Stanley Cup with seven points (two goals, five assists). The Leafs were bombed 6–0 in the first game of the finals but took the second game 4–0. Stewart scored one of the goals. That win at the Montreal Forum got the Leafs back on track, and they took the Cup in six games.

MAPLE LEAF CAREER HIGHLIGHTS

★ Signed as a free agent on March 6, 1942 by the Leafs
★ Member of two Stanley Cup teams (1942, 1947)
★ Named as an NHL First Team All-Star for the 1945–46 season
★ Recorded 133 points (81G, 52A) in 165 games as a Leaf

LEAF FACT:

Gaye Stewart won the Calder Trophy as the rookie of the year for the 1942–43 season, becoming the first Maple Leaf to win that award in the forties. Three other Leafs won the award in the same decade: Gus Bodnar (1944), Frank McCool (1945) and Howie Meeker (1947). In addition, Wally Stanowski (1940) was a finalist for the award. The Leafs won a total of five Stanley Cups in the decade.

50 | BILLY HARRIS

BORN: JULY 29, 1935 IN TORONTO, ONTARIO
POSITION: CENTRE
YEARS AS A LEAF: 1955–56 TO 1964–65
SWEATER #: 15
MAPLE LEAF MOMENT: OCTOBER 19, 1957

AS A SIX-YEAR-OLD BOY living in Toronto in 1942, Billy Harris was enthralled, as many other Canadians were, on the night of April 18 as the Maple Leafs played the Detroit Red Wings in the seventh game of the Stanley Cup finals. Harris' heroes won the game 3–1, and as the voice of Foster Hewitt trailed off the youngster fell asleep, dreaming of one day playing for the Maple Leafs. Few young boys ever realize that dream, but for Harris it was a goal he would achieve, and he would share in more than one Stanley Cup for the blue and white. Harris also remembered being inspired by a speech given by former Leaf great Syl Apps.

In the early fifties Harris was recruited by Stafford Smythe for the Leafs organization, and by 1950–51 he was playing Junior B for the Weston Dukes. He was promoted to the Toronto Marlboros Junior A team for the 1952–53 season and had 51 points in 56 games. The next year saw him score 25 goals and record 64 points in 59 games. He capped his junior career with a Memorial Cup in 1955 after a great regular season that saw him score 37 times in just 47 contests. A smooth skater and nifty puck handler, Harris had a style that was popular with the Leaf fans right from the start of his pro career. The Leafs hoped Harris could take over from Ted Kennedy at centre, but that was a little beyond his reach. However, one night early in the 1957–58 season, the Leafs might have thought Harris could fulfill his promise.

The Leafs were still in the process of rebuilding their team as the '57–58 campaign began, and they started the season with three straight losses. When the Boston Bruins came to town for a Saturday night contest on October 19, 1957, the Leafs resoundingly whipped them by a 7–0 score. The Leafs were in a fighting mood on this night and handed the Boston club its first loss of the season, before 13,100 fans at Maple Leaf Gardens. Leaf goalie Ed Chadwick played his best game of the year to date (30 saves), while Brian Cullen and Harris notched three goals apiece for the young Toronto club. Cullen opened the scoring, but it was Boston who outshot the Leafs 9–3 in the first period. Cullen added another in the second period, while Ron Stewart got another to give the Leafs a commanding 3–0 lead.

Harris stole the show in the third period with three goals, taking him to four on the season. His first two goals came just 30 seconds apart, scoring one on a backhand drive and the other on a deflection on a drive taken by Stewart. His third goal came in the final minute of play, as he bolted out of the penalty box to steal the puck and go in on a breakaway. His shot beat Don Simmons in the Boston net with just 22 seconds to play. The Gardens crowd gave him a large ovation and littered the ice with programs. When the game was over Leaf coach Billy Reay came onto the ice to celebrate his first-ever NHL victory by hugging Chadwick.

When Punch Imlach took over as coach of the Leafs he was bent on getting Harris out as a front-line player. Imlach would have been happy to trade "Hinky," but Smythe would not allow it, perhaps out of loyalty or because he knew Harris still had lots to offer in a supporting role. Imlach felt Harris

was too light at 157 pounds and probably not aggressive enough, even though he was an even six feet tall. Once Dave Keon and Red Kelly joined the team as centres, Harris was told that he was an extra forward and would play more only if there were injuries. He accepted his fate as a good team player and waited for an opportunity to show he could still contribute. Harris helped the Leafs make it to the finals in 1959 and 1960 and filled in admirably when the Leafs needed help to win three Stanley Cups.

MAPLE LEAF CAREER HIGHLIGHTS

★ Member of three Stanley Cup teams
★ Scored 22 goals and 30 assists in 1958–59 for the Leafs
★ Recorded 18 points (8G, 10A) in 62 playoff games
★ Recorded 287 points (106G, 181A) in 610 games for Toronto

LEAF FACT:

After the Leafs acquired Red Kelly in 1960, Billy Harris was often used as a reserve centre. On December 2, 1961, Harris filled in for Dave Keon between Dick Duff and George Armstrong. Harris scored three times on Chicago goalie Glenn Hall, and the Leafs won 6–4, while Toronto goalie Gerry Cheevers won his first NHL start. Harris finished the 1961–62 season with 15 goals and 25 points in 67 games.

51 | WALLY STANOWSKI

BORN: APRIL 28, 1919 IN WINNIPEG, MANITOBA
POSITION: DEFENCE
YEARS AS A LEAF: 1939–40 TO 1947–48
SWEATER #: 2, 3, 16 AND 20
MAPLE LEAF MOMENT: APRIL 14, 1942

DEFENCEMAN WALLY STANOWSKI first came to the attention of the Toronto Maple Leafs during the 1938 Memorial Cup final that was played at Maple Leaf Gardens. Stanowski was the star blueliner for the St. Boniface Seals when they came east to play the Oshawa Generals for the junior title. The Seals won the series in five games, and Stanowski's play was made up of spectacular rushes up the ice that caught the eye of all fans in the sold-out arena. One man watching very closely was Maple Leafs manager Conn Smythe. The shrewd Smythe made a deal with the New York Americans, who held Stanowski's playing rights, and the blueliner was sent to the minors for the 1938–39 season to play with the Syracuse Stars of the American Hockey League. Stanowski was brought up to the Leafs for the 1939–40 season and was picked to replace defenceman Jimmy Fowler. In his first game as a Leaf, Stanowski broke his ankle, so his season was reduced to just 27 games (two goals, seven assists). He put in a full season the next year, recording seven goals and 21 assists in 47 games.

Stanowski captured the imagination of the Toronto fans with his special way of winding up for a charge up the ice. His style of rushing the puck earned him the nickname "Whirling Dervish," and his good play earned him an All-Star Team selection for the 1940–41 campaign. Any defenceman who can take the puck out of danger is always a very valuable commodity, and Stanowki's game was built around trying to be creative on offence. His excellent skating skills and speed allowed him to hang on to the puck whenever he wanted. Stanowski was also very strong (at 5′11″, 180 pounds), which made him a feared bodychecker, but his penalty minute total was usually very low. The ankle injury flared up again the next season when he stepped on a glove during a fight. As a result he got into only 24 contests but came on strong during the playoffs with two goals and eight assists, helping the Leafs to win their first championship in many years. The 1942 finals against the Detroit Red Wings saw Stanowski paired on defence with Bingo Kampman, and they formed a formidable wall on the Leaf blue line. They were especially needed on the night of April 14, 1942, as the Leafs tried to win their second game of the finals against Detroit after losing the first three games of the series.

The Red Wings seemed determined to run the Leafs out of the building in the fifth game of the finals, held before 15,076 fans at Maple Leaf Gardens, but the Leafs came out strong. Detroit took three penalties in the first period and the Leafs took advantage to build a 2–0 lead. Stanowski and Syl Apps set up Nick Metz for the opening tally, then Stanowski got an unassisted marker at 15:24 of the opening frame. On his goal, Stanowski joined the attack as the Leafs swarmed the Detroit net, with Gaye Stewart, Pete Langelle and John McCreedy leading the charge. Stanowski jumped in, and his drive went into the net off the stick of a Detroit defenceman. The Leafs took complete charge of the game in the second when they scored five times to up the lead to 7–0.

Detroit finally got on the board in the third period, but Stanowski and Apps went to work again and set up Don Metz for a goal to make it 8–1. Apps got one more before Detroit added a couple late to make the final score 9–3 for Toronto. After the game the jubilant Leafs vowed they would be back home for the seventh game. "We'll win in Detroit on Thursday and back here on Saturday," goaltender Turk Broda predicted. The Leafs did just that and won their first Stanley Cup since 1931.

After a two-year stint in the Canadian army during the Second World War, Stanowski returned to the Leafs during the 1944–45 season. The Leafs finished third that year, but in the playoffs they beat Montreal and Detroit to win the Cup again.

MAPLE LEAF CAREER HIGHLIGHTS

★ Acquired by the Leafs in a trade with the New York Americans on October 17, 1937
★ Member of four Stanley Cup teams (1942, 1945, 1947, 1948)
★ Recorded 17 points (3G, 14A) in 60 playoff games
★ Recorded 94 points (20G, 74A) in 282 career games

LEAF FACT:

The 1940–41 season saw the Maple Leafs place three players on the NHL's First All-Star Team, marking only the second time this had happened in club history. Turk Broda was the goaltender, while Wally Stanowski was selected as a defenceman and Dave "Sweeney" Schriner made it as the left-winger.

52 | EDDIE SHACK

BORN: FEBRUARY 11, 1937 IN SUDBURY, ONTARIO
POSITION: LEFT WING
YEARS AS A LEAF: 1960–61 TO 1966–67; 1973–74 TO 1974–75
SWEATER #: 23
MAPLE LEAF MOMENT: DECEMBER 7, 1963

EDDIE SHACK WAS considered a top prospect in the New York Rangers system when he graduated from junior hockey. The six-foot-one, 200-pound left-winger scored 47 goals and totalled 104 points while playing his final season with the Guelph Biltmores of the OHA in 1956–57. Those numbers gave hope that Shack would have a big impact on Broadway, but it never happened for the rough-and-tough youngster. He never fit in while wearing the Ranger uniform, and the New York club tried to trade him to Detroit, but that deal fell through. Leaf coach and general manager Punch Imlach came to the rescue and sent Johnny Wilson and Pat Hannigan to the Rangers to complete a trade for Shack. It was the best thing that ever happened to the truculent winger, who found a home with the Leafs, mostly as a player who could come off the bench and give the team a much-needed spark. Toronto fans enjoyed his reckless approach and often chanted "We want Shack" whenever things got too dull. The game between the Leafs and the Chicago Black Hawks on the night of December 7, 1963, was anything but dull, and Shack played a prominent role.

The game was fast-moving and very physical, with the Toronto side determined to get a win against Chicago, who had beaten the Leafs four times already and had tied another contest. Backed by the superior goaltending of backup Don Simmons, the Leafs scored a goal in each period and shut out the Black Hawks 3–0 before more than 14,000 spectators at Maple Leaf Gardens. George Armstrong opened the scoring in the first period, while Frank Mahovlich scored a beautiful goal in the second. Shack chased down Elmer Vasko into the Chicago end, and when the Black Hawk defenceman unexpectedly tumbled to the ice, the Leaf winger was in all alone. Chicago netminder Glenn Hall did not go for a deke, so Shack simply whipped a shot into the short side for his fifth goal of the season with 3:33 gone in the third. It looked like the Leafs would coast the rest of the way, but Shack made sure the fans had a reason to stay until the end.

Just before the halfway mark of the final stanza, Shack got his stick up around the collar of Chicago tough guy Reggie Fleming and was called for high sticking. A few minutes later Fleming was on the ice with Shack and speared him just inside the Leaf blue line. Referee Frank Udvari caught the infraction and gave Fleming a five-minute major. Shack fell to one knee and looked to be hurt. Bob Baun was not going to stand idle while one of his teammates had been attacked in such a manner and skated over to the penalty box. He attempted to drag Fleming out of the sin bin and engage him in a fight. The officials intervened and then decided Fleming should be ejected. But that meant he would have to cross the ice to get to the dressing room. Fleming never made it, as Baun and Larry Hillman of the Leafs both pummelled the Chicago culprit. Soon all the players spilled out onto the ice, resulting in a major free-for-all that drew fines of $850 (including $25 each from 22 players in the game who had left the bench to join the fight).

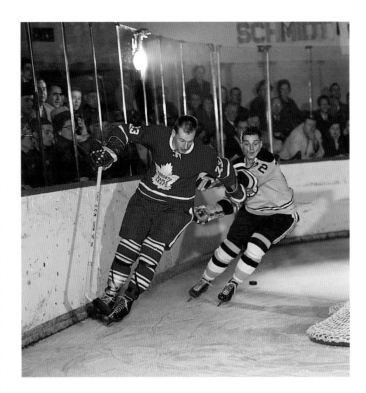

One of the main events in the brawling was a fight between Chicago's Murray Balfour and Toronto's Carl Brewer that ended up with the Leaf player going through an open gate at the Leaf bench. The wild scene saw Toronto Argonaut star running back Dick Shatto run down from the stands to come to the aid of Brewer.

The entire impetus for the brawl may have come from Shack, who told an interviewer before the game that Fleming was only a dangerous player from behind, and that he was pretty soft when confronted face to face. Whatever the reason, the game showed the Leafs were a tough team that stuck together.

MAPLE LEAF CAREER HIGHLIGHTS

★ Member of four Stanley Cup teams
★ Scored Stanley Cup-winning goal in 1963
★ Joined team again when contract purchased by the Leafs in June of 1973
★ Scored 99 goals and 195 points in 504 games

LEAF FACT:

One of the few athletes to have a song written about him, Eddie "the Entertainer" Shack had his ballad shoot to the top of the local hit parade when "Clear the Track, Here Comes Shack" was released during the 1965–66 season. The lyrics were written by hockey commentator and author Brian McFarlane, whose brother-in-law, Bill McCauley, composed the music.

53 GUS MORTSON

BORN: JANUARY 24, 1925 IN NEW LISKEARD, ONTARIO
POSITION: DEFENCE
YEARS AS A LEAF: 1946–47 TO 1951–52
SWEATER #: 3
MAPLE LEAF MOMENT: APRIL 1, 1948

DEFENCEMAN GUS MORTSON was another one of those players from the Canadian north to find fame and fortune as a Maple Leaf. He played junior hockey at St. Michael's and was on the 1945 Memorial Cup-winning team, one of the best junior squads ever assembled. The army discharged him because of a bad leg, but the Leafs signed him and inserted him into the lineup for the 1946–47 season when Toronto wanted to go with a younger team. He was paired with Jim Thomson, and the defensive duo became known as the Gold Dust Twins, since both of them hailed from the northern part of Ontario, an area known for its rich mining potential. Mortson was a blueliner with a mean streak and an ability to carry the puck out of his own end. He was a good skater and a fearless checker who let you know you were in for a battle if you dared to venture into the corner with him. Mortson and Thomson were the heart of the defensive-minded Leafs, and they helped lead the team to four Stanley Cups between 1947 and 1951.

In the 1947 playoffs, the Leafs faced the Canadiens in the Stanley Cup finals, and, in the third contest of the series, on the night of April 12, 1947, Mortson had a big hand in the Leaf victory. A great solo effort by Mortson got the Leafs an early 1–0 lead. Mortson skated around Ken Reardon of the Canadiens and then blasted a shot past Bill Durnan in the Montreal net, despite the fact he had torn ligaments in his wrist earlier in the first period. After the game Mortson said, "With my wrist hurting, the drive was a change of pace and it couldn't have worked out better." Both he and Thomson threw themselves in front of many Montreal drives, and Mortson played the entire game with his injury. He swept one puck away from the Toronto cage just as it was about to cross the goal line. The Leafs went up 3–0 before the Habs were able to respond with a pair, but a third-period tally by Toronto captain Ted Kennedy ended any hopes for a Montreal comeback. After the game, Leaf general manager Conn Smythe commented on his two defensive stars. "Those kids have only been scored on four times in eight games," Smythe noted. It would not be the last time their stellar work would be noticed, as the Leafs took the Cup in six games.

April 1, 1948, was another good night for Mortson. The Leafs were defending their championship against the Detroit Red Wings in the finals. It was the opening game of the series, and Mortson scored the winning goal in a 5–3 Leaf victory. His goal came at 14:32 of the second when he joined the attack and shot home a pass from Max Bentley, giving the Leafs a 4–1 lead. Mortson, who had also assisted on a Syl Apps goal in the first, then broke his leg when he and Thomson smashed into Jack Stewart of the Red Wings. His leg was fractured in two places, above the ankle and below the knee. He missed the rest of the playoffs and was expected to be in a cast for six to eight weeks. Despite the injury to one of their best defencemen, the Leafs went on to sweep the Red Wings in four straight to win their second consecutive Cup.

After the game was over Mortson described how he got hurt in the collision: "My skate turned in on me, stuck in

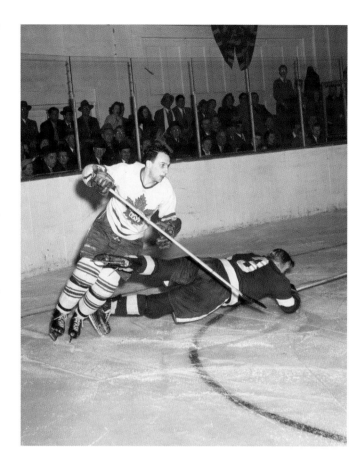

the ice and when Stewart rode into us, my whole weight came down on my leg. I could feel something go. Stewart just leaned on us. I'll get better — I hope."

Mortson did indeed get better and returned to the Leaf lineup for the 1948–49 season, playing in all 60 games and recording 15 points. The Leafs won their third straight Cup that year, and Mortson was also a member of the 1951 squad that won another championship. His career in Toronto ended when the Leafs sent him to Chicago in 1952.

MAPLE LEAF CAREER HIGHLIGHTS

★ Member of four Stanley Cup teams with Toronto
★ Led the NHL in penalty minutes twice as a Leaf
★ Named to the NHL's First All-Star Team in 1949–50
★ Recorded 92 points (21G, 71A) in 371 games as a Leaf

LEAF FACT:

Gus Mortson believed that Toronto traded him away to Chicago because he got angry at Leaf manager Conn Smythe after a game. He was with the Black Hawks for six years and was offered back to the Leafs at one point. Chicago wanted Tim Horton in return, but the Leafs wisely refused the offer. Mortson finished his career with Detroit in 1958–59.

54 | TOMAS KABERLE

BORN: MARCH 2, 1978 IN RAKOVNIK, CZECH REPUBLIC
POSITION: DEFENCE
YEARS AS A LEAF: 1998–99 TO PRESENT
SWEATER #: 15
MAPLE LEAF MOMENT: OCTOBER 28, 2006

WHEN NEW COACH Pat Quinn took over the Maple Leafs for the start of the 1998–99 season, one area he wanted to address was the blue line brigade. Toronto needed some new faces on defence, and Danny Markov, Yannick Tremblay and Tomas Kaberle were all going to be given a chance. Kaberle was not expected to make the Leafs coming out of training camp, but he showed he belonged and logged an amazing 29:13 minutes in his first game as a Leaf (a 2–1 win over Detroit). He also scored his first NHL goal against the Red Wings and finished his rookie year with four goals and 22 points in 57 games. Blessed with good bloodlines (his father was a good player for the Czech national team in his day and his brother won a Stanley Cup with Carolina in 2006), Kaberle is an amazing skater who handles the puck with great dexterity. He is not nearly as alert on defence as he should be, but the strength of Kaberle's game is to carry the puck and to lead or join the attack. When he does not play that way he can get into trouble, and at the start of the 2006–07 season the heavily scrutinized Leaf had a large contract to live up to, and that is not always easy. That was the position Kaberle found himself in when the Leaf rolled into Montreal on October 28, 2006.

To say that Kaberle got off to a slow start in '06–07 would be an understatement. The Leafs were trying to develop an identity under new coach Paul Maurice, and Kaberle was looking for his game (only two assists in the first 11 contests) when he exploded with a four-point night against the Canadiens. The 28-year-old defenceman got the Leafs off to a good start by assisting on Alexei Ponikarovsky's fourth goal of the season at 1:44 of the first period and then took a shot that got past Montreal netminder David Aebischer to give Toronto a 2–0 lead. Montreal got one back to shrink the Leaf lead to 2–1, but Kaberle scored once again on a backhand drive (that actually bounced off teammate Michael Peca) to restore Toronto's two-goal margin. The Habs cut the lead in the second period once again, but Kaberle led a rush into the Montreal end and threw the puck out in front from just beside the Canadiens' net. Somehow it bounced into the net and Kaberle had recorded his first-ever career hat trick. It was the first Leaf three-goal game by a defenceman since Borje Salming did it back in October of 1981!

But Kaberle's goal scoring was not over. The Habs came back to even the score at 4–4, and when overtime proved fruitless, the two teams lined up for the shootout. Maurice sensed Kaberle's stick might still be hot and chose him to be the Leafs' first shooter. He made a nice move on Aebischer before roofing a drive up into the top of the net, making it look easy in the process. The Leafs finally prevailed in the shootout (largely due to the good work of netminder J.S. Aubin) when Kyle Wellwood scored and they were credited with a 5–4 victory.

After the game Kaberle spoke about playing on the road to the media gathered around. "You guys [the media] were on us big-time, so it's nice to go on the road and get

away from it," he said. "Obviously, I'm not there to score hat tricks. I'm there to keep it simple in the back end and get passes to guys. That's my game. I'm just happy we got the two points." A new five-year contract (valued at $21.25 million) signed in the off-season meant that more would be expected of Kaberle. He was philosophical the next day when he added, "I wish we had all the answers. I was battling hard [prior to his big game in Montreal]. Sometimes you have good chances and the points just don't come. . . . But you have to keep playing." For the most part, Tomas Kaberle has played very well for the Maple Leafs.

MAPLE LEAF CAREER HIGHLIGHTS

★ Drafted 204th overall by Toronto in 1996
★ Scored a career-high 11 goals in 2002–03 and 2006–07
★ Recorded a career-best 67 points (9G, 58A) in 2005–06
★ Has recorded five seasons of 40 or more points as a Leaf (as of 2006–07)

LEAF FACT:

During the 2000–01 season the Maple Leafs had an opportunity to trade Tomas Kaberle as part of a package to Philadelphia for Eric Lindros, but general manager and coach Pat Quinn balked at the Flyers' request to include the defender in the deal. In the off-season prior to the 2006–07 campaign, it was rumoured that Kaberle was part of package offered by the Leafs to Edmonton for defenceman Chris Pronger, but that deal never materialized.

55 | DAVE ANDREYCHUK

BORN: SEPTEMBER 29, 1963 IN HAMILTON, ONTARIO
POSITION: LEFT WING
YEARS AS A LEAF: 1992–93 TO 1995–96
SWEATER #: 14
MAPLE LEAF MOMENT: MARCH 23, 1993

THE MAPLE LEAFS had one of those "nice" problems on their hands when they realized that goaltender Felix Potvin could play at the NHL level. Grant Fuhr had been the best Leaf player in 1991–92, but there was really no need to keep two top-flight goalies on one team when one could be traded for other help. After conferring with coach Pat Burns, Toronto general manager Cliff Fletcher decided the Leafs could acquire some scoring assistance by moving Fuhr to another team. The Buffalo Sabres were very interested and offered left-winger Dave Andreychuk (a 29-goal scorer at the time), back-up netminder Darren Puppa and a first-round draft choice (eventually used to select Kenny Jonsson) to complete the deal on February 2, 1993. The Leafs wanted to find a scoring winger for centre Doug Gilmour, and the big winger (6´4˝ and 220 pounds) fit the bill perfectly.

An imposing figure in front of the opposition net, Andreychuk had soft hands and a long reach that allowed him to scoop up many loose pucks. He was especially good on the power-play and could handle the heavy going in the slot area. Andreychuk worked hard to scoop up loose pucks and rebounds, and he was good at getting his shot off quickly. His play with the Leafs for the remainder of the '92–93 campaign was all the Leafs could have hoped for, as he scored 25 times, including his 50th of the year on March 23, 1993, in Winnipeg.

The Leafs started the game with a strong forecheck and scored two goals before the game was seven minutes old. Toronto took 10 shots on goal in the first period, and it was only the work of Jets goalie Bob Essensa that kept the score respectable. (Toronto would outshoot Winnipeg 42–24 on the night.) The Jets came out firing in the second and took a 3–2 lead before Gilmour tied the game up for the Leafs once again by scoring in the last minute of the period. Teemu Selanne gave the Jets the lead early in the third, but Andreychuk scored his 50th goal of the season to even the score once more. The goal came as Andreychuk took a pass in the slot and ripped a drive over Essensa's shoulder at 4:22 of the final frame. The Leafs got a goal from Dave McLlwain to secure a 5–4 victory and their fifth win in six games. The win made it a perfect night for Andreychuk, who also recorded his 800th career point with an assist during the game. The talk afterwards was about his milestone goal.

"It's nice to get it out of the way. I was a little nervous before the game, and it's the first time in a long time I've been like that. But scoring 50 is something I'll always look back on," Andreychuk said. The Leaf winger took an amazing 15 shots on goal during the game. "If you can't score once out of 15 shots, you're in trouble," he said of the mark that beat his previous one-game total by three shots. As for the 50th goal puck, Andreychuk said he planned to give it to his father, Julian. "He's supported me through thick and thin. He can put it on top of the TV and look at it all day."

Andreychuk became the third player to record his 50th goal of the year while wearing a Toronto uniform. "This is good for me because it means my career is still on the rise.

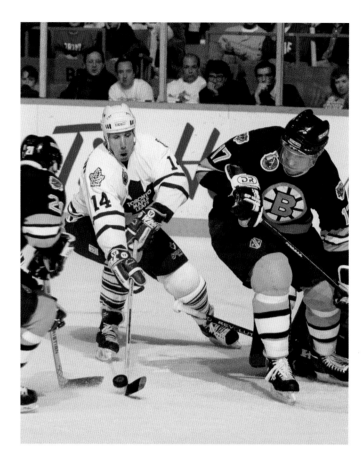

When you first start playing, you figure when you get to 30 [years old] your career will almost be over. Being traded has obviously helped. It's a new life with a new team," he said. Coach Burns said of the large winger, "He's a big horse. When the puck's around the goal, he's like a dog chasing a car."

The Leafs had a great playoff in the '93 postseason. Andreychuk scored 12 goals and totalled 19 points in 21 games. He followed that up by scoring 53 for the Leafs in 1993–94, the second-most in Leaf history for a single season.

MAPLE LEAF CAREER HIGHLIGHTS

★ Recorded 38 points (25G, 13A) in 31 games for the Leafs in 1992–93
★ Scored 53 goals and 99 points for the Leafs in 1993–94
★ Recorded 34 points (20G, 14A) in 46 playoff games
★ Recorded 219 points (120G, 99A) in 223 career games for Toronto

LEAF FACT:

Dave Andreychuk scored his 50th goal of the 1993–94 season against the San Jose Sharks, beating goalie Arturs Irbe at Maple Leaf Gardens on March 24, 1994.

56 | BOB NEVIN

BORN: MARCH 18, 1938 IN SOUTH PORCUPINE, ONTARIO
POSITION: RIGHT WING
YEARS AS A LEAF: 1957–58 TO 1963–64
SWEATER #: 11
MAPLE LEAF MOMENT: APRIL 9, 1963

BOB NEVIN WAS a product of the great Leaf development system in the fifties. He went into the Leaf chain with the Weston Dukes in 1953–54, then joined the Toronto Marlboros, where he produced 111 goals over three seasons of play (including 45 in 51 games during the 1956–57 season). He was on the Memorial Cup-winning team of 1956 as the Marlies beat the Regina Pats for the title. Many of the Marlboro players were just about ready to contribute to the Maple Leafs. Nevin played the 1957–58 season with the Marlies and got into four games with the Leafs that year. He played most of the next two seasons with Rochester of the American Hockey League (scoring 32 in his second year there) before he was deemed ready to be promoted to the big team.

The right-winger had good size at six feet and 190 pounds, and he knew how to use it well, although not in an aggressive manner. With 21 goals and 58 points in his first year, he quickly established himself as an NHL player. Nevin was a nice complement to centre Red Kelly and left-winger Frank Mahovlich, and the line was one of the best in the league during 1960–61. Only teammate Dave Keon kept Nevin from winning the rookie of the year award. In his next two seasons with the Leafs, Nevin made a major contribution to a pair of Stanley Cup wins. During the 1963 Stanley Cup finals, Nevin helped the Leafs get off to a great start against Detroit on the night of April 9, 1963.

The Leafs reached the finals by taking out the Montreal Canadiens in five games in the semi-finals. Most observers thought the first-place Leafs would do the same to the Red Wings to win their second consecutive championship. The series opened in Toronto, and Leaf winger Dick Duff set an NHL record with the fastest two goals to start a playoff game by scoring twice just 1:08 into the contest. Detroit goalie Terry Sawchuk did not look especially sharp on either of Duff's goals, although he bounced back to make some fine stops later in the game. Before the first period ended, the Leafs penetrated the Red Wing defence once again, as Nevin stole the puck from Detroit rearguard Howie Young at the blue line. The Leaf winger took the puck all the way in before backhanding a shot into the far side of the net past a beleaguered Sawchuk to make it 3–0.

However, the Red Wings got two goals from Larry Jeffrey in the second period to close the gap to 3–2 going into the third. It looked like the Leafs might blow the contest, but another marker by Nevin ended any Detroit hopes for a comeback. Bob Pulford let a drive go from the point that Nevin was able to redirect past Sawchuk to secure a 4–2 victory. The only bad thing to happen to the Leafs was the loss of star winger Frank Mahovlich to injury. It turned out the Leafs had no need to worry about playing without The Big M, since they beat Detroit handily in five games. Nevin finished the playoffs with three points (all goals) in 10 games.

Nevin's production had declined since his rookie year, and in 1963–64 he had only seven goals and 12 assists in 49 games. Sensing that the Leafs needed a change, coach and

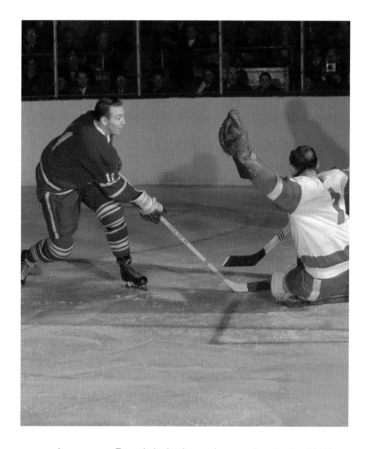

general manager Punch Imlach made a major deal with New York, sending Nevin to the Big Apple along with Dick Duff. Although he had been in the Leaf organization since his junior days, Nevin was philosophical about the deal. "You've got to expect these things when you're a professional athlete," he said. "That's the wonderful world of sport, I guess. They own your contract. It's their prerogative. You play where they say. Grin and bear it."

Nevin would excel in New York, playing seven years for the Rangers and being named team captain in 1964–65.

MAPLE LEAF CAREER HIGHLIGHTS

★ Played on two Stanley Cup teams with the Leafs
★ Scored 21 goals and 58 points as a rookie in 1960–61
★ Recorded 10 points (6G, 4A) in 27 playoff games
★ Recorded 155 points (55G, 100A) in 250 games as a Maple Leaf

LEAF FACT:

The trade that saw Bob Nevin go to the Rangers was a deal that was made for the current needs of the Leafs and the long-term needs of the New York club. It turned out as planned when, during the 1971 playoffs, Nevin returned to Maple Leaf Gardens and scored the winning overtime goal that knocked the Leafs out of the playoffs with a 2–1 victory in the sixth game of the quarter-finals.

57

JIM THOMSON

BORN: FEBRUARY 23, 1927 IN WINNIPEG, MANITOBA
POSITION: DEFENCE
YEARS AS A LEAF: 1945–46 TO 1956–57
SWEATER #: 2
MAPLE LEAF MOMENT: MARCH 24, 1948

DEFENCEMAN JIM THOMSON was one of the best student athletes to attend St. Michael's College in Toronto. He played hockey for the St. Mike's Majors for two seasons and was a top performer. Thomson then joined the Leafs as a 19-year-old in 1945–46. He played in five games for Toronto but spent most of the year in Pittsburgh, where he suited up for the Hornets of the AHL. The next season was Thomson's first full year with the Leafs, and he scored two goals and 14 assists in 60 games. The Leafs then took the Stanley Cup in the '47 playoffs, the first of three straight championships Thomson would anchor. One of the larger players in the NHL at the time at six feet and 190 pounds, Thomson was tough to play against (846 career penalty minutes with the Leafs) and often faced the opposition's best player. Thomson was the type of defenceman who looked after his own end first while defensive partner Gus Mortson lugged the puck up the ice. Thomson could pass the puck effectively, as his 29–assist total in 1947–48 indicates. He could handle the point on the power-play, although he was not a noted goal scorer by any means. (In six of his twelve seasons as a Maple Leaf, Thomson did not score a goal.) But he was a very valuable member of the team and the best defender in the club year after year. During one playoff game against the Boston Bruins, Thomson surprised everyone with a big goal when the Leafs needed it most.

The Leafs and Bruins began their semi-final series at Maple Leaf Gardens on the night of March 24, 1948. The Leafs had finished first overall during the 1947–48 season with 77 points, while the Boston club placed third with 59 points. Even though the Leafs were defending champions they were expecting a tough series from the Bruins. The Beantowners were determined to get off to a great start and jumped out to a 1–0 lead before Bill Ezinicki tied it for Toronto. The teams exchanged goals to keep the game even at 2–2 in the second period, but the Bruins scored two goals in the third to take a 4–2 lead, even though Toronto was outplaying the Bruins by a good margin, outshooting Boston 53 to 26. But Leaf captain Syl Apps was not going to stand still for a loss on home ice and got one back to draw Toronto closer at 4–3. The Leafs were accustomed to coming back during the regular season, and this night they were true to form. With under eight minutes to play, Thomson scored his first goal of the year (he had none in 60 regular season games) to lift the Leafs into a 4–4 tie. The game went into overtime, and the two clubs exchanged many chances before Nick Metz scored at the 17:00 minute mark to give the Leafs a hard-fought 5–4 win.

Naturally, Thomson was asked about his goal after the game. "Simply shoot when the goaltender's vision is blocked," he said with a smile on his face. He was also asked if he remembered what to do after scoring a goal. "I threw both hands up as high as I could," he replied.

The game marked the 10th time the Leafs and Bruins had played an overtime playoff game, with Toronto holding a 7–3 advantage. Although they lost, the Bruins were confident

they could still take the series. "Leafs were lucky," Bruins forward Grant Warwick proclaimed. "We'll wear them down." But Toronto manager Conn Smythe thought differently. "If we win this one, we'll take it all. The way those kids come back, nobody's going to beat them!"

Smythe was right, as the Leafs took the Bruins in five games and then won the Cup once again by beating Detroit in four straight games.

MAPLE LEAF CAREER HIGHLIGHTS

★ Member of four Stanley Cup teams with the Leafs
★ Twice selected to the NHL's Second All-Star Team
★ Recorded 223 points (15G, 208A) in 717 games as a Leaf
★ Recorded 15 points (3G, 13A) in 62 career playoff games

LEAF FACT:

When Ted Kennedy retired after the 1955–56 season, the Leafs named Jim Thomson as their new captain. But when Kennedy decided to come back during the 1956–57 season for his final 30 games as a Leaf, Thomson insisted that the 'C' be given back to Kennedy. Thomson was sold to Chicago in 1957 after his involvement in starting the players' union made Conn Smythe very angry with him and therefore Thomson never resumed his captaincy.

58 | TOD SLOAN

BORN: NOVEMBER 30, 1927 IN PONTIAC, QUEBEC
POSITION: CENTRE
YEARS AS A LEAF: 1947–48 TO 1957–58
SWEATER #: 11, 15 AND 20
MAPLE LEAF MOMENT: MARCH 10, 1956

ALTHOUGH HE WAS born in Quebec, Tod Sloan came to Toronto to attend St. Michael's College and play junior hockey for the Majors. His good play caught the eye of Leaf management, who were impressed with his ability to shoot a puck. Sloan helped the Majors to a Memorial Cup title in 1945 (17 goals in 14 playoff games) and then won the OHL's scoring title in 1945–46 (43 goals and 75 points). The Leafs signed him to a contract and then sent him to Pittsburgh of the AHL to give him some professional experience. He was in the minors for the better part of three seasons (including one in Cleveland) before he made it to the Leafs to stay in 1950–51. Sloan played with talented players like Ted Kennedy and Sid Smith for most of the year and scored 31 times. He saved his best performance for the '51 playoffs when the Leafs met the Canadiens in the final. In the last contest of the five-game series, Sloan scored two goals, the second coming in the last minute of play to give the Leafs a chance to win the Stanley Cup in overtime. Bill Barilko scored the extra-time winner, and Sloan's name was on the coveted trophy for the first time. Sloan scored 25 in the following season but then did not put up any notable numbers until the 1955–56 season, when he performed like an All-Star. He had a memorable night on March 10, 1956, when the Leafs hosted the New York Rangers.

Going into the Saturday night contest against the Rangers, Sloan had scored 36 goals, leaving him just one short of the Leafs' best single-season mark. New York jumped out to a 2–0 lead in the first period but did not play a defensive game. The Leafs, who needed the game to secure a playoff spot, got one back before the opening frame was done and then scored the next four goals to win the contest 5–2. Sloan's 37th of the year turned out to be the winning goal and tied him with Gaye Stewart for most goals in one season by a Leaf. It came when Sid Smith dug the puck out of the corner, and Sloan jumped in to take the loose disc to the front of the net before depositing a drive over the shoulder of Ranger netminder Gump Worsley into the top corner. The goal was the 10th game-winning marker for Sloan to that point in the season, and the Leafs had won only 23 games. Sloan posed with his record-tying puck after the game, and Toronto management decided he would earn a $1,000 bonus if he scored another to establish a new club mark. Sloan had received a $1,000 bonus for each of his 25th, 30th and 35th goals of the season under the bonus system the Leafs had set up before the year began.

"By then [the middle of the second period] I was getting desperate, and I wasn't going to pass up any shots," Sloan said after the game. "A few minutes before, Tim Horton set me up on a getaway, and I had Worsley all to myself. I had an opening of about six inches, tried to put the puck along the ice and missed from here to there." The shot that beat Worsley came from some distance, and some reporters wondered if Sloan had scored a lucky goal. "Fluke? In a way maybe," Sloan admitted. "I was surprised to see it go in. But they all count. For me and for the team."

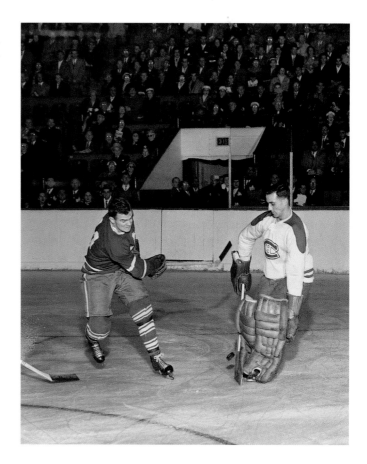

Sloan could not score another goal in the remaining three contests, but his team did make the playoffs as they edged out Boston by two points (61 to 59), earning fourth place in the standings. The Leafs met the second-place Red Wings in the semi-finals and were ousted in just five games. Sloan played two more years with the Leafs before he was sent to Chicago, where he won another Cup with the Black Hawks, in 1961, his last year in the NHL.

MAPLE LEAF CAREER HIGHLIGHTS

★ Signed as a free agent on April 30, 1946
★ Member of Stanley Cup team in 1951
★ Named to the NHL's Second All-Star Team for the 1955–56 season
★ Recorded 346 points (162G, 184A) in 549 games with Toronto

LEAF FACT:

The J.P. Bickell Memorial Cup was donated by the Maple Leafs' board of directors to honour the service of the man the trophy is named after for his efforts as a director. Since 1953, the trophy has been presented to a player at the discretion of the board, usually for a season of great play. Tod Sloan won the award for his play in 1955–56 when he scored 37 goals and totalled 66 points in 70 games played.

59 | BABE PRATT

BORN: JANUARY 7, 1916 IN STONY MOUNTAIN, MANITOBA
POSITION: DEFENCE
YEARS AS A LEAF: 1942–43 TO 1945–46
SWEATER #: 2, 4 AND 12
MAPLE LEAF MOMENT: APRIL 22, 1945

THE NEW YORK RANGERS considered defenceman Walter "Babe" Pratt one of the best prospects they had ever recruited when they signed him in October of 1935. He was in their farm system for only a brief time before he was called up to Broadway. Pratt was a Big Apple kind of character who enjoyed his celebrity status to the fullest. He was also a very good hockey player and helped the Rangers to the Stanley Cup in 1940, scoring three goals in 12 playoff games that year. Pratt always had his assist total in double digits, hitting a high of 24 in 1941–42. However, the New York club grew tired of his off-ice antics and dealt him to the Maple Leafs for Hank Goldup and Red Garrett on November 27,1943, after four games of the '43–44 season had been played.

The Leafs knew they were getting a player who marched to the beat of his own drummer and felt they would have to keep Pratt in check if he was going to be effective. They went as far as to make coach Hap Day his roommate on the road. It paid dividends. In his first 40 games as a Leaf Pratt recorded 37 points (12 goals, 25 assists). Pratt's best game during the season came on January 8, 1944, when he set a team record with six assists in one game during a 12–3 win over Boston. His fine performance was rewarded with a spot on the First All-Star Team and the Hart Trophy as the NHL's best player. Pratt's most memorable goal as a Leaf came in the 1945 playoffs, when the Leafs met the Detroit Red Wings in the finals. The Leafs won the first three games of the series (all shutouts by goalie Frank McCool) but then proceeded to lose the next three.

The Leafs had missed an opportunity to win the Cup in the sixth game on home ice on a Saturday night, losing 1–0 in overtime, and travelled to Detroit for the Sunday night game seven contest, held before 14,890 fans at the Olympia on April 22, 1945. If the Leafs felt down about their loss the previous night they did not show it, as they grabbed a 1–0 lead on a goal by Mel Hill at 5:38 of the first period when he knocked home a pass from Ted Kennedy. The goal stood up until the third period, when Detroit evened the score on a goal by Murray Armstrong, a one-time Leaf. The game remained tied until Syd Howe was whistled off for a penalty, giving the Leafs a power-play opportunity. An ailing Nick Metz got the puck over to Pratt inside the Red Wings' blue line, and he let go a shot that Detroit goalie Harry Lumley stopped but did not cover up. Pratt kept coming and poked the loose puck into the net to give the Leafs a 2–1 lead. Toronto's Elwyn Morris took a late penalty, but the Leafs held on the rest of the way. Red Wings fans had been hoping for a miracle finish, much like the Leafs had done to their team in 1942 when they came back from three games down to win the Cup. Pratt's goal ensured that was not going to happen, and the Maple Leafs won their third championship.

Pratt was good throughout the 1944–45 season (18 goals and 41 points in 50 games) and superb in the playoffs (two goals, four assists in 13 games), but he was never the same player afterwards. A contract dispute with the Leafs prior to the '44–45 season seemed to sour Pratt, who was

asking for a $7,000 raise but got $6,500 instead. "Hockey is my business and if I'm as valuable as this club thinks I am, then I'm playing according to dollar signs," he said. He played in only 41 games in 1945–46 due to a gambling-related suspension but still managed to record 25 points. The Leafs moved him to Boston for 1946–47, deciding that youth should be served. Pratt was a Bruin for just one season before he began toiling in the minor leagues for the balance of his career.

MAPLE LEAF CAREER HIGHLIGHTS

★ Member of Stanley Cup team in 1945
★ Named winner of the Hart Trophy in 1944
★ Elected to the Hockey Hall of Fame in 1966
★ Recorded 160 points (52G, 108A) in 181 games as a Leaf

LEAF FACT:

Babe Pratt's son Tracy played briefly for the Maple Leafs during the 1976–77 season. A defenceman like his father, the younger Pratt played in 11 games during the regular season (recording one assist) and in four playoff games.

60 | IAN TURNBULL

BORN: DECEMBER 22, 1953 IN MONTREAL, QUEBEC
POSITION: DEFENCE
YEARS AS A LEAF: 1973–74 TO 1981–82
SWEATER #: 2
MAPLE LEAF MOMENT: FEBRUARY 2, 1977

IAN TURNBULL WAS one of the most talented players the Maple Leafs have ever drafted. Gifted with great physical talent, the six-foot, 200-pound defenceman was also one of the strongest players to wear a Leaf uniform. The hard-shooting blueliner could skate as well as anyone in the NHL and could carry the puck with great authority. Turnbull started his career with the Leafs as a 19-year-old in 1973–74, the same year Borje Salming joined the team. The pair worked the points on one of the most devastating power-plays in the league for a number of years. When Turnbull was ready and focused to play he could cause havoc for any opposing team. Such was the case when the Detroit Red Wings came to play the Leafs on February 2, 1977, at Maple Leaf Gardens.

Turnbull entered the game against Detroit with only two goals in his last 37 games. By the end of the evening Turnbull had not only broken out of his slump but had set an NHL record for defencemen by scoring five goals in a 9–1 rout of the Red Wings. After a scoreless first period, Turnbull scored two goals to lead a five-goal outburst in the second by the home team. His first goal came on a wrist shot, while his second was scored on a breakaway on Detroit goalie Eddie Giacomin. The Red Wings switched to Jim Rutherford in net for the third period, but that proved to be futile, as the Leafs connected for four more goals. Turnbull's third goal of the night came on a hard slap shot, while the fourth bounced in off his body after teammate Stan Weir had taken a shot at the Detroit net. Turnbull's record-breaking final goal came on another breakaway with under two minutes to go in the game. Borje Salming (who earned three assists on the night) sprung his defensive partner with a perfect pass, and Turnbull made no mistake. The crowd of 16,422 gave him a standing ovation, as his teammates came off the bench to congratulate the 23-year-old defenceman. He had scored his five goals on only five shots.

Turnbull's goal total shot up to 16 with his five on the night, but he was also the Leafs' top plus/minus player on the season. "It was one of those nights when everything goes in. It was like a good day at the racetrack. I wish the track had been going this afternoon. I probably would have cleaned up," Turnbull joked after the game. "A couple of goals were easy and a couple of others were lucky," he said. Turnbull said the Leafs were using a different system since captain Darryl Sittler was out of the lineup with an injury, noting that the Leaf wingers were more checkers than puck carriers. That left room for the Toronto defencemen to jump into the attack. Turnbull indicated that he once scored five goals in a game as a junior but had never scored more than two in a game as a pro. He knew he had tied the record after his fourth goal and said he wanted to try for the fifth: "The whole idea was to head-man the puck, and everything went just as planned." Detroit coach Larry Wilson thought Turnbull "was the whole game. He did us in himself." Maple Leaf coach Red Kelly felt that Turnbull was overdue for some goal scoring. "I had no indication he was going to do it tonight, but I knew it wasn't far off."

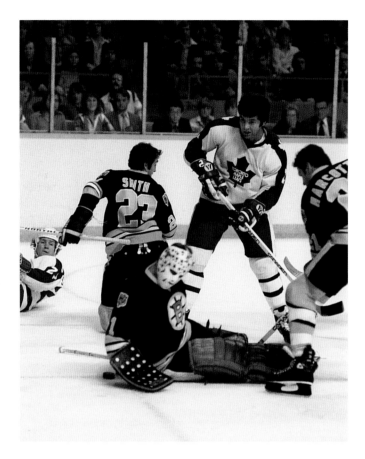

As great as this moment was for Turnbull, he played his best hockey for the Leafs in the 1978 playoffs when an injury to Salming forced him to raise his game to a new level. Turnbull did not disappoint during the series against the New York Islanders, and he scored a goal in the Leafs' 2–1 game seven victory.

MAPLE LEAF CAREER HIGHLIGHTS

★ Drafted 15th overall by the Leafs in 1973
★ Recorded 35 points (8G, 27A) as a rookie in 78 games
★ Recorded 50 or more points five times
★ Recorded 414 points (including 320 assists) in 580 games played

LEAF FACT:

Ian Turnbull (20 in 1976–76 and 22 in 1976–77) and Al Iafrate are the only two defencemen in Leaf history to score 20 or more goals in a season on two occasions; Turnbull is the only one to do it in consecutive years. He also holds the club record for points in a season for defencemen with 79 in 1976–77.

61 | BERT OLMSTEAD

BORN: SEPTEMBER 4, 1926 IN SCEPTER, SASKATCHEWAN
POSITION: LEFT WING
YEARS AS A LEAF: 1958–59 TO 1961–62
SWEATER #: 16
MAPLE LEAF MOMENT: APRIL 14, 1959

THE MONTREAL CANADIENS told left-winger Bert Olmstead that he was not going to be protected during the 1958 intra-league draft. The Habs were not going to meet the contract demands of the six-foot-two, 183-pound Olmstead, and the 32-year-old thought he might retire to try coaching. But the Maple Leafs thought Olmstead would be perfect for their young club, and Toronto coach Billy Reay (who had been a teammate of Olmstead's with the Canadiens) liked his work ethic. Even though Reay was replaced early in the 1958–59 season by Punch Imlach, Olmstead did not see his role change. A tireless checker and workhorse, he kept working with the younger players in the club, such as Bob Pulford and Frank Mahovlich. His dedication rubbed off on his teammates as the '58–59 season wore on. The Leafs recovered from a horrible start to make the playoffs on the last night of the season and upset the Boston Bruins in seven games in the semi-finals. The Leafs then met the Canadiens in the final, and they enjoyed one more shining moment on April 14, 1959, before the Habs rolled over Toronto for their fourth straight Stanley Cup.

Toronto kept the opening game at the Forum close for two periods — Olmstead helped set up a goal by Ron Stewart — but Montreal scored twice in the third to win 5–3. The Leafs vowed to play better for the balance of the series. Olmstead got another assist on the Leafs' only goal of the second game, but the Habs won the contest 3–1. Back in Maple Leaf Gardens for the third match, the Leafs played their best game of the finals. Toronto opened the scoring on a goal by Billy Harris late in the first period, but Montreal tied it before the intermission. Olmstead scored the only goal of the second, assisted on the play by Stewart and Pulford. Olmstead's overall play was very impressive, as he worked diligently along the boards and in the corners, causing all kinds of havoc in the Montreal end all game long. The Canadiens tied the score in the third period to force overtime, but the Leafs prevailed when Dick Duff beat Jacques Plante with a shot halfway through the first extra period.

The Leafs felt good about their first win in the finals since 1951. Duff said that he was thinking about trying to go around a Montreal defenceman on his winning rush, ". . . but then I realized I couldn't make it, so I just slapped it in." As for his goal, Olmstead was asked if he picked a hole. "No sir," he replied. "I don't pick holes. I just shoot at the net."

The Leafs' good feeling did not last very long, as the Habs came back to win the fourth game 3–2 despite a valiant effort by the hometown club. Olmstead took the defeat very hard, while Imlach bravely said, "They [the Canadiens] haven't won a thing yet. I'm proud of this team, but I'm not happy with the result." The Leaf coach was no happier at the end of the fifth game, as the Habs took the final contest 5–3. The Leafs fought until the final siren sounded, but they were not yet ready to upend the defending champions.

Fittingly, Olmstead scored the final goal of the game in the third period as the Leafs narrowed a 5–1 score to a more respectable 5–3. Montreal coach Toe Blake admired how the

Leafs refused to quit, while Montreal defenceman Tom Johnson respected the work of former teammate Olmstead. "If they had more like him, it might have been different. I'm glad they didn't have more like him."

Even though they did not win the Cup in '59, the Leaf club gained the confidence they needed for the future. Olmstead stayed with the Leafs until they reached the promised land in 1962. Then he was promptly put up for grabs again at the intra-league draft. Although the New York Rangers selected him, this time the future Hall of Famer decided to retire.

MAPLE LEAF CAREER HIGHLIGHTS

★ Member of Stanley Cup team in 1962
★ Recorded 52 points (18G, 34A) in 67 games during 1960–61 season
★ Recorded 165 points (56G, 109A) in 246 career games as a Leaf
★ Recorded 17 points (8G, 9A) in 29 playoff games for Toronto

LEAF FACT:

Bert Olmstead is the only player to win a Stanley Cup in the last contest he ever played for both Montreal (in 1958) and Toronto (in 1962).

62 | NICK METZ

BORN: FEBRUARY 16, 1914 IN WILCOX, SASKATCHEWAN
POSITION: LEFT WING
YEARS AS A LEAF: 1934–35 TO 1947–48
SWEATER #: 5, 10, 15, 17 AND 19
MAPLE LEAF MOMENT: MARCH 14, 1939

MAPLE LEAF SCOUTS spotted Nick Metz in western Canada when he played for the Notre Dame Hounds, and they brought him east to play junior hockey with the St. Michael's Majors. He was with the junior club for two seasons and then made the jump to the big team in 1934–35, when he played in 18 games for the Leafs (recording two goals and two assists). Metz's first game as a Leaf was on November 8, 1934, when he played on a line with Pep Kelly and Art Jackson, two teammates he had played with in junior when St. Michael's won the Memorial Cup earlier in the year. As a full-time Leaf in 1935–36 he scored 14 times, but it was clear he was not going to score much at the big-league level. Metz dedicated himself to being a very good defensive player and top penalty killer. However, he was not totally devoid of offensive skills, as a March 14, 1939, contest against the New York Americans clearly showed.

The game between the Americans and the Leafs, held at Maple Leaf Gardens before fewer than 9,000 fans, was much closer than the 7–3 Leafs' win would indicate. Toronto's Murph Chamberlain opened the scoring, but the Americans tied it early in the second period. A power-play opportunity seemed to turn the game around, as the Leafs scored three goals in quick succession. Metz scored the first of the three, assisted by Chamberlain and Gord Drillon. Metz and Chamberlain then set up Syl Apps to make it 3–1 for Toronto before Metz got another for the Leafs. Pep Kelly then scored for the home team when he was set up by Metz to make it 5–2 before the end of the second period. Metz added another goal at 5:18 of the third to give him three on the night for his first career hat trick and a total of five points, as the Leafs romped to their 18th win of the season. (Metz would record one other hat trick in his NHL career when the Leafs beat Chicago 8–2 on February 28, 1942.)

The game was important for the Leafs, who were fighting with the Americans for third place in the seven-team league. By the end of 1938–39, the Leafs edged out the New Yorkers for third spot by three points (47 to 44) and then beat the Americans in the first round of the playoffs two games straight in a best-of-three opening round. The Leafs shut out the Americans in both games by scores of 4–0 and 2–0. The Leafs then knocked off Detroit in the next round (2–1 in games) to make it to the finals against Boston. The Bruins beat the Leafs four games to one in the best-of-seven series. Metz was one of the best Leafs throughout the '39 playoffs, recording six points (three goals, three assists) in 10 postseason games.

The Leafs finally broke through to win the Stanley Cup in 1942, and Nick Metz and his brother Don were both instrumental in getting the Leafs past Detroit in a very difficult seven-game final. For Nick, it was his best-ever playoff, with eight points (four goals, four assists), while Don jumped into the Leaf lineup and contributed seven points (four of them goals) in the finals.

Nick Metz joined the Canadian army for two years between 1942 and 1944 but returned to the Leafs for the start of the 1944–45 campaign. He had generally recorded

around 20 points a season, but in 1944–45 he scored 22 times and totalled 35 points in 50 games. He helped the Leafs to the Stanley Cup in 1945 and 1947 and wanted to go out a winner after the 1947–48 season. The first-place Leafs met the Boston Bruins in the semi-finals of the '48 postseason, and Metz got the team off to a good start when the series opened on March 24, 1948, at Maple Leaf Gardens by scoring the overtime winning goal. The Leafs disposed of the Bruins and then romped past Detroit to give Metz a great retirement gift — another Stanley Cup title!

MAPLE LEAF CAREER HIGHLIGHTS

★ Member of four Stanley Cup teams with Toronto
★ Scored 11 or more goals eight times as Leaf
★ Recorded nine seasons of 20 or more points
★ Recorded 250 points (131G, 119A) in 518 career games as a Leaf

LEAF FACT:

Nick and Don Metz were by far the most successful brother act ever to play for the Maple Leafs. Between them they won nine (five for Don, four for Nick) Stanley Cups for Toronto. The only other set of brothers to win Cups with the Leafs were Art (1945) and Harvey Jackson (1932), who combined for two championships.

63 | GARY LEEMAN

BORN: FEBRUARY 19, 1964 IN TORONTO, ONTARIO
POSITION: RIGHT WING
YEARS AS A LEAF: 1983–84 TO 1991–92
SWEATER #: 4 AND 11
MAPLE LEAF MOMENT: JANUARY 8, 1990

ONE OF THE MOST gifted athletes to play for the Maple Leafs was right-winger Gary Leeman. Although he was not a big man at 5´11˝ and 175 pounds, Leeman had soft hands that allowed him to make good passes or whip a hard shot on goal. He could read the play easily, and that helped him jump into the holes to set up or score a goal. Leeman's skill set allowed him to be a very good defenceman in the Western Hockey League, an All-Star with the Regina Pats in 1982–83 when he recorded 24 goals and 62 assists. He also joined the Leafs for two games in the '83 postseason, giving him his first taste of NHL action. Toronto management was not exactly sure where Leeman fit in the bigger picture and let him go to the minors for some seasoning. He split the next two seasons between the St. Catharines Saints and the Leafs, and it was during that time that Leeman converted to forward position. He was in Toronto on a full-time basis starting in 1986–87, scoring 21 times in 80 games. He followed that with seasons of 30 and 32 goals, then had a breakout year in 1989–90 that few would have predicted. One of his best nights that season came against the Washington Capitals on January 8, 1990, during a game at Maple Leaf Gardens.

Under new coach Doug Carpenter, the Maple Leafs seemed to find an identity as a high-scoring club but also one that was weak on defence and in goal. The Leafs fell behind 2–0 to the Capitals but got one back from Daniel Marois before the first period ended. Toronto then scored the first three goals of the second period, including one by Leeman, to take a 4–2 lead. The teams traded goals until it was 6–5 for Washington late in the second period. Leeman then scored his second of the night to tie the game before the period was over. In the third period the Leafs scored two goals to win the contest 8–6, and Leeman notched the final goal of the contest to give him 28 for the season. The win gave the Leafs a 22–21–1 record on the year, marking the first time since 1977–78 that they had been over .500 this far into the season.

"I think we're surprising ourselves with our offence," said Leeman. "Now we know we can do it, and psychologically that's good for us. We're exploiting our best weapon, which is our offence." Leeman also agreed that the Leafs were not the best defensive club in the NHL, saying "I imagine the coaches are pulling their hair out." Centre Ed Olczyk, who played between Leeman and Mark Osborne, also commented, "As long as we get two points, that's all that matters. They don't ask how, they ask how many."

For Leeman it soon became a question of how many goals he would finish the season with, as the Leafs kept pouring pucks into opposition nets. (Only Calgary and Los Angeles that year would score more goals than Toronto's 337.) On March 28, 1990, Leeman became just the second Leaf to score 50 goals in one season when he beat New York Islander goalie Mark Fitzpatrick with a slap shot from the slot area. The Leafs lost the contest 6–3, but Leeman was still relieved that he had achieved the milestone.

"They've [Olczyk and Osborne] really been trying to get it for me and I appreciate it. Hopefully, they can just relax now and not try to set me up all the time," Leeman said. "But it's a great feeling. I remember telling my dad a couple of years ago that I felt I could score 50 goals in this league."

Leeman finished the season with 51 goals and the Leafs were exactly at the .500 mark with 80 points for the 1989–90 season, a breakthrough of sorts for a team that had not played to that level in many years.

MAPLE LEAF CAREER HIGHLIGHTS

★ Drafted 24th overall by the Leafs in 1982
★ Recorded 50 or more points four consecutive seasons (1986–87 to 1989–90)
★ Scored 51 goals and totalled 95 points in 1989–90
★ Recorded 407 points (176G, 231A) in 545 games as a Leaf

LEAF FACT:

Gary Leeman was the only Leaf player selected for the 1989 NHL All-Star Game that was played in Edmonton on February 7th. It was the first (and only) All-Star Game appearance for Leeman, who scored one goal and added one assist for the Campbell Conference in a 9–5 victory over the Wales Conference.

64 | STEVE THOMAS

BORN: JULY 15, 1963 IN STOCKPORT, ENGLAND
POSITION: LEFT WING
YEARS AS A LEAF: 1984–85 TO 1986–87; 1998–99 TO 2000–01
SWEATER #: 32
MAPLE LEAF MOMENT: APRIL 22, 2000

LEFT-WINGER STEVE THOMAS had a pretty good junior career with the Toronto Marlboros (51 goals, 105 points in his final year of 1983–84) but was not drafted by any NHL club. Size may have had something to do with it. Listed at 5′10″, 185 pounds, the player known as "Stumpy" had a strong desire to succeed and signed as a free agent with the Maple Leafs. It was one of the best free agent acquisitions the Leafs had ever made. Thomas was not quite ready to play in the NHL, so for the 1984–85 season he was sent to the Leafs' farm club in St. Catharines, where he earned American Hockey League rookie of the year honours, scoring 42 goals and 90 points in 64 games. He started the next season in the minors, but after scoring 18 goals and 32 points in 19 games, he was called up to the Leafs, where he produced 20 goals and 57 points in 65 contests. In the playoffs, Thomas scored six goals and had 14 points. He was in the NHL to stay.

In his first full season as a Leaf, Thomas scored 35 times and gained 62 points in 78 games. When a bitter contract impasse could not be resolved, the Leafs sent Thomas to Chicago in a multi-player deal in September of 1987. A wrong was righted when the Leafs brought Thomas back for the 1998–99 season and played him on a line with the talented Mats Sundin. Thomas once again thrived with a playmaking centre, scoring 28 goals and totalling 73 points in 78 games, a remarkable season for a player many thought was washed up. He added 12 points in 17 playoff games as the Leafs made it to the final four for the first time since 1994. Thomas played two more seasons for the Leafs (34 goals in that stretch) and helped kill the Ottawa Senators' playoff hopes during the 2000 postseason. Thomas scored a key overtime goal on April 22, 2000, to give the Leafs the series lead.

The first-ever playoff series between Toronto and Ottawa was tied at two games apiece with the fifth game to be played at the Air Canada Centre. The Senators took a 1–0 lead in the second period and then played back and frustrated the Leafs at almost every turn. Near the halfway point of the third, Garry Valk took a double minor for the Leafs, making the situation even bleaker for the Toronto side. But the Leafs were rejuvenated after killing off the penalty, and they shifted their plan a little, starting to shoot the puck into the Ottawa end. Their efforts paid off when Thomas took a pass from Sundin and unleashed a slap shot past goalie Tom Barrasso to even the score with only 4:30 to play.

The Leafs kept pressing, but the game went into overtime. The teams began the extra session by exchanging chances back and forth. Finally, Toronto's Sergei Berezin broke away with Thomas on a two-on-one break. Berezin put a perfect pass on Thomas' stick, and he redirected it past Barrasso on his backhand to give the Leafs a 2–1 victory.

After the game Thomas spoke about his return to the Leafs and how he wanted to do well in his second stint with Toronto. "I was fearful when I signed here. I knew there'd be a lot of pressure [with] people saying 'Why would you sign a 34-year-old player?' I use that to fuel myself. I didn't want to look bad in front of everybody. I don't think there's any better

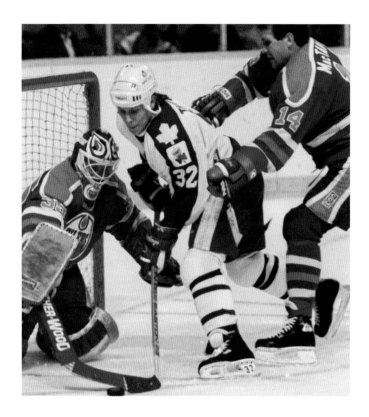

place to play hockey than Toronto when you're successful."

Leaf coach Pat Quinn offered this about Thomas: "It's not in my power to try and explain it, he just comes up with those big plays." Berezin talked about the winning goal: "I was looking for the shot, but they took away my room. I just looked for someone to be open and I'm glad it was Thomas. He's the perfect guy in overtime."

The Leafs eliminated the Senators with a 4–2 victory in the sixth game of the series.

MAPLE LEAF CAREER HIGHLIGHTS

★ Originally signed as a free agent May 12, 1984
★ Recorded four seasons of 20 or more goals as a Leaf
★ Recorded 60 or more points three times with Toronto
★ Recorded 291 points (118G, 173A) in 377 games for Toronto

LEAF FACT:

Leaf fans seem to enjoy eliminating the Ottawa Senators from the playoffs perhaps more than any other team since the new century began. Steve Thomas had a total of six goals and two assists when the Leafs knocked off the Senators for the first time in the 2000 playoffs. He scored two goals in the second game of the series, a goal and assist in the third contest, two more markers in the fifth match, and one more goal plus one assist in the sixth and final game.

65 VINCENT DAMPHOUSSE

BORN: DECEMBER 17, 1967 IN MONTREAL, QUEBEC
POSITION: LEFT WING
YEARS AS A LEAF: 1986–87 TO 1990–91
SWEATER #: 10
MAPLE LEAF MOMENT: OCTOBER 17, 1988

THE MAPLE LEAFS were surprised that Vincent Damphousse was still available when it came time for them to make their first selection at the NHL entry draft in 1986. He had closed his junior career with 45 goals and 110 assists for Laval in the QMJHL, a performance that put him on the potential draft list of every NHL team. Damphousse was the player the Leafs wanted all along, and they were delighted to take the Montreal native with their sixth overall choice. Only Damphousse and Joe Murphy (taken first overall by Detroit) made their respective NHL clubs to start the following season, and the Leafs got the benefit of having a rookie who would score 21 goals in his first year. (He also had 25 assists and played in all 80 games.) The six-foot-one, 190-pound left-winger (and sometime-centre) was not a great skater, but he could handle the puck exceptionally well, and he had the superior vision associated with top playmakers. His second season was not as productive from a goal-scoring point of view (he notched 12), but he upped his assist total to 36 to give him two more points than his first season. Everyone was wondering what Damphousse would do in his third year, but their concern was not necessary, as he posted new highs in goals (26) and assists (42). The night of October 17, 1988, at the Montreal Forum helped Damphousse get off on the right foot.

Like many NHL players, Damphousse wanted to excel when he came back to his hometown to play in front of family and friends. The Leafs were not expected to be a playoff contender for the 1988–89 season, but the club was a respectable 3–3 to start the year before their game against the Canadiens. In front of more than 16,000 spectators, Damphousse scored a goal in each period to lead the Leafs past the Habs by a 6–2 score. Rookie Derek Laxdal got the Leafs going when he beat Montreal netminder Brian Hayward from a long distance to give Toronto a 1–0 lead. Damphousse got his first of the night, followed by a Dan Daoust marker to close the opening frame, and his second of the night late in the second gave the Leafs a 4–1 lead. His signature goal of the evening was scored in the third against Patrick Roy, when Damphousse rocketed a slap shot past the recently inserted Montreal netminder.

After the game Damphousse admitted to being nervous. "It's always exciting playing here, but you get used to it a little. It's not like the first time. I was worried more for Daniel [Marois] than for me. I remembered my first game here and I thought of the butterflies I had in my stomach." As for the hat trick, Damphousse added, "It's a thrill of a lifetime. It's something I always dreamed of doing. The first hat trick is always special, something I'll be able to talk to my kids about."

Damphousse had found some success early in the season by centring a line with Marois on right wing and Dave Reid on the left side. "We just seem to complement each other. Dave is a hard worker, a solid two-way player. Danny, he just knows how to get open. And he can pass pretty well, too." He also thought the trio was anxious to impress. "We can't have any let-ups. There are guys in the wings waiting to take our jobs if we let up."

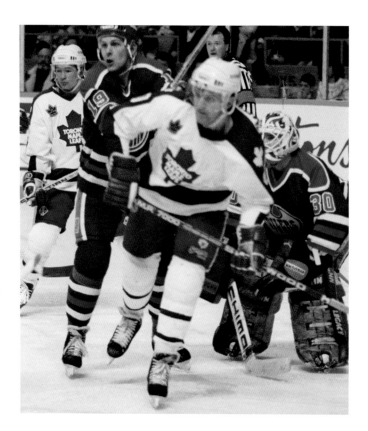

Leaf coach John Brophy said, "This was the biggest win we've had since I've come to Toronto. I know it's only October, but that was a great confidence builder."

The Leafs won four of their next five after this contest (the other game was a tie) giving hope to a Toronto uprising. The team eventually reverted to their expected form and finished the year out of the playoffs, but for one glorious night in Montreal everything seemed possible.

MAPLE LEAF CAREER HIGHLIGHTS

★ Recorded 46 or more points in each of his five seasons as a Leaf
★ Recorded 94 points (33G, 61A) in 80 games during the 1989–90 season
★ Scored four goals in 1991 NHL All-Star Game while representing the Leafs
★ Recorded 329 points (118G, 211A) in 394 career games with Toronto

LEAF FACT:

Of the 21 players selected in the first round of the 1986 NHL entry draft, four went on to play for the Leafs at some point in their career. Damphousse was their own choice, but through trades and free agent signings the Leafs also acquired Brian Leetch (selected ninth overall by the New York Rangers), Tom Fitzgerald (17th overall by the New York Islanders) and Ken McRae (18th overall by Quebec).

66 | GARY ROBERTS

BORN: MAY 23, 1966 IN NORTH YORK, ONTARIO
POSITION: LEFT WING
YEARS AS A LEAF: 2000–01 TO 2003–04
SWEATER #: 7
MAPLE LEAF MOMENT: MAY 4, 2002

LEFT-WINGER GARY ROBERTS was very happy to sign with the Maple Leafs as a free agent on July 4, 2000. He wanted to come home after spending the bulk of his career with the Calgary Flames (where he won a Stanley Cup in 1989) and the Carolina Hurricanes, a team he had joined after sitting out one year with a serious neck injury. The Leafs needed a player with his skill and fire. Roberts' work ethic and dedication to fitness rubbed off on many of his new teammates, and he would also lead in the dressing room as needed. In his first year with the blue and white he scored 29 goals and 53 points. During the 2001–02 season, Roberts scored 21 times and added 27 assists, but his real value shone through in the playoffs, when a depleted Leaf lineup needed a veteran to step up and lead the club. This was never more in evidence than on the night of May 4, 2002, when the Leafs battled the Ottawa Senators in the second game of their playoff series.

The Leafs barely managed to get past the New York Islanders in the first round of the playoffs in seven games but had to open the next round against Ottawa just two nights later. They were wiped out 5–0 in one of the worst games a Leaf team has ever played in the postseason. It was going to be difficult for the Leafs to advance any further, considering they were without captain Mats Sundin, forward Mikael Renberg and defenceman Dmitry Yushkevich not in the lineup due to injury. (They would also lose Darcy Tucker, Karel Pilar and Jyrki Lumme during the Ottawa series.) But players like Roberts and Alyn McCauley stepped into the void and gave the Leafs a chance. The second game of the series was played at the Air Canada Centre on a Saturday night that would turn into early Sunday morning before it was settled. The Leafs got off to a good start by taking a 2–0 lead on goals by Travis Green and Darcy Tucker before the game was nine minutes old. Ottawa scored one in the second and one early in the third to even the score, while the Leafs could not score any more during regulation play.

There was no scoring in the first overtime period and none in the second (despite one power-play opportunity for each team), taking the drama into a third extra period. Shayne Corson of the Leafs and Chris Neil of Ottawa were called for coincidental minor roughing penalties at 3:36, opening up some ice as the teams played four a side. Toronto's Robert Reichel was out with Roberts for a face-off in the Ottawa end. The puck stayed in the middle of the ice when Roberts pounced on the loose disc and put a shot between the legs of Ottawa netminder Patrick Lalime for a 3–2 Leaf win. The Leafs were as relieved as they were happy to take this must-win game.

Roberts spoke about the work of Leaf goalie Curtis Joseph (who stopped 54 shots on the night) as much as he did about the winning goal. "I missed on that one [a two-on-one rush] and thanks to Cujo [Joseph] I got another chance. Our whole team felt for him." (Joseph had been taking heat for his uneven performance in the playoffs to date.)

"Everybody has had to take on a little more of a leadership role, but I think Gary's on-ice skill and his ability to lead by example has shown itself," McCauley said of his teammate. "I guess you could say Gary has been thrust into being the captain without the 'C' on his sweater," he added. For his part Roberts said, "I'm just trying to lead by example, which I always try to do, and hopefully everyone in this room can elevate their game a little in the absence of Mats to help our team win hockey games."

On this night there was no doubt the leader of the Leafs had come through for his team.

MAPLE LEAF CAREER HIGHLIGHTS

★ Scored 20 or more goals three times as a Leaf
★ Played his 1,000th career game as a Leaf during the 2003–04 season
★ Recorded 40 points (14G, 26A) in 50 playoff games for Toronto
★ Recorded 157 points (83G, 74A) in 237 games as a Maple Leaf

LEAF FACT:

Gary Roberts recorded his 12th career hat trick while he was with the Leafs when Toronto beat the New York Rangers 6–3 at Madison Square Garden on December 6, 2001. Prior to that, the last Leaf to score three goals in one game on the road against the Rangers was Daniel Marois on February 17, 1989, during a 10–6 victory.

67 JOHN ANDERSON

BORN: MARCH 28, 1957 IN TORONTO, ONTARIO
POSITION: LEFT WING
YEARS AS A LEAF: 1977–78 TO 1984–85
SWEATER #: 10
MAPLE LEAF MOMENT: MARCH 24, 1985

THE TORONTO MAPLE LEAFS had not had two first-round selections at the entry draft since 1973 when they found themselves with two choices in 1977. The Leafs were selecting 11th (their own choice) and 12th (Pittsburgh's selection, acquired in a trade) that year. They were looking for some scoring and a defenceman. The Leafs selected winger John Anderson with their first choice and added defenceman Trevor Johansen with the next selection, both graduates of the Toronto Marlboros. Anderson certainly seemed like a good choice based on his junior career. The native of Toronto was a solid goal scorer (154 goals in 211 games) and in 1975 was part of the last Marlie team to win the Memorial Cup. He had good size at 5´11˝ and 190 pounds, but his main asset was his speed. Anderson was an excellent skater whose fast moves often got him into the open. He had soft hands in close with a good shot and a nose for the net. All these skills earned him plenty of goals and a reputation as an offensive player who was not going to be overly physical. He first played for the Leafs in 1977–78 (three points in 17 games) but spent most of that season with Dallas of the Central Hockey League, where he had 22 goals in 55 games.

Getting lots of ice time as a young player under Leaf coach Roger Neilson was not exactly easy, but Anderson managed 15 goals and 11 assists in 71 games in 1978–79. He was put on a line with two other young players, Rocky Saganiuk and Laurie Boschman, for the 1979–80 season, and Anderson contributed 25 goals in 74 contests. He then started to score consistently and put up seasons of 17, 31, 31 and 37 goals. The Leafs were a pretty poor team over all those years, but a line of Anderson plus newcomers Bill Derlago and Rick Vaive gave Leaf fans some entertainment when little was to be found. The 1984–85 season saw the Leafs win only 20 games (while losing 52), but the play of their big line gave them some good games to look back on, such as the night of March 24, 1985, in Detroit.

The Leafs were all but mathematically eliminated from the playoffs, but a late-season surge was keeping faint hopes alive. Scoring three goals on the power-play and one short-handed, the Leafs defeated Detroit 5–3. The line of Derlago, Vaive and Anderson was especially hot and did most of the damage. Derlago had one goal and three assists, while Vaive notched his 33rd of the season, but the star of the game was Anderson with three tallies to give him 25 on the year and seven goals in his last four games. "I don't want people to say we're a bunch of quitters," Anderson said. "People boo us at Maple Leaf Gardens. But it's not like we haven't been trying. We're a young team, some of the kids have a little experience now, and we're starting to go a little. It's helped to have a lot of ice time, and most teams give their good players a big workload." Anderson was likely making reference to the fact that he and both his linemates had been benched by coach Dan Maloney during the season.

Before the season was over, Anderson set a team record with at least one goal in 10 consecutive games. The final goal in the streak (a slap shot that beat goaltender Pete

Peeters) came on the last night of the year when the Leafs were walloped 5–1 by the Boston Bruins. Anderson scored a total of 14 goals over the 10-game period and finished the year with 32. The club record had previously been held by former captain Darryl Sittler at nine games, and Anderson was honoured to set a new mark.

"Because Darryl Sittler was such a great guy and a fine player, breaking a record of his is something a little special," he said. In a 20-win season, Anderson's goal-scoring exploits to close out the year provided one of the few highlights for the Leafs in '84–85.

MAPLE LEAF CAREER HIGHLIGHTS

★ Scored over 30 goals four straight seasons as a Leaf
★ Recorded 50 or more points five times as a Leaf
★ Produced 80 points (31G, 49A) in 80 games during 1982–83
★ Recorded 393 points (189G, 204A) in 534 career games with Toronto

LEAF FACT:

Even though he was established in Toronto (a chain of hamburger outlets with his name on it opened up in the area) and had played his entire career in one city, John Anderson was traded on August 21, 1985, to Quebec in exchange for defenceman Brad Maxwell, who would play in only 52 games for the Leafs. Anderson would go on to score 93 more goals with Quebec and Hartford before retiring from the NHL.

68 | HAROLD COTTON

BORN: NOVEMBER 5, 1902 IN NANTICOKE, ONTARIO
POSITION: LEFT WING
YEARS AS A LEAF: 1928–29 TO 1934–35
SWEATER #: 8, 11 AND 14
MAPLE LEAF MOMENT: MARCH 29, 1932

LEFT-WINGER HAROLD "Baldy" Cotton played his junior hockey in the Toronto area but signed as a free agent with Pittsburgh when he turned professional. He played minor league hockey in the steel town for two seasons before the Pittsburgh team joined the NHL as the Pirates. Cotton was with them for three seasons. His best year as a Pirate came in 1927–28, when he scored nine goals and 12 points in 42 games. Towards the end of the 1928–29 season Maple Leaf general manager Conn Smythe made inquiries about Cotton's availability. The five-foot-ten, 155-pound Cotton got wind of the discussions and made sure he had a good game the next time the Leafs and Pirates played each other, scoring one goal in the contest. Smythe liked that Cotton had a feisty nature and was willing to throw his body around. He was also a top checker and penalty killer. The Leafs had to add $9,500 along with the rights to Gerry Lowrey to complete the deal, but Smythe was more than pleased to add a player with the courage displayed by Cotton. Thrilled to be back in his home area, Cotton produced his best hockey with the Maple Leafs. He scored 21 goals in 1929–30 and always had double-digit assist totals in Toronto. Cotton was with the Leafs in 1931–32 when they won their first Stanley Cup. Even though he only scored five goals and 18 points during the season, in the first round of the playoffs Cotton played very well during a March 29, 1932, game against Chicago at Maple Leaf Gardens.

The Leafs had finished second in the Canadian Division and faced second-place Chicago of the American Division in a two-game total-goals series to start the '32 playoffs. In the first game, the Black Hawks shut out the high-scoring Leafs (Toronto had scored a league-high 155 goals) 1–0 behind the superlative goaltending of Charlie Gardiner. The teams returned to Toronto for the second game, and Leaf captain Hap Day got his team off to a good start by opening the scoring in the first period. Charlie Conacher added another to give the Leafs a 2–1 lead. As the Leafs kept up the pressure in the second period, the Black Hawks started to wilt. Toronto scored three consecutive times in the middle stanza to pull away. The Leafs got goals from Bob Gracie, Conacher and Frank Finnigan to make the overall series score 5–1. Cotton assisted on Finnigan's marker when he sprung his teammate with a pass that was taken into the Chicago zone. Finnigan took a shot that missed, but he grabbed the rebound before Gardiner could reach it and put a shot into a wide open net. Chicago scored in the third to cut the lead to 5–2, but Cotton scored another for the Leafs, assisted by Ace Bailey and Harold Darragh.

More than 13,000 fans left the Gardens happy that their team had knocked Chicago out of the playoffs with a 6–2 goal total. The Leafs then faced the Montreal Maroons in another two-game total-goals series. Toronto won the semi-finals by scoring four goals to Montreal's three, although it took an overtime marker by Gracie at the Gardens in the second contest to settle the issue. The Leafs then beat the New York Rangers in three straight games during a best-of-five series.

Cotton produced two goals and two assists during the seven games the Leafs played in the '32 playoffs.

Cotton had another decent year with Toronto in 1932–33 with 10 goals and 21 points in 48 games and had an 11-goal year in 1934–35, his last as a Maple Leaf. The Leafs sold him to the New York Americans in 1935, and he played with them for two seasons before his NHL career was over. Cotton coached the Toronto Marlboros for four seasons and was also named a goodwill ambassador for the Gardens. The Leafs made a mistake in not hiring Cotton as a scout, but the Boston Bruins hired him as one, and he stayed in that role for more than 25 years! Among his finds? Bobby Orr.

MAPLE LEAF CAREER HIGHLIGHTS

★ Acquired in a trade with Pittsburgh on February 12, 1929
★ Member of Stanley Cup team in 1932
★ Recorded 20 or more points five times as a Leaf
★ Recorded 156 points (68G, 88A) in 285 games with Toronto

LEAF FACT:

Hockey Night in Canada has been a big part of Maple Leaf history, and after his retirement Harold Cotton was one of the regulars on the "Hot Stove League," a recurring intermission feature, first on radio and then on television. Hockey analysts discussed the game being broadcast that night, as well as events around the NHL.

69 ERROL THOMPSON

BORN: MAY 28, 1950 IN SUMMERSIDE, PRINCE EDWARD ISLAND
POSITION: LEFT WING
YEARS AS A LEAF: 1970–71 TO 1977–78
SWEATER #: 12
MAPLE LEAF MOMENT: MARCH 8, 1975

ERROL THOMPSON PLAYED junior hockey in Halifax for three years between 1966 and 1969 before deciding to give up the game for a secure job and more education. He returned to P.E.I. and went to Charlottetown but did not give up on hockey altogether. He joined a senior hockey team called the Royals, and it was there that Leaf scout Johnny Bower discovered the swift skater. It was one of Bower's first forays into the scouting field after his retirement, and he suggested the Leafs take a chance on Thompson in the draft. Thompson played for the Royals only because he was asked to come out, and it came as quite a surprise to him that the Leafs would draft him 22nd overall in 1970. The Leafs switched him from defence to left wing and assigned him to their farm club in Tulsa for the 1970–71 season, where he scored 15 goals in 65 games for the minor league Oilers. He began the next season in Tulsa and upped his production to 21 goals and 21 assists in 46 contests, which earned him a promotion to the Maple Leafs for the following season.

In 1972–73, Thompson scored 13 times in 68 games while adding 19 assists. His game was built around his great skating ability. He had great speed and could turn it on at just the right moment, then unleash a blistering, heavy shot that earned him many goals. He had a stocky build (5′9″, 185 pounds) that helped him survive in the NHL, but he was not a very aggressive player. He struggled the next season with only seven goals in 56 games, but the 1974–75 season saw a breakthrough for Thompson with 25 goals and 42 points in 65 games. His best night of the season came on March 8, 1975, against the Minnesota North Stars.

The line of Thompson, George Ferguson and Lanny McDonald did most of the damage against the North Stars in a 5–3 Leaf victory. All three Toronto players had been hit with injuries during the regular season, and the Leafs were not enjoying one of their better years. But on this night Thompson was showing no ill effects from his cracked thumb, as he notched three consecutive Toronto goals (two of which came on the power-play). He opened the scoring at 7:44 of the first, beating North Star goalie Peter LoPresti after being set up by McDonald and Borje Salming. Minnesota tied the game before the end of the first, but Thompson scored twice in the second (including his 21st of the season) to give the Leafs a 3–1 lead. Minnesota came back to tie the game, but in the third period, Thompson and Ferguson worked hard to set up defenceman Rod Seiling for the game winner, and Blaine Stoughton added another to seal the win for the Leafs.

After the game Toronto coach Red Kelly remarked on the play of his best line on the night. "We'd lost a whole line and a pretty good one for a long time [because of the injuries]. Now that we've got set lines and can work with a set rotation, we're going places." The victory gave the Leafs their sixth straight win, although they were hardly playing the best teams in the NHL during the streak. The Leafs added another win to their consecutive string the next night against Washington and finished the year with a 31–33–16 record for 78 points.

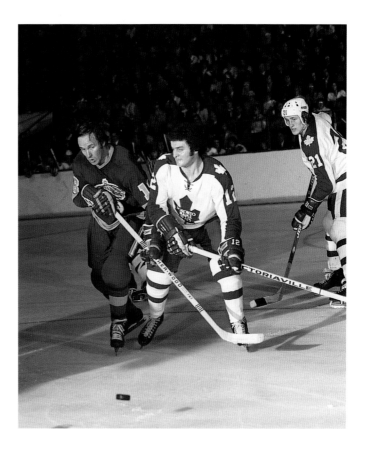

They salvaged a little measure of respect by knocking off the Los Angeles Kings in a best-of-three playoff series.

Things got even better for Thompson in 1975–76 when he was placed on a line with McDonald and Darryl Sittler. The line put up terrific numbers. Thompson, recognizable with his curly locks, playing alongside two future Hall of Fame players, contributed his share with 43 goals and 80 points. (Sittler had 41 goals and 100 points, while McDonald had 37 goals and 93 points.) Their points added up to the best totals for a line in Leaf history.

MAPLE LEAF CAREER HIGHLIGHTS

★ Played his first NHL game against Detroit on March 28, 1971 (a one-game call-up)
★ Scored 25 goals in 1974–75 and 21 in 1976–77
★ Scored 43 goals and 80 points in 75 games for the Leafs in 1975–76
★ Recorded 245 points (126G, 119A) in 365 games for Toronto

LEAF FACT:

Errol Thompson was not the first native of Prince Edward Island to score a hat trick in a National Hockey League game. Billy MacMillan scored three for Toronto on December 25, 1971 (the last time the NHL allowed games on Christmas Day), when the Leafs beat Detroit 5–2 at Maple Leaf Gardens.

70 GEORGE HAINSWORTH

BORN: JUNE 26, 1895 IN TORONTO, ONTARIO
POSITION: GOALTENDER
YEARS AS A LEAF: 1933–34 TO 1936–37
SWEATER #: 1
MAPLE LEAF MOMENT: MARCH 28, 1935

MUCH TO THE SURPRISE of Maple Leaf general manager Conn Smythe, he was offered Montreal netminder George Hainsworth in a trade. Before Canadien manager Leo Dandurand could change his mind, Smythe accepted the proposal and sent goalie Lorne Chabot in exchange. After seven stellar seasons in Montreal, the diminutive Hainsworth (5'6″ and 150 pounds) had suffered a bad 10–0 defeat to Boston during the season and then lost in the first round of the playoffs. Yet Smythe knew he was getting a quality netminder, since Hainsworth had won the Vezina Trophy (then awarded to the goalie who allowed the fewest goals) for the first three years it was given (1927, 1928 and 1929). He had also backstopped the Canadiens to two Stanley Cups (in 1930 and 1931) and had recorded an astounding 75 regular season shutouts for the Habs, including an NHL record 22 shutouts in 1928–29.

The Leafs liked the fact they were getting a technically sound netminder who built his game around being very efficient when he was making his many saves. Hainsworth was very good in his first season with the Leafs, posting a 26–13–9 record in the 48-game schedule. He was even better the next year, when he won 30 games for Toronto in 1934–35. The Leafs finished in first place in the Canadian Division with 64 points, which was the best record of any NHL team in '34–35. Toronto faced Boston in the first round of the playoffs and were counting on Hainsworth to continue his great work in net. The Bruins won the first game of the series on home ice by a score of 1–0, but the Leafs took the next game 2–0. Hainsworth was looking for his second consecutive shutout on the night of March 28, 1935, in a game at Maple Leaf Gardens.

The Leafs provided support for their netminder by scoring just 43 seconds into the contest on a goal by Bill Thoms, assisted by Frank Finnigan. The early goal forced the Bruins to go on the attack, but they got nowhere for the rest of the first period as Hainsworth stopped all of Boston's 11 shots on goal. The Bruins hemmed the Leafs in their own end for the better part of two minutes as the period was about to end, but the Toronto defence and goaltending were equal to the task. The Bruins used their momentum to further advantage at the start of the second period, and Hainsworth was forced to make a great stop on Max Kaminsky. Further fine saves on Red Beattie and Jim O'Neil of the Bruins seemed to inspire the Leafs to go back on the attack. Toronto defenceman Red Horner got the puck up to Nick Metz, who beat Boston netminder Tiny Thompson (a star goalie in his own right) with a shot to make it 2–0 for the Leafs. Boston superstar blueliner Eddie Shore then tested Hainsworth with a hard drive, but the Leaf goalie turned it aside to keep Toronto up by two.

The Bruins charged out for the third period, determined to beat Hainsworth. The line of Kaminsky, Gerry Shannon and Marty Barry threatened to do some damage, but they could get nothing by the Toronto netminder. When Shore was hurt by a Horner check, the steam went out of the Bruin attack, and the Leafs were able to add another goal by

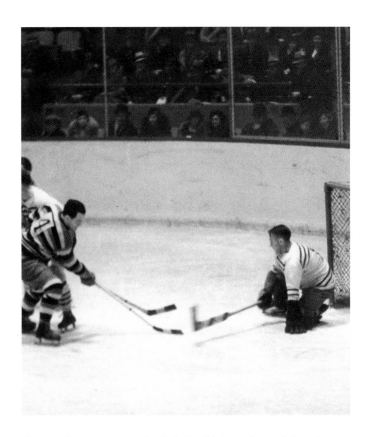

Harvey Jackson to make it 3–0 with less than eight minutes to play. The Bruins knew the game was over after the Jackson goal, and the Leafs cruised the rest of the way, giving Hainsworth his eighth and final career playoff shutout.

Toronto knocked out the Bruins with another victory to take the series 3–1, with Hainsworth giving up just two goals in the five games. The Leafs were hoping to reclaim the Stanley Cup they had last won in 1932, but the Montreal Maroons took the Cup in three straight games, outscoring the Leafs 10–4 in the process.

Hainsworth was with the Leafs three full seasons but was let go by the club when Turk Broda came along and became a fixture in the Toronto net for many years.

MAPLE LEAF CAREER HIGHLIGHTS

★ Acquired in a trade with Montreal on October 1, 1933
★ Recorded 19 regular season shutouts with the Leafs
★ Posted a 79–48–20 record in 147 games with Toronto
★ Elected to the Hockey Hall of Fame in 1961

LEAF FACT:

George Hainsworth faced the first nine penalty shots taken against the Maple Leafs (between 1934 and 1936), stopping the first seven but allowing the last two. The only other Leaf netminder to face almost as many penalty shots was Curtis Joseph, who allowed two goals on eight attempts (between 1998 and 2002).

71

MARCEL PRONOVOST

BORN: JUNE 15, 1930 IN LAC LA TORTUE, QUEBEC
POSITION: DEFENCE
YEARS AS A LEAF: 1965–66 TO 1969–70
SWEATER #: 3
MAPLE LEAF MOMENT: APRIL 29, 1967

WHEN THE MAPLE LEAFS lost to the Montreal Canadiens in the 1965 semi-finals, Toronto coach and general manager Punch Imlach thought it was time to make changes to his team, even though they had won three Stanley Cups in a row before their ouster. He worked out a deal with Detroit that saw Andy Bathgate, Billy Harris and Gary Jarrett go to the Red Wings in exchange for five players, including veteran defenceman Marcel Pronovost. (Imlach was always interested in experienced rearguards.) The acquisition of the workhorse blueliner became even more important when Carl Brewer decided he no longer wanted to play with the Leafs, and the club needed someone to take his place. Pronovost could withstand a lot of pain but got into only 54 games for the Leafs in his first season with the team due to injuries. He played in just 58 regular season games in 1966–67 in what was an up-and-down campaign for the team, but he was ready for the playoffs. Pronovost was paired on defence with one-time Red Wing Larry Hillman, as the Leafs got past first-place Chicago in the semi-final. In the final, Montreal was a tough opponent for the aging Leafs. However, the series was tied at two wins each when Toronto travelled to Montreal for the fifth game on April 29, 1967.

The situation looked bleak for the Leafs as they got ready to play the game that Saturday afternoon. The Habs had ripped the Leafs and netminder Terry Sawchuk for six goals in the fourth game, and Toronto could not turn to Johnny Bower due to injury. Sawchuk was battered and bruised, and the fast-skating Montreal forwards were giving the Leaf defence a difficult time. Things looked even worse when Leon Rochefort scored just 3:09 into the contest to give Montreal a 1–0 lead. But the savvy Leafs dug down and tied the game on Jim Pappin's power-play marker at 15:06 of the first.

The Leafs took the lead early in the second when Brian Conacher scored, but Red Kelly was called for a penalty halfway through the period. The Leafs' penalty-killing efforts proved the key point of the game, as Conacher got the puck loose when Yvan Cournoyer and Bobby Rousseau could not corral it at the Leaf blue line. Pronovost broke away on a solo rush. He let go a low shot from just inside the Montreal blue line that eluded netminder Rogie Vachon for a short-handed tally, stunning the Forum faithful. A goal by Dave Keon padded the Leafs' lead to 4–1 by the end of the second. Backed by the superlative netminding of Sawchuk (who made 37 saves), the Leafs then checked the Habs into the ice for the third period and took the series lead 3–2. The three stars of the game were all Leafs: Sawchuk, Pronovost and Tim Horton.

Kelly, upset that he had been assessed a penalty by referee Bill Friday, had a cheeky response for the official when Pronovost scored his goal. "I told Friday that it proved the penalty was a fake," said Kelly, who thought Montreal's Bobby Rousseau had taken a dive. For his part Pronovost decided to keep things simple: "I was aware of [Ron] Ellis on

the other wing, and maybe the goalie was, too. I didn't pick a spot or anything, I just shot."

It was the most important goal Pronovost scored as a Leaf (his only one in the playoffs), and it helped to get his name on the Stanley Cup for a fifth time in his career.

MAPLE LEAF CAREER HIGHLIGHTS

★ Acquired in a trade with Detroit on May 20, 1965
★ Member of Stanley Cup team in 1967
★ Played in all 70 games in 1967–68, recording 20 points
★ Recorded 48 points in 223 games as a Leaf

LEAF FACT:

Two other players acquired in the deal that brought Marcel Pronovost to Toronto were contributors to the 1967 Stanley Cup triumph. Autry Erickson dressed for three games during the finals, while Larry Jeffrey (who had 11 goals and 28 points in 56 games in '66–67) only played in the semi-final versus Chicago before being injured.

72 | AL IAFRATE

BORN: MARCH 21, 1966 IN DEARBORN, MICHIGAN
POSITION: DEFENCE
YEARS AS A LEAF: 1984–85 TO 1990–91
SWEATER #: 33
MAPLE LEAF MOMENT: FEBRUARY 7, 1990

WHENEVER THE MAPLE LEAFS took a big defenceman with their first-round draft choice the expectation level was high. Such was the case with Al Iafrate, who was listed at 6'3" and 220 pounds and was expected to be a leader on the Leaf defence for many years to come after he was selected fourth overall in 1984. Instead of letting an immature 18-year-old return to play junior hockey, the Leafs rushed the blueliner into their starting lineup, where he played in 68 games during the 1984–85 season (scoring five goals and 21 points). It was clear that Iafrate was a large man who could move fast, and that he had an impressive shot when he got it off. It was just as clear that he lacked direction and seemed to be determined only at certain times. Despite possessing all the tools necessary to be a star, Iafrate languished on a poor team for the next two seasons, though he did manage 30 or more points in each year. Iafrate had a breakthrough in 1987–88, when he tied a club record (held by Ian Turnbull) for goals by a defenceman (22) and had 52 points, but he slumped back to 13 goals the next season, playing as inconsistently as the rest of the team. The 1989–90 season would turn out to be Iafrate's best with the Leafs, as he produced a 63-point campaign which was highlighted by his performance against the St. Louis Blues on February 7, 1990.

The Leafs owned the Blues for almost the entire '89–90 season. In the previous seven meetings between the two clubs, Toronto had won six games while St. Louis had managed just one 6–4 victory, which had come the night before this contest was to take place at Maple Leaf Gardens. The Toronto club came out determined to regain their dominance over the Blues. Iafrate and Ed Olczyk set up Gary Leeman for the opening goal of the contest, which came on a power-play. Iafrate then set up Scott Pearson and Lou Franceschetti for goals in the second period before potting one himself on another Leaf man-advantage situation. St. Louis managed to keep Iafrate's point total to four the rest of the way, but the Leafs scored three more in the final period to complete the rout of the Blues 7–1.

"We were driving to the net and we hadn't done that [the previous night in St. Louis]," Iafrate said. "And [goalie Allan Bester] kept us in there. A lot of games [against the Blues] could have gone either way, but we've had great goaltending against them." He also said the Leafs knew they were fortunate to be up a goal after the first period: "Nobody had to say anything when we came in the dressing room. We all knew we weren't playing well and knew we'd had a terrible period."

Toronto coach Doug Carpenter noticed that Iafrate took charge of the game when his team needed a boost. "We just came in and put our heads together. We knew we had to play better and we went out and did it," the first-year Leaf coach said. "As for Iafrate, he just keeps getting better and better. When I'd used to scout you would look for the four S's: size, strength, speed and skill. He's got all of them," Carpenter praised.

Near the end of the '89–90 campaign, Iafrate suffered a serious knee injury that knocked him out of the playoffs.

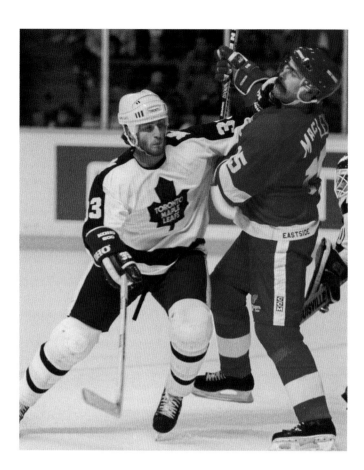

The Leafs crumbled without a defenceman capable of carrying the puck out of their end with some speed and lost a playoff series in five games to the same Blues they had dominated during the regular season.

The sensitive Iafrate had trouble recovering from his injury and was traded away to the Washington Capitals just 42 games into the 1990–91 season. He earned a place on the NHL's Second All-Star Team in 1992–93.

MAPLE LEAF CAREER HIGHLIGHTS

★ Selected fourth overall by the Leafs in 1984
★ Scored over 20 goals twice (1987–88 and 1989–90) for the Leafs
★ Recorded 30 or more points five consecutive seasons
★ Totalled 250 points (81G, 169A) in 472 career games in Toronto

LEAF FACT:

The 1989–90 season featured one of the most exciting offence-oriented Leaf teams in club history. Al Iafrate was a big part of the Leaf attack, and when he recorded more than one point in a game that year the team had a record of 12–2–2. He also won the "hardest shot" portion at the NHL All-Star Game Skills Competition held in Pittsburgh in February of 1990.

73 | DAVE ELLETT

BORN: MARCH 30, 1964 IN CLEVELAND, OHIO
POSITION: DEFENCE
YEARS AS A LEAF: 1990–91 TO 1996–97
SWEATER #: 4
MAPLE LEAF MOMENT: APRIL 27, 1993

DAVE ELLETT'S FATHER, Bob, was a long-time minor league hockey player, and he certainly passed on some of his hockey skills and knowledge to his son. The smooth-skating Ellett attended Bowling Green University (54 points in 43 games in his final season there) and caught the eye of the Winnipeg Jets, who selected him 75th overall in the 1982 entry draft. The six-foot-two, 205-pound defender joined the Jets for the 1984–85 season (spending no time in the minors) and produced a respectable 38 points in 80 games played. His hard drive from the point allowed Ellett to score goals in the double digits every year he was with the Jets, including a 22-goal season in 1988–89. He had 17 the next season, but by 1990–91 the Jets were looking to add some scoring up front. When the Leafs made Ed Olczyk available the Jets sent Ellett to Toronto, completing a two-for-two trade. The Leafs were thrilled with their part of the deal, as they had finally landed a defenceman to build around. Ellett's role started to change, however, as Leaf coaches wanted him to join the attack as opposed to leading it, though the talented blueliner still managed to score 18 times during the 1991–92 season. It was in the 1993 postseason that Ellett really started to show his true value to the team. The night of April 27, 1993, was a good example of how important Ellett was to the Leafs.

The Leafs' opening-round series against Detroit was a classic that would go seven games. The Red Wings wiped out the Leafs in the first two games with 6–3 and 6–2 wins, but the Leafs bounced back on home ice to tie the series with 4–2 and 3–2 wins. The fifth game back at the Joe Louis Arena did not start well for the Leafs, who found themselves down 2–1 after the first period. Detroit scored two goals early in the second to make it 4–1, and it looked like another rout was on. The Leafs were very sloppy and ineffective in their own end. Even Ellett struggled defensively. But then he jumped up to score two goals before the period was over. Suddenly, Toronto was back in it. Ellett's first marker came from a long distance and somehow bounced by Tim Cheveldae in the Red Wing net. It may have been a fluky goal, but it got the Leafs going in the right direction. His second of the night, on the power-play from a shot at the point, gave the Toronto side some momentum going into the third.

Captain Wendel Clark scored to tie the contest in the third period, and the Leafs buzzed around looking for the go-ahead goal. Neither side could score before the end of regulation, but just over two minutes into extra time, Clark set up Mike Foligno right in the slot, whose shot went right through Cheveldae's legs for the winner. The Leafs mobbed Foligno and now had a 3–2 lead in the series going back to Maple Leaf Gardens.

"It's the biggest goal of my career," Foligno said. "I got the puck and just tried to put it on net." Leaf coach Pat Burns said he stopped trying to match lines with the Red Wings. "I just said to hell with it. Let's just get going," Burns recounted. Centre Peter Zezel noticed the change as well: "We had no continuity. So Pat just started rolling over four lines." Winger Bill Berg sounded a cautionary note: "We got a lucky break

tonight. But if we come back here [for a seventh game], we'll be playing right into their hands."

The Leafs were hammered 7–3 in the sixth game but came back to Detroit to win a very exciting contest 4–3 in overtime, with rookie Nikolai Borschevsky scoring the series winner. Ellett finished the '93 playoffs with 12 points (4G, 8A) in 21 games, and in the 1994 postseason he had 18 points in 18 games. Ellett's playoff performances in '93 and '94 were the highlights of his time as a Maple Leaf.

MAPLE LEAF CAREER HIGHLIGHTS

★ Acquired in a trade with Winnipeg on November 10, 1990
★ Recorded 30 or more assists four times as a Leaf
★ Scored 18 goals and 51 points in 1991–92
★ Recorded 223 points (51G, 172A) in 446 games for Toronto

LEAF FACT:

Dave Ellett joked that the Maple Leafs had thrown Doug Gilmour into the deal that sent the two over to New Jersey on February 25, 1997, but Toronto general manager Cliff Fletcher did pretty well, getting Alyn McCauley, Jason Smith and Steve Sullivan back in the trade. All three players the Leafs received were still active in the NHL during the 2006–07 season, but not for Toronto, who had nothing left to show for any of them!

MIKE WALTON

BORN: JANUARY 3, 1945 IN KIRKLAND LAKE, ONTARIO
POSITION: CENTRE
YEARS AS A LEAF: 1965–66 TO 1970–71
SWEATER #: 15 AND 16
MAPLE LEAF MOMENT: NOVEMBER 15, 1967

MIKE WALTON WAS another of the many talented players the Maple Leafs recruited from Northern Ontario. The Kirkland Lake native joined the Toronto Marlboros for the 1963–64 season, and the slick centre scored 41 goals in 53 games for the Marlies that year. He then added another 12 in the playoffs, as the very skilled club took the '64 Memorial Cup. He spent the 1964–65 campaign with the Tulsa Oilers and was promptly named the rookie of the year when he scored 40 goals and totalled 84 points in 68 Central Hockey League games. Walton then moved to the American Hockey League for the next season and scored 35 goals and 86 points to take the rookie of the year award in that circuit as well. He also played in six games for the Leafs in 1965–66 and acquitted himself well with one goal and four points.

Although he was on the small side (listed at 5'10" and 175 pounds), Walton could skate very fast and had the ability to unleash a hard, accurate drive. Many in the Leaf organization felt they had found a feistier Dave Keon, but Walton could not stick with the big team for the 1966–67 season, splitting time between Toronto and Rochester. He was with the Leafs when they took the Stanley Cup in '67, but he was still not a regular on the team when the 1967–68 season began. A three-goal game against the Boston Bruins on November 15, 1967, gave the Leafs something more to think about.

Walton told anyone who would listen that he could be a regular NHL player if given a chance. Toronto coach Punch Imlach was restricting Walton to power-play duties and to fill in for other centres in case of injury. He had four goals in the first 15 games of the '67–68 season (all with the extra man), but Dave Keon was out with an injury as the Bruins came to play at Maple Leaf Gardens. Walton was slotted between wingers George Armstrong and Wayne Carleton and earned many scoring opportunities throughout the game. Bob Pulford opened the scoring for the Leafs early in the game, and Walton added another marker just 31 seconds later when he beat Bruins defenceman Ted Green to a puck and let go a hard wrist shot that eluded Gerry Cheevers in the Boston goal. The Bruins got one back to make it 2–1, but then Jean-Paul Parise, playing his first and only game as a Leaf, got the puck into Boston territory before sliding a pass over to Walton, who whipped a backhand drive past Cheevers for his second of the night. Walton scored his third of the evening in the second period when he kept whacking at a loose puck in front of the Bruins' net. He had carried the puck over the Boston blue line and got through to deke Eddie Johnston (who was now in goal for the Bruins), but his shot hit the post. He took another swipe at the puck and then again as he was being knocked down to his knees before the disc cleared the goal line. Derek Sanderson scored a late goal for Boston, but the Leafs hung on to a 4–2 victory and regained first place in the process.

Walton was named the first star of the game by Foster Hewitt and received a loud ovation from the Toronto fans. "That was great, just great pulling off a win against those guys without [Frank] Mahovlich, Keon and [Allan] Stanley,"

Walton said, smiling as he held the puck from his third goal. "And our line didn't give up a goal. I was really happy about that." He also spoke about the goal that gave him that hat trick: "I was dizzy with joy when the light went on. I've had a few hat tricks as a pro, two at Tulsa and one I think with Rochester, but this was the big one. I'd have been mad if I had missed it."

The game seemed to be a springboard for Walton, who went on to lead the Leafs with 30 goals and 59 points in '67–68 — the best of his five seasons in Toronto.

MAPLE LEAF CAREER HIGHLIGHTS

★ Member of Stanley Cup team in 1967
★ Recorded 7 points (4G, 3A) in 1967 playoffs
★ Scored 20 or more goals three times as a Leaf
★ Recorded 191 points (84G, 107A) in 257 games for Toronto.

LEAF FACT:

Mike Walton is the only Maple Leaf player ever to take penalty shots in consecutive games. He scored against Roger Crozier of Detroit on March 9, 1968, at the Gardens but was stopped by Jack Norris of the Black Hawks the next day in Chicago.

75 BILL DERLAGO

BORN: AUGUST 25, 1958 IN BIRTLE, MANITOBA
POSITION: CENTRE
YEARS AS A LEAF: 1979–80 TO 1985–86
SWEATER #: 19
MAPLE LEAF MOMENT: DECEMBER 5, 1981

WHEN THE MAPLE LEAFS sent Dave "Tiger" Williams and Jerry Butler to Vancouver they were thrilled to get back not one but two first-round draft choices. Rick Vaive was the Canucks' first selection (fifth overall) in 1979, while five-foot-ten, 190-pound centre Bill Derlago was taken fourth overall by Vancouver in 1978. Leaf general manager Punch Imlach, back in Toronto for the second time in his career, was looking to reshape the team with younger, faster players who could provide some offence. Both Vaive and Derlago fit the bill, and the deal turned out to be one of the few Imlach made during this stint as the Leafs' boss that turned out well for his team.

Derlago was an offensive machine during his junior days with the Brandon Wheat Kings. In three years with the Kings, he never recorded fewer than 100 points, and he had 96 and 89 goals respectively over his final two years. He played in nine games for the Canucks in 1978–79 (notching eight points) and then had 28 points in 54 games for Vancouver before the surprise deal with the Leafs. He scored 17 points in 23 games in Toronto to finish the year. The next year the Leafs were hoping Derlago would put up top numbers in his first full season with the team, and he responded with 35 goals and 74 points in 80 games. That same year, 1979–80, the Leafs won 35 games and made the playoffs, and one year later they won 28 and still made the postseason, although they were knocked out in the first round both years.

By the time the 1981–82 season began the Leafs had gone through tremendous changes in their roster and would go through even more before Imlach became too ill to continue in his role. (Some say owner Harold Ballard dismissed him.) Toronto was hoping to see their youngsters develop in 1981–82, but they lacked direction and would only win 20 games by the end of a season that was filled with more turmoil. One bright spot was the play of Derlago, and on the night of December 5, 1981, he showed more of the promise the Leafs had traded for.

The Washington Capitals were not exactly a team loaded with talent as they came to play the Leafs on a Saturday night at Maple Leaf Gardens. The line of Derlago, Vaive and John Anderson led the way as Toronto pounded the Caps 9–4. The Leafs were physical and aggressive on the forecheck all night long, and it paid off early as Vaive scored just 3:10 into the contest. Derlago then scored the next two goals to give the Leafs a 3–0 lead before the 12-minute mark. But the Capitals got back into the wide open contest by scoring twice before the first period was over. Washington tied the score in the second period, but the Leafs got markers from Darryl Sittler, Rene Robert and rookie Ernie Godden (who scored his first NHL goal) before the Caps responded with one from Dennis Maruk to make the score 6–4. However, Vaive (assisted by Derlago) and Dan Maloney scored before the middle frame was over to make it 8–4. Derlago scored his third of the night early in the final stanza to salt away the Leaf victory, which featured many scraps before it was over.

"That hat trick was a long time coming, more than three years," Derlago said after the game. "I thought we were moving the puck out of our end quite well at times. I thought [defenceman Jim] Benning did a big job in handling and moving the puck."

Toronto coach Mike Nykoluk said, "We have to check in the corners and along the boards to be effective. We also have to use our speed to some advantage. Well, we did those and got a win we needed."

The hard-shooting Derlago would finish the year with 34 goals and 84 points for a team highlight in what was otherwise a dismal '81–82 campaign for the Leafs.

MAPLE LEAF CAREER HIGHLIGHTS

★ Acquired in a trade with Vancouver on February 18, 1980
★ Recorded 60 or more points four times as a Leaf
★ Scored a career-high 40 goals in 1983–84
★ Recorded 334 points (158G, 176A) in 378 career games with Toronto

LEAF FACT:

Despite his nearly point-per-game performance as a Maple Leaf, Bill Derlago was dealt to Boston on October 11, 1985 in exchange for centre Tom Fergus. In 357 games as a Leaf, Fergus recorded 297 points (118 goals and 179 assists), making it a good exchange for Toronto.

RIGHT-WINGER LORNE CARR played junior hockey in Calgary and senior hockey in Vancouver. The New York Rangers, who owned his professional rights, sent him to Buffalo of the International Hockey League for a couple of seasons, beginning in 1931. He played in 14 games for the Rangers in 1933–34 but could not score a goal or record a point, so back he went to the minors to play in Philadelphia and Syracuse. The Rangers eventually sent the five-foot-eight, 161-pound Carr to their cross-town rival, the New York Americans. Carr enjoyed success with the Americans for a number of seasons and would score between 13 and 19 goals most years. He loved playing with Dave Schriner and Art Chapman while with the Americans, but eventually both those players left the team, and by the end of the 1940–41 season Carr was unhappy. Maple Leaf manager Conn Smythe saw an opportunity to add a quality player, and he was also able to reunite Carr with Schriner, whom he had acquired earlier.

Carr had his best years with Toronto, helping the Leafs regain the Stanley Cup in 1942. He was outstanding in the finals against Detroit, recording five points (including two assists) in the deciding contest of a seven-game series. In 1942–43 he scored 27 goals and 60 points, then did even better the following year with a career-best 36 goals and 74 points in a 50-game season. Carr recorded 46 points in 47 games during the 1944–45 season and was also effective in the postseason when the Leafs met the Montreal Canadiens in the semi-finals. The Leafs started the series with a 1–0 win at the Forum and met the Habs there again on the night of March 22, 1945.

As defending Stanley Cup champions, the Canadiens did not want to go back to Toronto down by two games, but it was the Leafs who showed more desire in this game. All three Toronto markers came on the power-play. Ted Kennedy opened the scoring at 4:07 of the first period when he beat Bill Durnan in the Montreal net. The Canadiens came storming out for the start of the second period and were rewarded with a goal by Butch Bouchard at 8:15 of the middle stanza. The Montreal crowd went wild and showered the ice with all sorts of debris. The Leafs regained their composure during the delay to clean up the ice and were determined not to lose their advantage. They scored twice before the second period was over on goals by Carr (assisted by Schriner) and Nick Metz to take a 3–1 lead into the third period. Montreal tried to get back into the game, but a late goal by Elmer Lach was all they could muster past Frank McCool, the rookie netminder occupying the Leaf net. It was a bitter loss for the Habs, who thought they had one of their best teams ever. Montreal had finished first in '44–45 with 80 points, losing only eight games, while the Leafs had finished in third place with 52 points, winning 24 and losing 22 games.

Montreal won the next game 4–1 at Maple Leaf Gardens, but Toronto took the fourth contest 4–3 in overtime. Although Montreal whipped the Leafs 10–3 back in the

Forum, Toronto closed out the series with a 3–2 win on home ice. Carr had a great series against the Habs, scoring three goals and adding two assists over the six games — a big reason why the Leafs were able to pull off the upset. The Leafs then went on to beat Detroit in seven games to claim another Cup for Carr.

Carr played one more season with the Leafs, but his production dropped off to five goals and 13 points in 42 games during the 1945–46 regular season. He did, however, score his 200th career goal on November 7, 1945, during a game against the Boston Bruins. The Leafs decided to go with a youth movement the following year, and Carr went into retirement.

MAPLE LEAF CAREER HIGHLIGHTS

★ Member of two Stanley Cup teams with Toronto
★ Named to the NHL's First All-Star Team twice as a Leaf (1943 and 1944)
★ Led the Leafs in goals scored twice (1942–43 and 1943–44)
★ Recorded 226 points (105G, 121A) in 236 games with Toronto

LEAF FACT:

For a player who scored just under a point a game in his career as a Maple Leaf, the trade that brought Lorne Carr to Toronto was quite one-sided. The Leafs "loaned" four players to the New York Americans' minor league team for one year. The Leafs later sent Jack Church and cash to New York to complete the deal. None of the other players in the deal were even close to the calibre of Carr.

77

RON
STEWART

BORN: JULY 11, 1932 IN CALGARY, ALBERTA
POSITION: RIGHT WING
YEARS AS A LEAF: 1952–53 TO 1964–65
SWEATER #: 12
MAPLE LEAF MOMENT: APRIL 11, 1963

WHEN RON STEWART began playing hockey in his hometown of Calgary, former Leaf Dave "Sweeney" Schriner was one of his coaches. Perhaps Schriner persuaded Stewart that he had to come to Ontario if he was to have a real shot at playing professional hockey, so he joined the Toronto Marlboros for the 1949–50 season. The sturdy right-winger (six feet, 197 pounds) played two seasons with the Marlies (33 goals in 104 games), but he was sent to the Barrie Flyers during the 1951–52 campaign. He was then added to the Guelph Biltmore Mad Hatter team for the 1952 Memorial Cup playoffs. He had an impressive 10-goal, seven-assist performance in just 12 games as the Guelph club took the junior title in a sweep of the Regina Pats.

Stewart was ready for the NHL and was signed by the Leafs on October 6, 1952. He never played a game in the minors, making the Toronto club on his first try, and had 13 goals and 22 assists during the 1952–53 season. For the next five seasons, Stewart consistently scored 14 or 15 goals a year and pushed his point total to 39 by the 1957–58 season. The Leafs were not a great team during Stewart's first years in the NHL, but he had enough skill to stay around until the team improved. Stewart's main strength was his effortless skating style. He was also a relentless checker, and he could play that way all season long. Once the Leafs realized Stewart was not going to be a big goal scorer, they made him a checking winger who could on occasion pop in the odd goal. Stewart also suffered his share of injuries (broken jaw, ribs and shoulder) but played through them to help the Leafs win three straight Stanley Cups. He made a major contribution to the cause on the night of April 11, 1963.

The Leafs had taken a one-game lead against the Detroit Red Wings during the 1963 Stanley Cup finals and were looking to hold their home-ice advantage as they skated out for the second game. Ed Litzenberger opened the scoring for the Leafs in the first period before the game was six minutes old. Litzenberger, filling in for an injured Frank Mahovlich, then set up Stewart for a marker before the opening frame was over. Litzenberger spotted Stewart in alone behind the Detroit defence, and Stewart swiftly moved in on the Red Wing net, manouevring Terry Sawchuk out of position before depositing a backhander into the net. Toronto made it 3–0 on a goal by Bob Nevin, but Gordie Howe got one back for Detroit. Norm Ullman of Detroit was then called for holding, and the Leafs took advantage on the power-play. Stationing himself to the right of the Detroit net, Stewart was able to swat home a pass from teammate Billy Harris to give Toronto a 4–1 lead. Howe scored once again in the third to narrow the score, but the Leafs checked closely to win the game 4–2 and take an insurmountable two-game lead to Detroit.

In the Leaf dressing room, coach Punch Imlach said he was fortunate to have such good bench strength on his team. "It pays a coach to be lucky and have solid, versatile players on the bench," he said of players like Stewart and Litzenberger (who had a three-point night). It was a different story in the Red Wing room. "They got us disorganized with

that close checking, and no matter what we did with our lines, there didn't seem to be any reserve," Detroit coach Sid Abel lamented after the game. "This is a tired hockey club," Abel said of his team. "The Leafs played a big game. They had the puck most of the night, and when they didn't have possession they were pressuring us into mistakes. I think three days' rest will snap us back to form. If it does this series is far from over."

Abel was right for one night, but the teams ended up splitting the two games at the Olympia. The Leafs then came home to claim their second straight Cup with a 3–1 victory.

MAPLE LEAF CAREER HIGHLIGHTS

★ Member of three Stanley Cup teams with Toronto
★ Scored 21 goals in 1958–59 for the Leafs
★ Recorded 28 points (10G, 18A) in 82 playoff games
★ Recorded 368 points (186G, 182A) in 838 games as a Leaf

LEAF FACT:

Like many other players who were with the Maple Leaf organization in the fifties and sixties, Ron Stewart tried his hand at coaching once his career was over. He coached the New York Rangers for 39 games (15–20–4) in 1975–76. He then took over the Los Angeles Kings for the 1977–78 season and had a respectable record of 31–34–15 in 80 games. The Kings faced the Leafs in the '78 playoffs during a best-of-three preliminary round playoff series. The Leafs won the series 2–0, and the first contest featured a hat trick by usually low-scoring Toronto centre George Ferguson in a 7–3 romp. Stewart did not coach in the NHL again.

78 | CAL GARDNER

BORN: OCTOBER 30, 1924 IN TRANSCONA, MANITOBA
POSITION: CENTRE
YEARS AS A LEAF: 1948–49 TO 1951–52
SWEATER #: 17
MAPLE LEAF MOMENT: APRIL 16, 1949

WHEN A CENTRE the size of Cal Gardner (6´1˝, 175 pounds) comes with some skill, the professional hockey scouts are always going to pay close attention. Gardner showed a real ability to score, so the New York Rangers gave him $100 to be on their negotiation list. When he was with the Winnipeg Rangers in 1942, he helped that team to the Memorial Cup title with 11 goals in 10 games (defeating the Oshawa Generals in the finals). Gardner then served a stint in the Canadian navy before reporting to the Rangers' farm club, the New York Rovers, for the 1945–46 season. In just 40 games for the Rovers, Gardner led the Eastern League with 41 goals and 73 points.

Gardner developed nicely there, as the Rangers had hoped, and he was named the most valuable player in the league. Gardner spent the next two years in New York, but the Rangers were disappointed with his goal production (seasons of 13 and seven were not enough), so he was dealt to the Leafs, who needed a centre owing to the retirement of Syl Apps. In order to get Gardner, the Leafs had to give up a quality defenceman in Wally Stanowski but felt the centreman's potential was worth the risk. (It also helped that the Leafs picked up defenceman Bill Juzda in the transaction.) The Leafs were a much better team than the Rangers, which meant that Gardner did not have to be a star in Toronto. His first year with the Leafs in 1948–49 saw him score 13 times and add 22 assists. Gardner then had a strong playoff with seven points in nine games. He saved his most memorable goal for the night of April 16, 1949, when the Leafs had a chance to clinch the Stanley Cup.

The '48–49 Leafs had finished in fourth place with a mark of 22–25–13 for 57 points during the 60-game regular season, despite the fact they were two-time defending champions. Toronto knocked out Boston in five games in the semi-finals and then met first-place Detroit (75 points during the season) in the final. The Leafs took the first two games in Detroit by 3–2 and 3–1 scores and then won the first game at Maple Leaf Gardens by a 3–1 margin. The Red Wings looked like they might be able to prolong the series when they took a 1–0 lead in the first period of the fourth game. The Leafs tied the game on a goal by rookie Ray Timgren and then took the lead on Gardner's first goal of the finals with only 15 seconds remaining in the second period. The play started when Leaf winger Bill Ezinicki, playing without his stick and challenged by Red Wing blueliner Jack Stewart, kicked the puck ahead to defenceman Jim Thomson, who then hit a streaking Gardner with a pass. Gardner raced down the side that Stewart had vacated and made a shift with his body that seemed to throw Detroit goalie Harry Lumley out of position. Gardner put the puck where Lumley left an opening, and the Leafs had a 2–1 lead. A third-period goal by Max Bentley sealed the Leaf victory and earned the Leafs their third straight Cup, the first team in NHL history to do so.

After the game was over, Ezinicki commented on the game-winning goal by Gardner. "I've been playing hockey for about 15 years, and that's the first time I ever figured on a

goal by kicking," he said. "Stewart did our club a favour by trying to push me around. He wouldn't give me a chance to get my stick, so I just kicked the puck. It landed on Thomson's stick and he made a pass to Gardner."

Manager Conn Smythe entered the Leaf dressing room and congratulated each of the players. "You did it," he shouted across the noisy room. "You did something never done before. You've taken that Cup three years in a row." Long-time trainer Tim Daly didn't understand what all the fuss was about. "I don't know why you guys are so excited at winning the Stanley Cup. We do it every year."

MAPLE LEAF CAREER HIGHLIGHTS

★ Member of two Stanley Cup teams (1949 and 1951)
★ Scored Stanley Cup-winning goal in 1949
★ Scored 23 goals and 51 points in 66 games for the Leafs in 1950–51
★ Recorded 153 points (58G, 95A) in 219 games for Toronto

LEAF FACT:

Cal Gardner was on the ice for the famous Bill Barilko goal that won the Stanley Cup in 1951, but Conn Smythe told him he was in prime position to score the winner. Gardner had stayed back a little to make sure Maurice Richard was being checked, and he had to convince Smythe that was the reason he missed scoring the goal or else he was going to be fined $1,000!

79 | ALEX MOGILNY

BORN: FEBRUARY 18, 1969 IN KHABAROVSK, USSR
POSITION: RIGHT WING
YEARS AS A LEAF: 2001–02 TO 2003–04
SWEATER #: 89
MAPLE LEAF MOMENT: APRIL 30, 2002

ALEX MOGILNY WAS only a Maple Leaf for three seasons, but he may have been one of the most talented players ever to wear the blue and white. Mogilny joined the Leafs as a free agent when the New Jersey Devils decided they could no longer afford his contract demands. The superbly skilled Russian did not really want to leave the Devils (with whom he had won a Stanley Cup in 2000), but he did believe the Toronto club was on the verge of a championship as well. The Leafs knew all about Mogilny's abilities after he tied an NHL record with four points (one goal, three assists) in one period against Toronto in the 2001 playoffs during a 6–5 Devil victory. He joined the Leafs for 2001–02 after a 43-goal season for New Jersey, but as a result of an injury he appeared in only 66 games, scoring 24 times (and totalling 57 points). Much was expected of the easy-going Mogilny in the playoffs, and on the night of April 30, 2002, he delivered in a crucial game.

The Leafs, who recorded 100 points during the regular season, drew the New York Islanders in the first round of the playoffs. Toronto was expected to win the series and took the first two games at home by 3–1 and 2–0 scores. However, the plucky Islanders won the next two at home, and the Leafs also lost captain Mats Sundin for the rest of the series due to a hand injury. Toronto won the fifth contest 6–3, but the Isles refused to die and evened the series at three games each. The only thing higher than the scores was the body count as both clubs lost key players to various ailments.

It all came down to one game at the Air Canada Centre. The New York club scored the opening goal early in the game on a power-play, but Gary Roberts tied it for the Leafs before the first period was over. Mogilny then went to work. Leaf rookie defenceman Karel Pilar carried the puck back into his own end while goalie Curtis Joseph rushed to the bench for an extra attacker during a delayed penalty call on the Islanders. The Leafs got the puck up the ice and Darcy Tucker fed a pass to Mogilny, who then relayed the puck to Robert Reichel. He passed back to Mogilny, who fired a low wrist shot from the slot past New York netminder Chris Osgood.

Mogilny passed the puck more often than he shot after he joined Toronto, but he made no mistake with this drive. The Leafs seemed to play a little more relaxed now that they had the lead. Centre Travis Green scored when he scooped up a giveaway and fired a shot over Osgood's glove to make it 3–1 for Toronto. However, a New York goal at 4:23 of the third made it close again, and only the brilliant netminding of Joseph held the surging Islanders off the board. The sellout crowd of 19,519 let out a huge sigh of relief when Mogilny got his second of the game, putting a shot into the empty net from the Islander blue line at 19:20 of the final period to clinch the series for the Leafs.

"We just beat them to the finish line," said Leaf Alyn McCauley of a series that was filled with great controversy, questionable hits, fighting and one suspension. "We were staggering but we got there." McCauley filled in at centre in

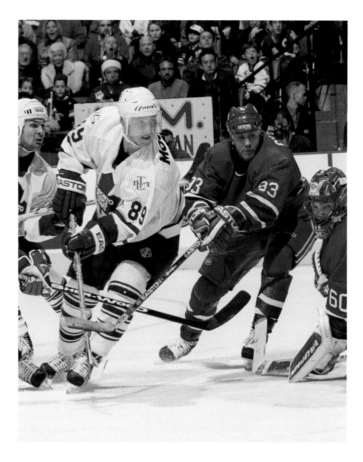

a match that saw both Sundin and Shayne Corson absent from their normal roles. "From top to bottom everyone stepped up at some point," commented Green. "It was awesome."

No one was more awesome that night than the enigmatic Mr. Mogilny.

MAPLE LEAF CAREER HIGHLIGHTS

★ Signed as a free agent by Toronto on July 3, 2001
★ Named winner of the Lady Byng Trophy in 2003
★ Recorded 79 points in 73 games in 2002–03
★ Scored 65 goals and 166 points in 176 games as a Leaf

LEAF FACT:

The Leafs have never fared well against the Philadelphia Flyers in the playoffs, winning only one of six series. The two teams met in the Conference quarter-final in 2003, and the Leafs opened the series with a 5–3 win when Alex Mogilny scored a hat trick in Philadelphia, but the Flyers took the series in seven games.

80 **ED OLCZYK**

BORN: AUGUST 16, 1966 IN CHICAGO, ILLINOIS
POSITION: CENTRE
YEARS AS A LEAF: 1987–88 TO 1990–91
SWEATER #: 16
MAPLE LEAF MOMENT: APRIL 12, 1988

THE MAPLE LEAFS had been pursuing centre Ed Olczyk for some time but were not able to land him until they completed a trade with the Chicago Blackhawks in September of 1987. It cost the Leafs plenty to acquire the big (6′1″, 200-pound) pivot in the deal that saw them give up Rick Vaive, Steve Thomas and Bob McGill in exchange for Olczyk and former 50-goal scorer Al Secord. Olczyk was originally drafted third overall by Chicago in 1984, but the pressure that went with being a local hero seemed to be holding the youngster back. Given a more prominent role in Toronto, Olczyk found his scoring touch with the Leafs, but the team remained in a state of disarray under poor coaching and wretched management.

As bad as the Leafs were during the eighties, they still managed to make a few appearances in the playoffs because other teams in their division somehow managed to be worse. In 1987–88 the Minnesota North Stars dipped to 51 points, one less than the Leafs produced over the 80-game regular season. The Leafs were matched up in the first round with the Detroit Red Wings, who finished first in the Norris Division under coach Jacques Demers. The Leafs were heavy underdogs and played that way for the most part, though they did manage a win in the opening contest. Detroit took the next three and humiliated the Leafs 8–0 on home ice. Toronto fans had seen enough and pelted the ice with everything they could get their hands on over the course of the third period. Even a Leaf sweater was rolled up and tossed onto the ice. It was an embarrassing sight for the once-proud franchise.

Nobody knew what to expect from the Leafs in the next game, to be played in Detroit on April 12, 1988, but Olczyk almost single-handedly won the game for the Leafs by scoring three goals — his first career hat trick — in a 6–5 upset victory to prolong the series. Olczyk scored a short-handed marker 3:44 into the contest and added another on the power-play at the midway mark of the second period. He completed his heroics with an overtime winner just 34 seconds into the extra session when he fired a low shot past surprised goalie Greg Stefan. "It's a great feeling, the kind you dream about," Olczyk said afterwards. "I knew when I hit it, it felt good," he recounted about his overtime winner, which was the first extra-time goal of his career. As he was mobbed by his teammates after the goal, the hero of the night could not retrieve the puck, and one of the unhappy Red Wings threw it into the stands of the Joe Louis Arena. Olczyk also showed some grit by taking several stitches near his eye (the result of an errant stick) in the first period, but he returned to the game.

"What took place — people throwing jerseys and pucks and eggs — is unheard of in Toronto. It hurt a lot; it hurt the guys," Olczyk commented after the game. "If we're gonna go out we want to do it at least with a little class and distinction. I don't want to live with the memory of what happened Sunday night [in Toronto]. I don't think any of these guys do."

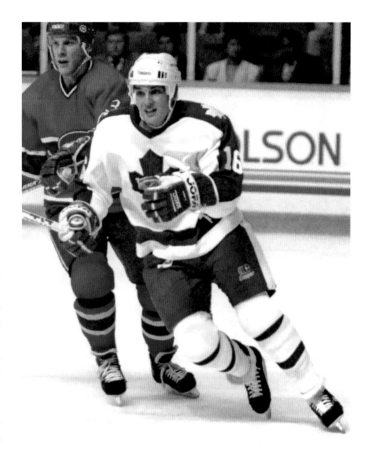

Two days later the Leafs were eliminated by the Red Wings, who ousted them with a 5–3 victory at Maple Leaf Gardens. Thanks to Olczyk's efforts the pride of the Maple Leafs was restored, if only for one evening during a long decade.

MAPLE LEAF CAREER HIGHLIGHTS

★ Acquired in a trade with Chicago on September 4, 1987
★ Scored 42 goals in 1987–88
★ Led the Leafs in points in two seasons (75 in 1987–88 and 90 in 1988–89)
★ Recorded 267 points in 257 games as a Leaf

LEAF FACT:

In 1989–90 Ed Olczyk tied a team record held by former captain Darryl Sittler with at least one point in 18 consecutive games. Olczyk was thrilled to receive a phone call from Sittler when he equalled the mark. "It's an honour to share the record with him," Olczyk said.

81

GUS BODNAR

BORN: APRIL 24, 1923 IN FORT WILLIAM, ONTARIO
POSITION: CENTRE
YEARS AS A LEAF: 1943–44 TO 1946–47
SWEATER #: 8 AND 21
MAPLE LEAF MOMENT: OCTOBER 30, 1943

Gus Bodnar

GUS BODNAR PLAYED all his junior hockey in his home town of Fort William (later amalgamated with Port Arthur to form Thunder Bay) and then signed with the Leafs for the 1943–44 season. The 20-year-old centre came to the Leafs' training camp unsure if he could make the team, but he was on the roster for opening night at Maple Leaf Gardens. During the training camp Bodnar had been knocked out by Bucko McDonald, and the five-foot-eleven, 160-pounder learned a lesson quickly, keeping his head up the rest of his days in the NHL. Bodnar was a good offensive player and could score or set up goals, although he was a better playmaker than goal scorer. He was a Maple Leaf for only three full seasons but managed to get his name on the Stanley Cup twice (1945 and 1947) before he was dealt to Chicago. His best season as a Leaf was his first, when he scored 22 goals and added 40 assists for 62 points, taking the Calder Trophy as the NHL's best rookie. The opening game of his rookie year is still memorable, as Bodnar set a rookie record that has yet to be broken. The record took place on October 30, 1943, when the Leafs opened the '43–44 campaign on home ice against the New York Rangers.

The Rangers had finished last in the NHL in 1942–43 and were destined to finish sixth again in '43–44, while the Leafs were a third-place club in both seasons of wartime hockey, which featured 50-game schedules. With many of the regular NHL players serving in different capacities in the effort to win the war, both teams were forced to use youngsters. Coach Hap Day took a chance and started Bodnar's line for the opening face-off. Bodnar took the opening draw at centre ice against Kilby McDonald of the Rangers. The puck went to Toronto defenceman Elwyn Morris, who fed it over to Bob Davidson. Bodnar then took a pass from Davidson, split the Ranger defence and walked in to beat Ken McAuley in the New York net. Only 15 seconds had passed. No rookie since has started an NHL career with a goal in his first game that quickly. Bodnar's memorable night was by no means finished. He helped Lorne Carr score to start the second period and then scored another goal himself in the third period (assists on this tally went to Davidson and Babe Pratt) to give the Leafs a 5–0 lead. Toronto cruised to a 5–2 victory, with the Rangers adding a couple of meaningless goals to close out the contest.

The Leafs were knocked out of the playoffs in '44 by the Montreal Canadiens in five contests, but the two teams met once again in the 1945 postseason. This time it was the Leafs who came through with a series win in six games. Bodnar had his best playoff year with the Leafs in '45 with four points (three goals, one assist) in 13 games, as the team won the Stanley Cup with a game-seven victory over Detroit in the finals. Despite his good performance as a Leaf (44 points in 1944–45 and 37 points in 1945–46), Bodnar found himself in the minors for a portion of the 1946–47 season (39 games with the Leafs and 15 games with Pittsburgh of the American Hockey League). He got called up to the Leafs for one playoff game in the finals against

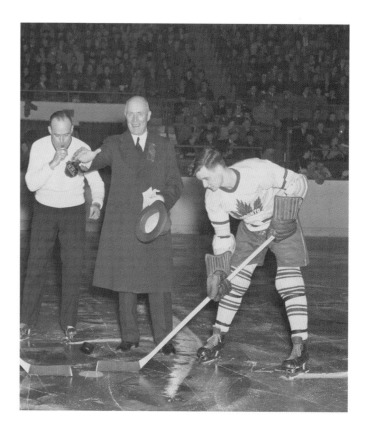

Montreal, so he had his name inscribed on the Cup once more.

Bodnar started the 1947–48 season in the minors again before being sent to Chicago in the deal that saw Max Bentley become a Leaf. He was with Chicago for the next seven years and made the playoffs only once during that time. Bodnar's days as a Black Hawk will be best remembered for setting up Bill Mosienko for three goals in an NHL record 21 seconds during a game against the Rangers. He played for Boston in his final NHL season and finished his career with 396 points in 667 games. He returned to the Leaf organization and coached the Toronto Marlboros to the Memorial Cup in 1967.

MAPLE LEAF CAREER HIGHLIGHTS

★ Member of two Stanley Cup teams
★ Scored 22 goals and 60 points in 1943–44
★ Named winner of the Calder Trophy in 1944
★ Recorded 153 points (48G, 105A) in 187 games as a Leaf

LEAF FACT:

On their way to winning the Stanley Cup in 1945, the Maple Leafs faced the defending champion Montreal Canadiens in the semi-finals. Gus Bodnar scored an overtime winning goal on March 27, 1945, at the Gardens to give Toronto a 3–1 lead in games. Montreal won the next game, but the Leafs took the sixth game 3–2 to win the series.

82 | JIM PAPPIN

BORN: SEPTEMBER 10, 1939 IN COPPER CLIFF, ONTARIO
POSITION: RIGHT WING
YEARS AS A LEAF: 1963–64 TO 1967–68
SWEATER #: 17 AND 18
MAPLE LEAF MOMENT: MAY 2, 1967

JIM PAPPIN WAS one of the many prospects that were developed by the Leafs' junior club, the Toronto Marlies. The six-foot, 190-pound right-winger spent two years as a Marlie and scored a total of 57 goals over that time, including 40 in 48 games in his final junior season of 1957–58. He then spent the next three seasons in the minors and proved himself to be a good goal scorer, with 34 goals for the Rochester Americans in 1962–63. He played in 50 games for the big club the following year and scored 11 times. Pappin was also with the team when the Leafs won the Stanley Cup in 1964 and was dressed for 11 of the 14 games the Leafs played in the playoffs. For the next three years he shuttled back and forth between Toronto and Rochester, as he was never able to please coach Punch Imlach enough to stick in the NHL. In 1966–67, Pappin played in six games for the Americans but played in 64 for the Leafs and scored 21 times. Late in the season, Pappin was put on a line with Bob Pulford and Peter Stemkowski, and the trio caught fire. They were the Leafs' best offensive line throughout the playoffs. That situation continued on the night of May 2, 1967, when Toronto had the chance to clinch the Cup on home ice.

It was something of a miracle that the Leafs were in a position to win the Cup when no one expected them to get past Chicago in the semi-final. Pappin had seven points (3 goals, 4 assists) in the six-game series against the Black Hawks and had already scored three goals against Montreal in the final. The game was expected to be a close-checking one, and the teams did not score a goal in the first period. Ron Ellis got the Leafs on the board in the second period, and it looked like the 1–0 lead would hold going into the third. But late in the middle stanza, Pappin got control of the puck along the boards in the Montreal end and drifted a shot at the Canadien net. The puck deflected off the skate of Montreal defenceman Terry Harper past netminder Gump Worsley. Suddenly, the Leafs had a 2–0 lead. Montreal was not about to give up, and former Leaf Dick Duff finally beat Terry Sawchuk in the Toronto net to make it 2–1. When Pappin took a slashing penalty with over half the third period played, he sweated for two minutes while he sat in the box. The Leafs killed it off and then won a key face-off in their own end with Worsley on the bench and 55 seconds on the clock. Toronto worked the puck out of their end to captain George Armstrong, who put it into the empty net to ensure a 3–1 victory.

Pappin was soaked in champagne in the Leaf dressing room after the game and confessed to not being sure what happened on what turned out to be the winning goal (which had originally been credited to Stemkowski). "We just kept plugging, that's all," Pappin said. "I lobbed the puck across the goal. It went off [Harper's] skate. Pete told the referee right away, but they gave him credit for it." For his part Stemkowski wanted to make sure Pappin got credit for the marker because his linemate wanted to have the most goals scored in the playoffs. "Pappy wanted to beat out Béliveau," Stemkowski said.

When Pappin saw Montreal writers approaching he quipped, "You've got Expo, so let us have the Stanley Cup." It was a line Coach Imlach might have used, since the Leaf mentor made it his personal mission to keep the Stanley Cup out of a display case at "Man and His World," the world's fair held in Montreal to celebrate Canada's 100th birthday.

One year later Pappin was back in Imlach's bad books with 13 goals in 58 games. A demotion to Rochester was in order once again. Pappin was dealt away to Chicago in May of 1968 in what turned out to be a terrible trade for the Leafs.

MAPLE LEAF CAREER HIGHLIGHTS

★ Member of Stanley Cup team in 1967
★ Scored Stanley Cup-winning goal in 1967
★ Scored 21 goals in 1966–67
★ Totalled 100 points (54G, 46A) in 223 career games

LEAF FACT:

Even though the Maple Leafs have won 11 Stanley Cups, only two Toronto players have ever led the playoffs in scoring. The first was Ted Kennedy in 1948 (14 points). The second was Jim Pappin in 1967 (15 points).

83 | JAMIE MACOUN

BORN: AUGUST 17, 1961 IN NEWMARKET, ONTARIO
POSITION: DEFENCE
YEARS AS A LEAF: 1991–92 TO 1997–98
SWEATER #: 34
MAPLE LEAF MOMENT: JANUARY 2, 1992

WHEN THE MAPLE LEAFS were shellacked 12–1 by the Pittsburgh Penguins on December 26, 1991, it looked like the team had hit rock bottom. Two more losses (5–4 to Detroit on December 28 and 5–2 to Quebec two days later), and Leaf general manager Cliff Fletcher knew he had to do something dramatic to shake up his team. He had started the 1991–92 season (his first with Toronto) with a blockbuster deal involving the Edmonton Oilers, but that did not seem to give the club a new direction. Nobody expected Fletcher to complete a 10-player swap with the Calgary Flames, but that's exactly what happened on January 2, 1992. "This is a trade of great magnitude which I felt had to be made with a team that has won 10 of its first 40 games," Fletcher said. Their terrible record had the Leafs ranked 21st in a 22-team league. The player deal set a record for the most players involved in a single trade during the season. Toronto gave up some youth, but they were thrilled to get scoring centre Doug Gilmour, a young prospect in Kent Manderville, an experienced goalie in Rick Wamsley, plus a pair of defencemen, Ric Nattress and Jamie Macoun, who could step right into the lineup.

Macoun was the more talented of the two blueliners acquired, although both had played for the Stanley Cup–winning Calgary club in 1989. Macoun did not really think a professional hockey career was possible for him, but he attended Ohio State University for three seasons and played hockey while continuing his education. He was signed as a free agent by the Flames and joined the Calgary club for the last part of the 1982–83 season. Without ever playing a single contest in the minors, Macoun quickly established himself as an NHL defenceman. At 6′2″ and 200 pounds, Macoun was ideal for the defensive side of the game, but he was not devoid of offence, scoring a total of 19 goals and 76 points in his first three years. A good skater in the early years of his career, Macoun always showed up to play, and he could play hurt if needed. He missed the entire 1987–88 season after a car accident that nearly cost him his life, but he bounced back to help the Flames take the championship in '89.

The success of the Flames led many of the players to demand better contracts, and Calgary management was not sure they would be able to meet those requirements. Gilmour was the most vocal about his displeasure regarding his contractual status, but all the players who came to the Leafs in the deal had some issues with Calgary general manager Doug Risebrough. Macoun was no exception, though he did his best to keep his dispute as low-key as possible. The Flames were one game below the .500 mark at that point in '91–92 and, like the Leafs, felt they had to make some changes. The Flames moved their contract hassles to Toronto, but the reality was that they received inferior quality in Gary Leeman, Michel Petit, Alexander Godynyuk, Craig Berube and Jeff Reece. Risebrough did his best to put the right spin on the deal, but the general consensus was that Fletcher had fleeced the team that once employed him. By contrast, four of the players the Leafs received owned Stanley Cup rings.

When he was informed of the deal, Macoun was at the hospital with his wife, Karen, who was giving birth to their son. "When I first saw my child at the hospital, I hoped that I would be staying here at least a couple of years," Macoun said. "But to use the old cliché of traded players, it's nice to be going to a team that wants me."

Macoun also scored a goal in his debut with Toronto (in a loss to Chicago), as did Gilmour (in a loss to Detroit). The Leafs soon became a much better team and nearly made the playoffs in 1992. The deal turned the team around, and Toronto was a Cup contender in both 1993 and 1994.

MAPLE LEAF CAREER HIGHLIGHTS

★ Scored a goal in his first game as Leaf on January 4, 1992
★ Recorded 30 points (3G, 27A) in 82 games during the 1993–94 season
★ Played his 1,000th career game as a Maple Leaf during 1996–97
★ Recorded 101 points (13G, 88A) in 466 games with Toronto

LEAF FACT:

The Maple Leafs were out of contention during the 1997–98 season and decided to move Jamie Macoun to the Detroit Red Wings, who needed a veteran defenceman for the playoffs. Macoun, who won another Stanley Cup with Detroit, was dealt for a fourth-round draft choice. Not many fourth-round selections make it to the NHL, but by the 2006–07 season, Alexei Ponikarovsky was an important member of the Leafs.

84 | TODD GILL

BORN: NOVEMBER 9, 1965 IN CARDINAL, ONTARIO
POSITION: DEFENCE
YEARS AS A LEAF: 1984–85 TO 1995–96
SWEATER #: 3, 11, 23 AND 29
MAPLE LEAF MOMENT: APRIL 20, 1994

TODD GILL REALLY developed as a hockey player when he was captain of the Windsor Spitfires of the Ontario Hockey League, where he was prepared for the NHL by coach Wayne Maxner. The Maple Leafs liked what they saw in the six-foot, 185-pound defenceman and selected him 25th overall in 1984. Gill played in 10 games for the Leafs in 1984–85 and then another 15 for Toronto the following season that also saw the youngster get his first taste of playoff action (a seventh-game showdown between the Leafs and the St. Louis Blues in the 1986 postseason). Gill then spent time in the minors (with St. Catharines and Newmarket) before joining the Leafs for good in 1986–87. It was not always an easy road for Gill after he became a full-time Leaf, as his mistakes tended to be costly ones. He nearly left Toronto when Doug Carpenter coached the club, but he persevered and saw better times (with a simplified game) under mentors Tom Watt and Pat Burns. When Burns teamed him with defenceman Dave Ellett, Gill's game improved tremendously, and he became a very valuable member of the team. This proved to be the case on the night of April 20, 1994, when the Leafs hosted the Chicago Blackhawks in a playoff game.

It was fitting that one of Gill's best moments as a Leaf came against Chicago, since he had suffered one of his worst at the hands of the Blackhawks in 1989, when Troy Murray stole a puck from Gill to score a goal that put the Leafs out of the playoffs and sent Chicago to the postseason instead. The Leafs had done well in the 1993 playoffs and were hoping for more of the same in 1994 when they faced the Blackhawks in the opening round. They won the first game in convincing style 5–1, but the second contest proved to be much tougher. The teams battled through 60 minutes of scoreless hockey as the fans at Maple Leaf Gardens were treated to a superb goaltending display by Felix Potvin of the Leafs (32 saves) and Ed Belfour of the Blackhawks (37 stops). Potvin's diving save to take away a sure goal from Chicago's Paul Ysebaert was truly spectacular, causing the crowd to leap up and show their appreciation for the second-year netminder.

After 2:15 of overtime, the Leafs kept the puck in the Chicago end, and the puck came to Gill at the point. He let go a slap shot that went all the way through to beat Belfour and give the Leafs a 1–0 victory and a 2–0 lead in the series. The Blackhawk netminder complained loudly that he was interfered with by Leaf forward Wendel Clark, but replays clearly showed there was no contact. "I saw Wendel in front and shot the puck at him," Gill said. "I think Belfour was more concerned about Wendel than me and it hit the inside of his skate and went in." He also spoke about his past troubles with the Blackhawks. "I've had some tough times in Chicago. I wished it had happened there [scoring the winning goal]. But this is the greatest feeling in the world. I didn't care who got the goal. The main thing was we won." Gill also took the time to give credit to the Leafs' goalie. "He's worth every cent he makes. That save he made [on Ysebaert] was a game-

breaker. It allowed us to stay in the game," Gill said of Potvin.

Gill's revenge against Chicago was complete when the Leafs took the series in six games. (The last contest, a 1–0 win for Toronto, marked the final NHL game played at Chicago Stadium.) Toronto went on to beat San Jose in seven games before losing to Vancouver. Gill stayed with the Leafs until he was traded to the Sharks in 1996.

MAPLE LEAF CAREER HIGHLIGHTS

★ Drafted 25th overall by the Leafs in 1984
★ Twice scored a high of 11 goals in one season
★ Recorded 20 or more points in eight seasons as a Leaf
★ Scored 59 goals and 210 assists in 639 career games

LEAF FACT:

Todd Gill led all Leaf defencemen with 31 points (4G, 27A) in 1986–87, his first full year with the team. His best season with Toronto came in 1992–93 when he had 43 points (11 goals, 32 assists) in the regular season and added 11 points in 21 playoff games.

85 | DARCY TUCKER

BORN: MARCH 15, 1975 IN CASTOR, ALBERTA
POSITION: LEFT WING
YEARS AS A LEAF: 1999–2000 TO PRESENT
SWEATER #: 16
MAPLE LEAF MOMENT: NOVEMBER 4, 2006

WHEN THE MAPLE LEAFS acquired Darcy Tucker from the Tampa Bay Lightning they were hoping he would bring an edge to their hockey team. The five-foot-ten, 170-pound Tucker already had a reputation for being one of the top antagonists in the NHL, and he enjoyed that recognition. "I love going into a rink and being the most hated guy on the ice," he said just after the deal was made. "Who wouldn't?" That was exactly the kind of attitude the Leafs were looking to add and the reason why they gave up skilled forward Mike Johnson plus defensive prospect Marek Posmyk in the trade. "He has a real edge to him," Toronto coach Pat Quinn said of the newest Leaf. "He's a great competitor who will sacrifice his body. You need those kinds of guys, and we didn't have enough of them."

Tucker also had a winning background with three Memorial Cup titles to his name (all won with the Kamloops Blazers of the WHL) and one gold medal when he represented Canada at the World Junior Championships in 1995. Tucker had been drafted by the Montreal Canadiens 151st overall in 1993, but after one and a half seasons as a Hab, he was dealt to Tampa Bay. He scored 21 times for the Lightning in 1998–99 and had 14 the next season before he came to Toronto, where he scored seven times in 27 games to finish the 1999–2000 campaign. The feisty Tucker then posted seasons of 16, 24, 10, 21 and 28 goals for the Leafs and had become a more complete player by the time the 2006–07 season began. He got off to a great start in '06–07 and was especially hot on the power-play as the Leafs pulled into Buffalo on November 4, 2006.

Since the HSBC Arena opened in Buffalo, the Leafs had posted a dismal 4–17–3 record there going into this contest. The Sabres went into the game not having lost in regulation play to start the '06–07 campaign, but the Leafs beat the Buffalo squad at its own game and came away with a convincing 4–1 win. The Sabres opened the scoring, but Leaf captain Mats Sundin tied it before the first period ended. In the second stanza, it was all Leafs, as they scored three straight times to take a three-goal lead. Tucker got the game-winning goal on a power-play when he swatted home a cross-ice pass from Sundin while standing just off to the side of the net. It was Tucker's 10th goal (the most of any Leaf player) of the young season (this was the Leafs' 16th game of the year), and most of them were scored with the man advantage. Jeff O'Neill and Sundin, with his second of the night, rounded out the Leaf scoring and sent the many Toronto fans who loyally trek to Buffalo home happy for a change.

"You have to evolve with the game, and I think I've adapted fairly well to the new rules and the way the game is being called now," Tucker said when asked if he is now more about skill and less about brawn. "I think Don Cherry said it well. When I play with a certain edge, that's when I play my best. I go out there and I play hard and I play with a tenacious effort. Sometimes that makes other people angry. I just go out and play."

Buffalo coach Lindy Ruff, a long-time Tucker hater, found nice words to say about the Leaf left-winger. "Right

now, he's a goal scorer. You have to give him credit. It might surprise some, but he's a key piece to their offensive puzzle."

Playing for a new contract, Tucker realized he had to make the most of his chances. "I get the opportunity to produce, so I better do it. That's the bottom line. You have to go out and do what you're asked to do. Our power-play has been good for me."

Tucker has been good for the Maple Leafs since the day he arrived in Toronto.

MAPLE LEAF CAREER HIGHLIGHTS

★ Acquired in a trade with Tampa Bay on February 9, 2000
★ Recorded over 100 penalty minutes three times as a Leaf
★ Scored 28 goals and 61 points for the Leafs in 2005–06
★ Recorded 285 points (130G, 155A) in 457 games with Toronto (as of May 2007)

LEAF FACT:

Soon after Darcy Tucker was acquired in a trade, he scored two short-handed goals in one game when the Leafs visited the Vancouver Canucks and won the March 6, 2000, contest 6–5 in overtime on a goal by Mats Sundin.

86

ANDY BATHGATE

BORN: AUGUST 28, 1932 IN WINNIPEG, MANITOBA
POSITION: RIGHT WING
YEARS AS A LEAF: 1963–64 TO 1964–65
SWEATER #: 9
MAPLE LEAF MOMENT: APRIL 25, 1964

ALL MAPLE LEAF FANS and players were shocked on February 22, 1964, to learn that wingers Dick Duff and Bob Nevin had been dealt to the New York Rangers. The Leafs had not been a very consistent team during the 1963–64 season, but Duff and the youthful Nevin had both been major factors in the Leaf teams that had won the Stanley Cup in 1962 and 1963. Leaf general manager Punch Imlach felt his team was not going to repeat if he did not shake up his lethargic squad, and he had always coveted right-winger Andy Bathgate, so he made the very unpopular deal. The Leafs also got veteran Don McKenney in return, but they had to give up promising youngsters in Rod Seiling, Arnie Brown and Bill Collins to complete the deal. The Rangers made the trade for their future and coach Red Sullivan acknowledged that the New York club would miss Bathgate, who had scored 276 career goals at the time of the trade. "Andy will do two things that'll make a tremendous difference for the Leafs," Sullivan stated. "He's an expert on the power-play, where the Leafs need help, and he has an excellent shot. With those improvements they'll be awfully hard to beat," he concluded. Sullivan's prediction was right on, as the Leafs won nine games after the deal was made and finished in third place. The Leafs managed to slip past first-place Montreal in the semi-final and then battled Detroit to a 3–3 series tie before coming home for game seven of the finals. On April 25, 1964, the Stanley Cup would be decided before more than 14,000 fans at Maple Leaf Gardens.

The only goal that the Leafs needed on the night was scored by Bathgate just 3:04 into the contest. Bathgate took advantage of a miscue by Detroit defenceman Al Langlois at the Leaf blue line. Langlois mishandled the puck on a Gordie Howe pass, and Bathgate stole the disc to go in alone on Red Wing netminder Terry Sawchuk. The Leaf winger knew Sawchuk had trouble lifting his left shoulder, so he aimed his hard wrist shot from about 25 feet out right at that spot and scored, giving the Leafs a 1–0 lead. The game stayed that way until early in the third period when Dave Keon relieved the tension in the building by making it 2–0. Frank Mahovlich set up Red Kelly and George Armstrong for two more goals, and the Leafs won their third straight world championship 4–0. The line of Bathgate, Kelly and Mahovlich saved their best game of the series for this evening, while goalie Johnny Bower turned back 33 Detroit shots. Bathgate's winning goal was the second game-winner of the series for the newly acquired Leaf, and he had totalled nine points in 14 playoff games.

In the dressing room after the game, Bathgate posed for pictures with the Cup and expressed both joy and relief as he sipped champagne from the old mug. "I feel jolted," Bathgate said. "It's an accomplishment I can't quite realize. It happened so fast, in two months up from the struggle in the valley to the top of the world. I'm just thankful to be here. It's not only the first time I've ever been on a Stanley Cup winner," the one-time Hart Trophy winner continued, "it's the first time I've ever been in the final …. This [the Leafs] is a big club with older fellows. It seems the pressure made them go better."

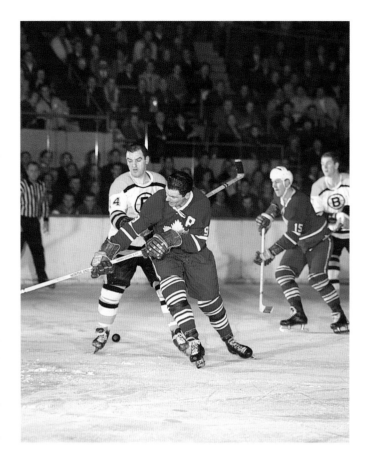

Despite his good performance in the playoffs, Bathgate never did get going in 1964–65 and feuded publicly with Imlach. He was dealt to Detroit in May of 1965, but he had fulfilled his role in helping the Leafs win the Stanley Cup.

MAPLE LEAF CAREER HIGHLIGHTS

★ Recorded 18 points in 15 games to finish the 1963–64 season
★ Scored two game-winning goals in the 1964 playoffs
★ Recorded 45 points in 55 games during the 1964–65 season
★ Totalled 63 points in 70 games as a Leaf
★ Elected to the Hockey Hall of Fame in 1978

LEAF FACT:

Everyone remembers Andy Bathgate's winning goal in game seven of the 1964 finals, but he also scored another important marker in the series. The Leafs were down two games to one when they played the fourth game of the series at the Detroit Olympia. The score was tied 2–2 in the third period when Bathgate let go a blistering slap shot, just as he crossed the Red Wing blue line, that overwhelmed netminder Terry Sawchuk to give Toronto a 3–2 lead. The Leafs won the game 4–2 and tied the series 2–2.

87

FERN FLAMAN

BORN: JANUARY 25, 1927 IN DYSART, SASKATCHEWAN
POSITION: DEFENCE
YEARS AS A LEAF: 1950–51 TO 1953–54
SWEATER #: 3 AND 12
MAPLE LEAF MOMENT: APRIL 1, 1951

WHEN THE MAPLE LEAFS lost their hold on the Stanley Cup in 1950, the management of the team felt it was time for changes. Coach Hap Day was moved into the role of assistant general manager, and former Leaf great Joe Primeau took over behind the bench. But some players were also moved out, including defenceman Garth Boesch and forward Don Metz, who retired. Then, on November 16, 1950, to help fill the gap left by the loss of Boesch on the blue line, the Leafs sent stalwarts Bill Ezinicki and Vic Lynn along to Boston for defencemen Fern Flaman and Leo Boivin, with forwards Phil Maloney and Ken Smith also coming to the Leafs. The key acquisition for the Leafs was the hard-hitting Flaman. The Leafs were then able to boast a blue line that consisted of Jim Thomson, Gus Mortson, Bill Barilko, Bill Juzda and Flaman. This rock-solid group of five led the Leafs back to being Stanley Cup contenders in the spring of 1951. The Leafs saw the rugged five-foot-ten, 190-pound Flaman as a little raw and perhaps too aggressive (though the Leafs did not mind this too much) for their very disciplined style of play. Flaman was a smooth skater, and he was known for his ability to get in close and throw punches when he got into a fight. He soon fit into the Leaf system, and in 39 games during the '50–51 season Flaman scored two goals and eight points with 64 penalty minutes. He would score very rarely but got a goal in the '51 playoffs against his former club in the first round of the playoffs on the night of April 1, 1951.

The Bruins had walked into Toronto and surprised the Leafs with a 2–0 win in the first game of the semi-final series. The second contest, held on a Saturday, ended in a 1–1 tie when it was decided that the game could not continue after midnight. (No sporting events were allowed on a Sunday in Toronto at the time.) This made the next contest in Boston an important one for the Leafs. They responded to the challenge by defeating the Bruins 3–0 to even the series. Cal Gardner opened the scoring for Toronto in the second period of what was a very rough contest. Flaman made it 2–0 for the Leafs when he ripped a 60-foot drive that Bruin netminder Jack Gelineau did not even see. Max Bentley got the Leafs' third goal of the night in the final period, and the Leafs checked the Bruins closely the rest of the way. Flaman was a big help to Leaf goaltender Turk Broda, who earned the shutout. The Leaf blueliner blocked many shots and hit Boston star Milt Schmidt with such force that Schmidt injured his knee.

The next game on April 3 was more of the same as the Leafs defeated Boston 3–1 to take a 2–1 lead in the series. Flaman was paired with Jim Thomson on defence, and they were a very effective duo for the entire game. Flaman helped to set up a goal (although he was not credited with an assist) when he took a drive that Gelineau turned aside. The rebound went right to Bentley, who made no mistake for the game-winning tally. After the second contest in Boston was over, Leaf general manager Conn Smythe said, "We got all the breaks." Really, though, it was the outstanding work of Broda in net and the stellar efforts of all the Leaf defencemen

that did the trick. The Leafs took the series in five and went on to play Montreal in the finals, winning the Stanley Cup in another five-game series.

The next three seasons saw Flaman rack up 110, 110 and 84 penalty minutes (and a couple of goalless years) before the Leafs decided he should be moved. Foolishly, in July 1954 the Leafs made an ill-advised trade and gave Flaman back to Boston for centre Dave Creighton (who would score a grand total of six goals over his entire Leaf career). Flaman played another six solid seasons for the Bruins and helped them to consecutive finals appearances in 1957 and 1958.

MAPLE LEAF CAREER HIGHLIGHTS

★ Acquired in a trade with Boston in November 1950
★ Member of Stanley Cup team in 1951
★ Recorded 31 points (4G, 27A) in 228 career games with Toronto
★ Elected to the Hockey Hall of Fame in 1990

LEAF FACT:

Two members of the Maple Leafs' Stanley Cup-winning team of 1951 went on to captain other teams once they left Toronto. Fern Flaman was the Boston Bruins' captain between 1955 and 1961, while Gus Mortson captained the Chicago Black Hawks from 1954 to 1957. Two other players on that championship team, Jim Thomson and Sid Smith, would be named captain of the Leafs for one season each.

88

LARRY HILLMAN

BORN: FEBRUARY 5, 1937 IN KIRKLAND LAKE, ONTARIO
POSITION: DEFENCE
YEARS AS A LEAF: 1960–61 TO 1967–68
SWEATER #: 2 AND 22
MAPLE LEAF MOMENT: JANUARY 18, 1961

MAPLE LEAF COACH and general manager Punch Imlach had a knack for picking up veteran players from other teams who came to Toronto and added something significant to his team. Red Kelly, Bert Olmstead and Allan Stanley were the most celebrated of these acquisitions, but there were others, including Al Arbour, Kent Douglas, Gerry Ehman, Larry Jeffrey, Ed Litzenberger and Don Simmons. Defenceman Larry Hillman, who had a hand in helping the Leafs win Stanley Cups in the sixties, was another. Hillman began his NHL career with the Detroit Red Wings in 1954–55, after playing his junior career in Windsor and Hamilton, and was on a Stanley Cup-winning team as a rookie (playing in three games of the '55 playoffs). The robust six-foot, 185-pound blueliner then spent the next two years playing for the Red Wings or their minor league teams but was claimed by two different teams in the 1957 intra-league draft, ending up with Boston for the next three years. Hillman's strength was moving the puck up the ice quickly, and he had the size to handle some of the NHL's bigger players, even though he was not the greatest skater. Imlach took the rights to Hillman in the summer of 1960, after Hillman was named winner of the Eddie Shore Award as the top defenceman in the American Hockey League, having played the 1959–60 season with the Providence Reds. He appeared in 62 games for Toronto in 1960–61, tallying 13 points, and scored his first goal as a Leaf on January 18, 1961, when Toronto tangled with New York at Maple Leaf Gardens.

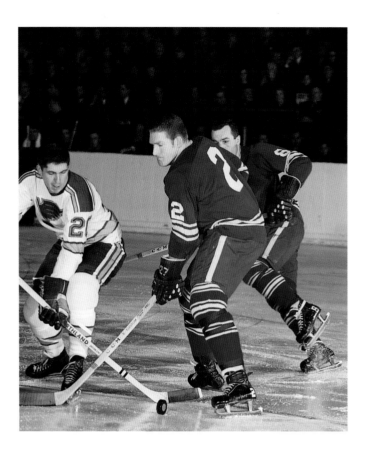

Hillman was starting for the Leafs in this contest because regular defenceman Carl Brewer was out of the lineup. He got even more ice time when blueliner Tim Horton got involved in a major brawl in the first period with New York's Lou Fontinato. The bench-clearing fight started when Fontinato and Toronto's Bert Olmstead kept up their feud when they stepped out of the penalty box. Horton did not like what was happening to his teammates and jumped off the bench to get at Fontinato. Five major fights took place during the brawl, but the fisticuffs seemed to ignite the Leafs, who were down 3–0 at the time. A different Leaf team came out for the second, and Hillman led the attack, scoring just past the halfway mark of the period. On a power-play, Hillman let go a hard slap shot from the left point that got by Gump Worsley in the Ranger goal. New York restored their three-goal lead, however, before the second period was over.

The third period was all Leafs, as they scored three times to earn a 4–4 tie. Dick Duff got the Leafs rolling in the final frame, then Red Kelly got the next two (his second goal in the final minute with goalie Johnny Bower on the bench) to get the Leafs the draw. Hillman continued his fine play by setting up Kelly's first goal but would be fined $25 for joining the fight in the first period. Afterwards, all the talk centred on the brawl. "I'm really getting too old for that sort of thing," Horton said. "But once it's done, it's done. I went out there alright."

New York's Red Sullivan had this view of the proceedings: "Horton touched it off. I mean it was just another fight until he roared out there. Then we had to go, too. You just can't sit there while something like that is going on."

Hillman was with the Leafs when they won the Cup in 1964. He was also a very important part of the Leafs' 1967 championship when he was teamed with Marcel Pronovost to give the Leafs their most consistent defensive pairing. In the 1967 playoffs, when Hillman played his best hockey as a Maple Leaf, he had three points and did not record a single penalty in 12 playoff games. He and Pronovost were not on the ice for an opposition goal-against at even strength for the entire playoffs.

Hillman played one more season with the Leafs before he was picked up by Montreal in a trade. He promptly found himself on another Cup winner in 1969!

MAPLE LEAF CAREER HIGHLIGHTS

★ Member of two Stanley Cup teams with Toronto
★ Recorded three seasons of more than 20 points with the Leafs
★ Recorded 28 points (3G, 25A) in 1965–66 with Toronto
★ Recorded 88 points (13G, 75A) in 265 games as a Leaf

LEAF FACT:

Larry Hillman was never afraid to drop the gloves and fight when he had to, taking on Montreal tough guy John Ferguson on more than one occasion. He also fought with Reggie Fleming, a noted hardrock with the Chicago Black Hawks.

89

KENT DOUGLAS

BORN: FEBRUARY 6, 1936 IN COBALT, ONTARIO
POSITION: DEFENCE
YEARS AS A LEAF: 1962–63 TO 1966–67
SWEATER #: 19
MAPLE LEAF MOMENT: APRIL 18, 1963

WHEN DEFENCEMAN KENT DOUGLAS won the Calder Trophy in 1962–63 it was unusual to see the NHL's top rookie award go to a 27-year-old — even in the era of the Original Six. The Leafs sent five players in June of 1962 to Springfield of the American Hockey League to acquire the rights to Douglas, who had just won the award for the best defenceman in the AHL. Springfield boss Eddie Shore at first demanded $50,000 for the highly sought-after Douglas but eventually settled for the players instead. The Leafs wanted Douglas to fill the role of fifth defenceman on the team and help out on the power-play. Douglas delivered as advertised in his first year with Toronto, scoring seven goals and 22 points while playing in all 70 games. On many nights Leaf coach Punch Imlach felt Douglas was the best defender on his club. The Leafs finished first in '62–63, then brushed off the Montreal Canadiens in five games during the semi-finals. They had Detroit down three games to one in the final. The Red Wings were trying to stay alive as they came to Toronto for the fifth game of the series at Maple Leaf Gardens on April 18, 1963.

It was a much closer contest than anyone might have expected. Toronto opened the scoring when Dave Keon scored a short-handed marker late in the first period with defenceman Allan Stanley in the penalty box. Veteran Alex Delvecchio tied the score for Detroit in the second stanza, while Red Wing netminder Terry Sawchuk kept the Leafs off the scoreboard. It looked like the game was heading for overtime when the Leafs got a face-off in the Detroit end. Leaf centre Bob Pulford won the draw back to Douglas who ripped a drive at the Detroit net. The shot was deflected by Eddie Shack in front of the Red Wing goal past a startled Sawchuk and into the net. The Leafs hung on for the last six minutes and were fortunate when Red Wing centre Norm Ullman missed an opportunity to tie the score in the final minute. Pulford took a penalty at 18:07 and Detroit pulled Sawchuk for an extra attacker, but Keon scored his second short-handed marker of the night with just five seconds to play to end any Detroit hope for a comeback. The normally sedate Toronto crowd let out a large roar and threw debris all over the ice in celebration of a 3–1 triumph. The Leafs had won their second straight Stanley Cup.

Pulford later described how the game-winning goal came about: "I told Douglas to be ready, that I would beat their defenceman [Doug Barkley] for the face-off in the Wings zone."

"Bob did a perfect job," Douglas said. "I fielded the puck with my skate and was able to put tremendous force into my shot. Fortunately, it hit Shack's stick and went past Sawchuk. Shack also chimed in on the winner: "I was cruising near the goal and the puck hit the stick on the handle and went in. I never saw it. All I wanted to do was get out of the way."

For Douglas, who had been part of three championship teams with Springfield, ending the season with a championship was becoming a springtime ritual. "This is the fourth straight season I've had the bubbly and I didn't want to miss

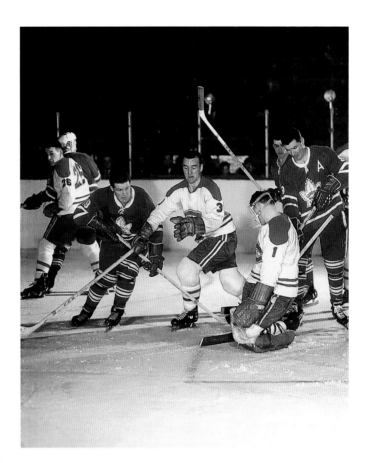

it. Like Punch, I've never missed the playoffs and I don't intend to start now. It's just too much fun."

Douglas was also with the Leafs for their Stanley Cup-winning seasons of 1963–64 and 1966–67, although he did not participate in the playoffs in either year, having been sent down to the minors. He was selected by the California Seals in the expansion draft of 1967.

MAPLE LEAF CAREER HIGHLIGHTS

★ Acquired in a trade with Springfield, June 7, 1962
★ Member of Stanley Cup team in 1963
★ Winner of the Calder Trophy in 1963
★ Scored 20 goals and 85 points in 283 games

LEAF FACT:

On April 1, 1965, Kent Douglas became the first player to be tossed out of a playoff game since Maurice Richard was thrown out of a postseason contest in 1947. Douglas got the boot for clubbing Dave Balon in the head with his stick at the Montreal Forum and had Richard, who was sitting in the stands as a spectator, come after him swinging his fists as the Leaf defenceman left the ice. Douglas was fined $100 and suspended for the next game.

90 ED BELFOUR

BORN: APRIL 21, 1965 IN CARMAN, MANITOBA
POSITION: GOALTENDER
YEARS AS A LEAF: 2002–03 TO 2005–06
SWEATER #: 20
MAPLE LEAF MOMENT: OCTOBER 10, 2002

ALL MAPLE LEAF FANS were very disappointed when goaltender Curtis Joseph decided to leave the team and join the Detroit Red Wings as a free agent. Joseph had just taken the Leafs to their second appearance in the Eastern Conference final in four years, and he had been the backbone of the team for all those seasons. Leaf management did not hesitate to find a replacement quickly, and they turned to another established veteran when they signed Ed Belfour to a free-agent deal starting with the 2002–03 season. Even though he was 37 years old, Belfour still believed he had plenty to offer a contending team, and he also had an illustrious hockey resumé to show off. He was a former rookie of the year (in 1991 with Chicago), a Vezina Trophy recipient on two occasions, a three-time Jennings Trophy winner, as well as a Stanley Cup champion (with Dallas in 1999). Skeptics pointed to his mediocre 21–27–11 record with the Dallas Stars in his final season there as a major concern, but the Leafs felt they were getting one of the most competitive goalies in the game who had plenty left in the tank.

The five-foot-eleven, 202-pound netminder was perhaps the most technically sound goalie in the NHL, and his economy of movement as he made stop after stop was truly amazing to watch. He was also one of the top puckhandlers among all goaltenders, which made him part of the attack, and that would suit the questionable Leaf defence just fine in their own end. Still, no one was quite sure what to expect when the Leafs went to Pittsburgh to open the season on October 10, 2002.

All those who doubted Belfour could rest easy at least for one night. The Leafs' new netminder had appeared somewhat shaky during the preseason but had no difficulty shutting down Mario Lemieux and the rest of the Penguins. Belfour was not overly busy in the first two periods but was forced to make quality saves in the third period, and 33 stops overall, to preserve a 6–0 shutout in his first appearance as a Maple Leaf. It marked the only time in club history that a goalie playing in his first game as a Leaf had recorded a shutout. The Leaf attack was paced by Mats Sundin and Alex Mogilny, who both scored twice, while Karel Pilar and Nik Antropov added singles. Sundin, Mogilny and their linemate Darcy Tucker each finished the contest with four points. The newly organized threesome got the Leafs going with a goal on a five-on-three advantage less than six minutes into the contest, scoring on Pittsburgh goalie Johan Hedberg. The game featured many penalties, as the NHL was trying to implement a new standard of officiating that even the Leafs did not like despite their six-goal outburst. The Leafs finished the game with nine minor penalties to five for the Penguins.

In the dressing room after the game Belfour talked about his transition to his new team. "In the preseason, you're working out the bugs, getting used to the guys and breaking in the equipment," he said. "Sometimes it doesn't work out like you'd want it to in the preseason. You try and get better every day, and our hard work paid off. I really

appreciate the hard work the guys did in front of me. They kept the chances down."

Leaf coach Pat Quinn expressed his concern that the Leafs were just trading scoring chances with the Penguins, and he had hoped the new season would have meant a different Leaf team when it came to defensive responsibilities. Try as he might, Quinn was not able to get his club to play well in their own end. That meant Belfour was going to see plenty of rubber during the season.

Belfour responded well to the challenge and won 37 games in '02–03, helping get the Leafs into the playoffs, where they were ousted by the Philadelphia Flyers in a seven-game series.

MAPLE LEAF CAREER HIGHLIGHTS

★ Signed as a free agent by the Leafs on July 2, 2002
★ Won 93 games for the Leafs over three seasons
★ Recorded 17 shutouts with Toronto
★ Named winner of the Molson Cup for the 2002–03 and 2003–04 seasons

LEAF FACT:

On December 19, 2005, Toronto netminder Ed Belfour won his 448th career game to surpass the great Terry Sawchuk on the all-time goaltender wins list, placing him second only to Patrick Roy. Belfour got the milestone win when the Leafs beat the New York Islanders 9–6 at the Air Canada Centre. "It took forever," Belfour said. "The guys played unbelievable. It took nine goals, but I'm really thankful."

91 | JOE KLUKAY

BORN: NOVEMBER 6, 1922 IN SAULT STE. MARIE, ONTARIO
POSITION: LEFT WING
YEARS AS A LEAF: 1946–47 TO 1951–52; 1954–55 TO 1955–56
SWEATER #: 8, 17 AND 19
MAPLE LEAF MOMENT: APRIL 8, 1949

JOE KLUKAY BEGAN playing hockey in his hometown in 1941–42 and then went to Stratford, Ontario, to play junior the next season. Scoring 11 goals in 14 games, the six-foot, 182-pound left-winger captured the attention of the Maple Leafs, who signed him in March of 1943. (He played in one playoff game for Toronto that year.) The next couple of seasons saw him serve in the Canadian navy during the last two years of the Second World War. He was assigned to Pittsburgh of the American Hockey League for the 1945–46 season, where he scored 26 goals and totalled 49 points in 57 contests, which would prove to be his best professional hockey totals.

The Leafs were impressed enough to get him into 55 games the following season, recording 29 points (nine goals, 20 assists). The Leafs won the Stanley Cup in Klukay's rookie year, and it became clear that his role was to be a top defensive player and an extraordinary penalty killer, often in tandem with teammate Nick Metz. He could be counted on for about 15 goals and 30 points a season, but Klukay's true value was preventing goals by the opposition. The Leafs won the Cup again in 1948 and were trying for a third straight title when they faced the Detroit Red Wings in the 1949 finals. In the first contest of the series, played on April 8, 1949, at the Detroit Olympia, Klukay shone in an offensive role for a change.

The fourth-place Leafs had knocked off the Boston Bruins in the semi-finals and were hoping to get off to a good start in the first game of the series against Detroit, but it was the Red Wings who got the first goal of the game when George Gee beat Turk Broda in the Toronto net. However, Ray Timgren and Klukay exchanged passes in the Red Wing zone to set up Max Bentley for the equalizer. The same three forwards were on the ice for the Leafs when they took the lead on defenceman Jim Thomson's goal in the second period. It looked like the Leafs might take the 2–1 lead the rest of the way, but Detroit evened the score on a rare goal by Bill Quackenbush with a little over seven minutes to play. Neither team could get another before overtime, but the Leafs appeared to be the hungrier team in the extra session. It took 17:31 of overtime to settle the issue, but it was Klukay who was the Leaf hero when Thomson and Timgren set him up for the winner. Thomson broke up a Detroit attack, trapping two Red Wings and getting the puck up to Timgren, who relayed it to Klukay in the Detroit zone. Klukay's shot bounced and went over Lumley's shoulder and into the net. The Red Wing goalie lost his glove in a futile attempt to make the save. The Leafs jumped over the boards to mob the hard-working Klukay.

Afterwards, Klukay commented on his big goal. "That's only my second playoff goal [of the '49 playoffs]," he said, too modest to talk about his great defensive work that helped keep the Red Wings' top line of Gordie Howe, Ted Lindsay and Sid Abel away from the Leaf net, especially after the game was tied 2–2. The Leafs would go on to sweep Detroit, a team that had finished nearly 20

points ahead of them during the regular season.

The Leafs were denied a fourth straight Cup in 1950 (losing out to the Red Wings) but came back to win the championship in 1951. Klukay had his best-ever playoff in the '51 postseason with seven points (three goals, four assists) in 11 games and had his name engraved on the silver trophy for the fourth time in five years. After one more year with Toronto, Klukay was dealt to Boston in 1952 (the Leafs got Dave Creighton in return) but was reacquired in 1954 in exchange for defenceman Leo Boivin, a future Hall of Famer. Klukay played two more years with the Leafs before retiring.

MAPLE LEAF CAREER HIGHLIGHTS

★ Signed as a free agent by the Leafs on March 15, 1943
★ Member of four Stanley Cup teams with Toronto
★ Scored 15 goals in one season twice as a Leaf
★ Recorded 170 points (76G, 94A) in 416 games with Toronto

LEAF FACT:

Many Maple Leaf players have had great nicknames over the years, but few could match the one given to Joe Klukay, who was known as the "Duke of Paducah."

92 | JIM McKENNY

BORN: DECEMBER 1, 1946 IN OTTAWA, ONTARIO
POSITION: DEFENCE AND RIGHT WING
YEARS AS A LEAF: 1965–66 TO 1978–79
SWEATER #: 18 AND 25
MAPLE LEAF MOMENT: FEBRUARY 25, 1967

ANYONE WHO SAW Jim McKenny play junior hockey for the Toronto Marlies would have said he was a "can't miss" NHL star. The five-foot-eleven, 192-pound defenceman loved to carry the puck up the ice and either dish it off to a teammate for a shot on goal or let go a drive that would often find the net. He helped the Marlboros win the Memorial Cup in 1964 (totalling eight points in 12 playoff games) and had 14 goals and 40 points in 42 games during his final year with the junior club in 1965–66. His play in junior was so good that McKenny was often compared to Bobby Orr!

As was often the case with star juniors during the six-team era, McKenny got called up to the Leafs for two games during the '65–66 campaign and played his first contest against the Boston Bruins, replacing Kent Douglas in the Toronto lineup. It was obvious he was a little nervous during his debut. He did not handle the puck with his usual deftness, although he generally acquitted himself well. The green rearguard did not see much of the ice after Johnny Bucyk scored early in the second period. "You better keep your head up in this league," McKenny said after the game. "Sometimes I had three guys coming at me so fast I couldn't see." McKenny then went to the minors with Tulsa and the Rochester Americans, earning a Calder Cup championship with the Americans in 1967–68. However, McKenny had scored his first NHL goal when he came up to the Leafs for six games during the 1966–67 season.

The Detroit Red Wings were in town to play the Leafs on February 25, 1967. McKenny, who had joined the Leafs for the previous three games, was scheduled to play. McKenny had been called up because of an injury to Bob Baun, but on this evening the young defenceman was filling in for the injured Allan Stanley. The Leafs had Terry Sawchuk in goal, and he recorded his 99th career shutout as Toronto beat Detroit 4–0. The veteran goalie was especially sharp, making 39 saves while Bob Pulford supplied two goals for the Leafs' attack. Brian Conacher scored his 14th of the season and the Leafs had a 3–0 lead before the second period was over. McKenny scored the fourth and final goal of the game when he grabbed a Frank Mahovlich rebound off the boards and slapped home a low drive from the left point that beat Detroit goalie George Gardner. McKenny was also strong on the defensive side of the game and got a cheer from the Gardens crowd by knocking down Detroit's Howie Young with a solid bodycheck. This was ironic, since McKenny was nicknamed "Howie" for his striking resemblance to the Red Wing bad boy.

McKenny's performance certainly did nothing to change his status as one of the Leafs' top prospects. The win was the fourth straight for Toronto under coach King Clancy, who was filling in for an ailing Punch Imlach. This victory put Toronto, who were struggling to maintain a playoff position, a full eight points ahead of Detroit. The Leafs went on to capture the Stanley Cup in the 1967 playoffs, helped in a small way by their young defenceman.

MAPLE LEAF CAREER HIGHLIGHTS

★ Recorded six consecutive seasons of 30 or more points
★ Recorded 44 points in 73 games during his first full season (1969–70)
★ Recorded a career-high 52 points (11G, 41A) in 1972–73
★ Totalled 329 points in 604 career games as a Leaf

LEAF FACT:

The first-ever NHL draft was held in 1963 and Jim McKenny was the Leafs' third selection, 17th overall. McKenny played with the Neil McNeil Maroons for the 1962–63 season and then joined the Toronto Marlboros for the next season. The other Leaf draft choices in '63 included Walt McKechnie (6th overall), Neil Clairmont (12th overall) and Gerry Meehan (21st overall). Meehan also played for the Maroons.

93

BRIAN GLENNIE

BORN: AUGUST 29, 1946 IN TORONTO, ONTARIO
POSITION: DEFENCE
YEARS AS A LEAF: 1969–70 TO 1977–78
SWEATER #: 24
MAPLE LEAF MOMENT: APRIL 6, 1972

BRIAN GLENNIE'S STELLAR junior career was high-lighted by the Toronto Marlboros winning the Memorial Cup in 1967. The six-foot-one, 197-pound defenceman was destined to be a large part of the Maple Leafs' future, since many of the old Toronto rearguards were set to retire as Glennie was ready to turn professional. However, Glennie decided he wanted to play for his country first and joined the Canadian National Team for the 1967–68 season. He represented Canada at the 1968 Winter Olympics in Grenoble (one point in seven games) and won a bronze medal. Glennie then joined the Leaf farm system the following year. He split the 1968–69 season between Rochester (AHL) and Tulsa (CHL) before joining Toronto for the 1969–70 season, when he scored one goal and added 14 assists as a rookie.

Glennie was not expected to provide much in the way of points (22, in 1973–74, was his highest total as a Leaf), but he was often paired with an offensive defenceman such as Jim McKenny. That meant Glennie was responsible for taking care of matters in the Leaf end of the ice first. Although he was a slow skater, Glennie was a hard-hitting defender who forced the opposition to keep their heads up at the Toronto blue line. The Leafs certainly needed Glennie's physical presence when they faced the Boston Bruins in the first round of the 1972 playoffs. Boston won the first game of the series 5–0, but the Leafs were determined to even the series on the night of April 6, 1972, at the Garden.

A gritty and resolute group of Leafs showed up and defeated the Bruins 4–3 in overtime to even the series. No one gave the Leafs much of chance against the powerful Bruins, but stellar goaltending by Bernie Parent and a stout defence led by Glennie and McKenny, along with Brad Selwood and Mike Pelyk, did the trick. (Regular defencemen Rick Ley and Bob Baun were benched for most of this contest.) "It has been a long time since we went with two pairs," explained Pelyk. "I was gasping a lot." The Bruins actually took a 2–0 lead in the first period on goals by Fred Stanfield and Phil Esposito. Dave Keon got the Leafs back in the game with a goal early in the second, and McKenny tied it up before Johnny Bucyk gave the Bruins the lead once again. A third-period goal by Toronto's Guy Trottier set the stage for overtime, and former Bruin Jim Harrison scored at 2:58 of extra time to shock all the Boston fans.

Leaf coach King Clancy (filling in for the ailing John McLellan) was ecstatic after the game. "I want to tell you, not many teams come here and win. Our guys played great," he enthused. "And we have two great goaltenders [Parent and Jacques Plante]." Former Boston coach Harry Sinden was at the game, and he singled out Glennie for special praise. "Brian Glennie was the solid guy on their defence. Man, did he dish out some solid checks." Bruin winger Ken Hodge was a particular target of Glennie's bodychecks all series long.

The glory was short-lived for the Leafs, as the Bruins came to Toronto and took a pair of victories by scores of 2–0 and 5–4. The Toronto side fought valiantly in the fifth game of the series but ultimately lost 3–2, despite another great effort

by Parent in the Leaf net. After the series was over Esposito commented on the Leafs' desire. "Give them credit. They made us earn everything, and I'm glad to see the last of them, especially Brian Glennie, for this season."

The Leafs said that Glennie played well despite a bad shoulder and a nagging groin injury. His outstanding efforts did not go unrewarded. Glennie was selected for Team Canada for the September 1972 Summit Series by Sinden, who coached the All-Star squad against the Soviet Union.

MAPLE LEAF CAREER HIGHLIGHTS

★ Member of Team Canada for 1972 Canada-Russia series
★ Recorded double-digit assist totals in five years with Toronto
★ Recorded 559 penalty minutes as a Leaf
★ Recorded 110 points (12G, 98A) in 554 games as a Leaf

LEAF FACT:

Brian Glennie was captain and the most valuable player of the 1967 Toronto Marlboro team that won the Memorial Cup. Other players who were on that team and went on to play at least one game with the Leafs were Doug Acomb, Mike Byers, Chris Evans, Tom Martin, Gerry Meehan and Mike Pelyk.

94 DMITRY YUSHKEVICH

BORN: NOVEMBER 19, 1971 IN YAROSLAVL, USSR
POSITION: DEFENCE
YEARS AS A LEAF: 1995–96 TO 2001–02
SWEATER #: 26 AND 36
MAPLE LEAF MOMENT: MAY 17, 1999

WHEN LEAF GENERAL MANAGER Cliff Fletcher sent three draft choices (including a first-round selection in 1996) to the Philadelphia Flyers for defenceman Dmitry Yushkevich and a second-round draft choice, it certainly raised a few eyebrows. None of the draft choices turned out to be significant on either side, but the Leafs certainly gained the benefit of having a good defenceman in their lineup for seven seasons. He started out well with his new team (with coach Pat Burns comparing him to one-time Maple Leaf hardrock Bob Baun), but it was not always so easy for Yushkevich in Toronto where much was expected from the stocky five-foot-eleven, 208-pound blueliner. The Leafs were not very good for a few years, and Yushkevich had to deal with a chronic knee injury. But then Pat Quinn took over as the coach of the team and in his first season guided the Leafs to the Eastern Conference final. The playoffs were the highlight of Yushkevich's time as a Maple Leaf. He played a big role in shutting down one of the best players in the league when Toronto faced Jaromir Jagr and the Pittsburgh Penguins in the second round of postseason play. On the night of May 17, 1999, the Leafs headed into Pittsburgh's Civic Arena with a chance to close out the Penguins in six games.

The game started badly for the Leafs, who found themselves down 2–0 after one period and would have been further behind if not for the work of goalie Curtis Joseph. But the gritty Toronto club clawed back into the game and took a lead on goals by Garry Valk, Lonny Bohonos and Sergei Berezin, only to see the Pens tie it up on a goal by Jagr. The game went into overtime when the Leafs lined up for a face-off in the Pittsburgh zone less than two minutes into the extra session. Centre Yanic Perreault won the draw and sent the puck over to Berezin, who let go a shot at Penguin goalie Tom Barrasso. Barrasso made the save, but the puck dropped to the ice in front of him. Valk saw the loose disc and managed to nudge it into the net for a 4–3 victory. The Leafs now had a spot in the conference final.

After the game was over the Leafs felt the key to winning the series was controlling Jagr. "It's not exhausting physically playing against Jagr. It's so exhausting mentally. Playing against him since game one was very tough mentally for me," Yushkevich said in the happy Leaf dressing room. "We were not sharp at the beginning of the game. And Cujo [Joseph] stood on his head. Jagr played great tonight. He definitely led their team. What can I say? We beat him." He further added, "We came in [the dressing room] before overtime, I knew we would win. This team has so much character, but I didn't know how much until tonight when the guys put right a game that was going wrong."

Yushkevich was teamed with youngster Danny Markov for this series, and the Leafs' defensive pairing drove Jagr to distraction. They were on the ice every time Jagr appeared and were in the superstar's face all series long. Disgust and frustration were clearly registered on Jagr's face when he was called for a penalty in the final contest. After Valk's game winner ended the series, Markov gave the military salute that

Jagr was using whenever he scored a goal to the Penguins and their fans. It put an exclamation point on the Leaf victory.

MAPLE LEAF CAREER HIGHLIGHTS

★ Acquired in a trade with Philadelphia on August 30, 1995
★ Recorded 20 or more points three times as Leaf
★ Recorded 12 points in 44 playoff games
★ Played in 506 career games as a Leaf, recording 135 points (25G, 110A)

LEAF FACT:

When the NHL All-Star Game made its return to Toronto in 2000, Dmitry Yushkevich was selected to play for the World All-Star Team. He scored a goal on Leaf teammate Curtis Joseph, who was in net for the North American All-Star Team. Yushkevich also had an assist for his team, which won the game 9–4. Pat Quinn was behind the bench for the North American team.

95

RUSS COURTNALL

BORN: JUNE 2, 1965 IN DUNCAN, BRITISH COLUMBIA
POSITION: CENTRE
YEARS AS A LEAF: 1983–84 TO 1988–89
SWEATER #: 9, 16 AND 26
MAPLE LEAF MOMENT: NOVEMBER 23, 1985

THE ONE POSITIVE about the Leafs' poor record during the decade of the eighties was that they had the opportunity to draft good prospects: Jim Benning (sixth overall in 1981), Gary Nylund (third overall in 1982), Gary Leeman (taken 24th in '82), Russ Courtnall (seventh overall in '83), Al Iafrate (fourth overall in '84), Wendel Clark (the very first player taken in '85), Vincent Damphousse (sixth overall in '86) and Luke Richardson (seventh overall in '87). Leafs management chose to let these players develop at the NHL level (with the exception of Leeman), and that meant many long nights during the first five seasons of the eighties. Under coach Dan Maloney, the Leafs' development was painfully slow, and the start of the 1985–86 season was no exception. But on a Saturday night in November, against a poor Detroit Red Wing club, the young Leafs started to show that something good might be developing.

The '85–86 season saw the Leafs win just three games by the time the Red Wings paid a visit to Maple Leaf Gardens on November 23, 1985. An inept Detroit club actually led the game 2–0 before the Leafs began to take out their season's frustrations and dominate all aspects of the game. Leading the Leafs to a 9–3 romp was swift-skating centre Russ Courtnall, who scored three goals and added three assists. Courtnall went into the game, after missing a few games with a sore throat, with only one goal to his credit (scored on his first shot on goal in the first contest of the year, 14 games earlier). He was put on a line with Greg Terrion and Gary Leeman. Courtnall's second goal was a thing of beauty, as he slipped the puck between the skates of bewildered Detroit defenceman Mike McEwen while stepping around his opponent to slip a backhand shot into the net past Greg Stefan in the Red Wings' net. In addition to his hat trick, Courtnall assisted on goals by Terrion, Leeman and Miroslav Frycer. His play delighted the 16,234 fans in attendance, who finally had something to cheer about. The win gave the Leafs a 3–2–3 record over their last eight games and let everyone have a better feeling about this young team.

Maloney suggested that one key to Courtnall's improved performance was the fact he was able to observe from the press box for a few games while recovering from his sickness. The Leaf youngster did not disagree with his coach. "It was almost like going to school watching games from up there. I keyed in on what our centres were doing and what the centres on the other team were doing, and I really learned a lot," he said. "I couldn't understand why I wasn't scoring more, but after watching those games while I was out, I learned that I had to use my head more than going 90 miles an hour every second I was on the ice," he continued. Courtnall also commented on the pressure of being a Maple Leaf. "We felt loose and relaxed. We joke around but still manage to stay on the serious side. When we don't get uptight, we improve. Maybe I was putting pressure on myself." For one night in November of 1985, Leaf fans and Courtnall could dream of a better future.

The Leafs went on to make the playoffs after the 1985–86 season and upset Chicago in the first round by sweeping the Blackhawks 3–0 in the best-of-five series. They took St. Louis to seven games before a tight 2–1 loss in the final contest of the next round. Courtnall contributed nine points in 10 postseason games, and it looked like he was going to be a big part of the Leafs' future. However, he was dealt away just three years later to the Montreal Canadiens in one of the worst trades ever made by the Leafs.

MAPLE LEAF CAREER HIGHLIGHTS

★ Drafted seventh overall by the Leafs in 1983
★ Recorded three 20-goal seasons with Toronto
★ Scored 29 goals and recorded 73 points in 79 games during 1986–87
★ Totalled 218 points in 309 games as a Leaf

LEAF FACT:

The Leafs have been widely criticized for their drafting record, but a closer look can sometimes reveal a different story. In 1983 it was expected the Leafs would select Andrew McBain (who next went to Winnipeg, 8th overall), but they took Russ Courtnall instead. Career numbers for Courtnall show 1,029 NHL games played, with 297 goals and 447 assists for 744 points. McBain played in 606 NHL games, scoring 129 goals and 172 assists for 301 points.

TO SAY THAT the trading of Lanny McDonald caused tremendous turmoil in the Maple Leaf dressing room would be a vast understatement. The entire team was upset that McDonald and defenceman Joel Quenneville were being sent to the Colorado Rockies for Wilf Paiement and Pat Hickey, but Leaf general manager Punch Imlach had no qualms about making the swap on December 29, 1979. Many felt that Imlach was trading away his star right-winger because he could not deal centre Darryl Sittler, a player the manager had clearly targeted for ridicule.

The Leafs were getting back a potential star in Paiement. Selected second overall by the Kansas City Scouts (the team location and name prior to their move to Colorado), the 24-year-old had accumulated 119 goals and 131 assists in his four-year NHL career before the deal, including seasons of 41 and 31 goals. The rugged six-foot-one, 210-pound winger not only had good size, but he also possessed a good shot and an edge to his play that kept the opposition honest. He was also incredibly strong. Few dared to challenge him.

As much as the Leafs and their loyal fans missed the colourful McDonald, Paiement quickly showed that he could help the club, and he found good chemistry on a line with Sittler. That was certainly evident on the night of January 12, 1980, as the Leafs hosted the Vancouver Canucks.

The game against the Canucks was a wide-open affair. Paiement, playing on a line with Sittler and Dave Williams, scored at 12:48 of the first when he was set up by Sittler and defenceman Carl Brewer. The Canucks tied it before the end of the period, but the Leafs came out firing to start the second and got two goals from Sittler and one from Paiement to take a 4–1 lead. Paiement assisted on both of Sittler's markers. On his own goal, he slapped home a shot after great work by Williams to get the disc over to the right-winger, who was open next the Vancouver net occupied by Glen Hanlon. The Canucks battled back to make it 4–3 by the end of the second. Then Laurie Boschman scored to make it 5–3 for the Leafs almost nine minutes into the third period. Vancouver got closer at 5–4, but Paiement completed the hat trick with his third of the night on a pass from Sittler with less than five minutes to play.

After the game Paiement refused to be drawn into a comparison about his play and that of McDonald. "I don't like comparisons because I'm Wilf Paiement, nobody else. Don't expect me to be Lanny McDonald. I'll tell you something: I'm going to produce for this club. In Colorado I was never with one line for a complete game and that's important — knowing your linemates. Sometimes one second in the timing of a play makes all the difference. That's easier to have when you've played together. I've got to give Darryl a lot of credit for the goals. He's been around several years and he's one of the best centres in the league as far as I am concerned."

For his part, Sittler had just started to play well again after giving up the team captaincy (right after the trade was

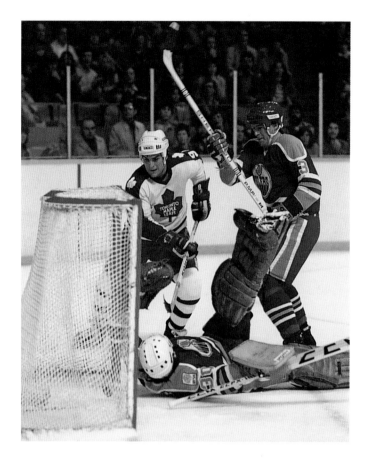

completed) and focusing just on hockey. He added this about his new linemate. "Wilf puts as much as he can into his game. Like Lanny, nothing comes easy, he has to work."

Coach Floyd Smith commented, "The whole line played very well and I'm going to keep it together."

Paiement certainly did end up producing during his short time as a Maple Leaf: 48 points in 41 games after the deal and a club record for right-wingers with 97 points in his first full year in Toronto.

MAPLE LEAF CAREER HIGHLIGHTS

★ Acquired in a trade with Colorado on December 29, 1979
★ Recorded three hat tricks as a Maple Leaf
★ Scored 40 goals and totalled 97 points in 1980–81
★ Recorded 203 points (78G, 125A) in 187 games for Toronto

LEAF FACT:

Perhaps it was because Wilf Paiement had scored only 18 goals by March 9, 1982, that he was traded away, somewhat inexplicably, by Leaf general manager Gerry McNamara. In return the Leafs acquired Miroslav Frycer from the Quebec Nordiques, who went on to play 329 games for Toronto and record 268 points (115G, 153A).

97 | JACQUES PLANTE

BORN: JANUARY 17, 1929 IN SHAWINIGAN FALLS, QUEBEC
POSITION: GOALTENDER
YEARS AS A LEAF: 1970–71 TO 1972–73
SWEATER #: 1
MAPLE LEAF MOMENT: DECEMBER 19, 1970

AT THE START of the 1970–71 season the Maple Leaf squad featured some quality veteran forwards like Dave Keon, Norm Ullman, Ron Ellis and Paul Henderson. They also had some youngsters on the club like Darryl Sittler, Jim Harrison, Brian Spencer, Billy MacMillan and Gary Monahan. But the Leafs were especially vulnerable on defence, where they had greenhorns like Rick Ley, Mike Pelyk, Jim McKenny, Jim Dorey, Brian Glennie and Brad Selwood. Veteran blueliner Bob Baun was brought back to Toronto to provide some leadership, but the man the Leafs were counting on the most was one of the best goalies of all time: Jacques Plante.

After a stellar career with Montreal (which included six Stanley Cups), Plante put in good years with the New York Rangers and the St. Louis Blues before becoming available to the Leafs in the summer of 1970. Leaf general manager Jim Gregory wanted Plante to help the young blueliners develop and learn from one of the cagiest veterans ever to play in goal. The Leafs gave Plante a good contract that featured a deferred salary component and set him up in an apartment that was air-conditioned, since Plante claimed his asthma acted up in Toronto. It took awhile for the Leafs to get going in the '70–71 campaign, but Plante soon proved he was well worth the time and money the Leafs spent on him. One such occasion was the night of December 19, 1970, when the expansion Buffalo Sabres came to town.

The Sabres were coached by one-time Leaf manager Punch Imlach and had humiliated the Leafs right on Maple Leaf Gardens ice one month earlier in the season when they won the first-ever meeting between the two clubs 7–2. (Earlier in December, the Leafs did bounce back to beat the Sabres 4–0 in Buffalo with Bruce Gamble in net.) But this Saturday night contest in Toronto was going to be different for the hometown team. Plante and Buffalo goalie Joe Daley kept the game scoreless until the third period, when Keon took a pass from Monahan and made it 1–0 at 5:22, and then Henderson added another at 11:06 to give the Leafs a two-goal lead. Plante made 24 stops to earn his second shutout of the season and covered up for mistakes made by his young defencemen. Veteran blueliner Baun racked up the Sabres' Gerry Meehan with a thunderous check at centre ice, but the Leafs needed Plante's good work to keep the Buffalo squad off the board. The Gardens crowd showed their appreciation for the veteran netminder.

"I think I play better now than I ever did," Plante said later. "Maybe I should say I am a more complete goalie than I was. You know those three seasons when I didn't play? [He was retired from 1965 to 1968.] I learned things about goaltending that I never could see when I was playing. Players who came in on the wrong wing used to get goals against me they didn't deserve because I was playing them wrong. Another change I made when I came back was the way I played the man who was shooting from the backhand. I used to try to slide across the face of the goal with him. Now, I move further out. That way I cut down his angle." Plante, who was approaching his 42nd birthday, also admitted he could

not play in back-to-back games very often. Gamble played the next night in Buffalo after Plante's shutout and won the game 4–2, giving the Leafs a six-game winning streak.

Whatever changes Plante made to his game, they were definitely effective during the '70–71 regular season, as he won 24 games while losing 11 and tying four. The Leafs made the playoffs with a solid fourth place finish (after missing out the year before) by accumulating 82 points, and Plante's play was a big reason for that success.

MAPLE LEAF CAREER HIGHLIGHTS

★ Acquired by the Leafs from St. Louis on May 18, 1970
★ Named to the NHL's Second All-Star Team for 1970–71 season
★ Recorded seven shutouts with the Leafs and had a 2.46 goals-against average
★ Played in 106 games for Toronto and posted a 48–38–15 record

LEAF FACT:

During the 1970–71 regular season Jacques Plante shared two shutouts. The first came on January 2, 1971, when the Leafs set a club record for the highest-scoring shutout ever by beating Detroit 13–0; Bruce Gamble played the third period of the game. The second came on March 24, when Toronto beat California 6–0 and the recently acquired Bernie Parent shared the whitewash with Plante.

98 | MARK OSBORNE

BORN: AUGUST 13, 1961 IN TORONTO, ONTARIO
POSITION: LEFT WING
YEARS AS A LEAF: 1986–87 TO 1993–94
SWEATER #: 12 AND 21
MAPLE LEAF MOMENT: JANUARY 9, 1993

TORONTO NATIVE MARK OSBORNE had two different stints with the hometown Maple Leafs between 1987 and 1994. The Leafs first acquired the superbly conditioned six-foot-two, 205-pound left-winger in March of 1987 when they sent Jeff Jackson to the New York Rangers in exchange for Osborne. As a rookie with the Detroit Red Wings, Osborne had scored a goal in his first NHL game and posted a very good first season with 26 goals and 67 points. He was traded to the Rangers but was having trouble on Broadway. Ranger general manager Phil Esposito felt Osborne would find his game with the Leafs. Esposito was right, as Osborne had 15 points in 16 games to finish the '86–87 season. For the next three seasons Osborne had point totals of 60, 48 and 73, and became a consistently reliable player in the process. The Leafs were faltering badly in 1990–91 when he was dealt to Winnipeg in a major trade. Late in the next season of 1991–92, the Leafs wisely reacquired Osborne in a deal swung by general manager Cliff Fletcher. The 1992–93 season saw Pat Burns take over as coach of the Leafs, and Osborne was a perfect fit for a new coach who stressed strong two-way play. Burns developed a top checking line that consisted of Peter Zezel, Bill Berg and Osborne, who was by this time best suited for this role. Although they did not score many goals, the line was quite capable of getting a big tally at the right moment. Such was the case when the Leafs played in Montreal on January 9, 1993.

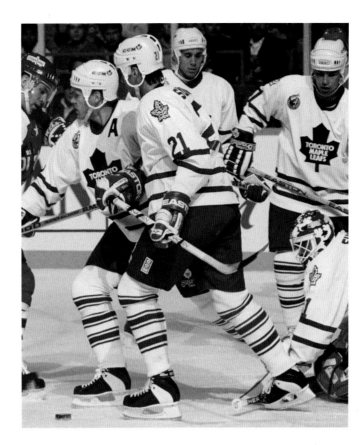

All the talk prior to this Saturday night contest was about the return of Burns to the Forum where he had coached the fabled Canadiens for four successful seasons (including one appearance in the Stanley Cup final). The Leafs were starting to develop as a team under Burns and were quite anxious to get a victory for their coach in his old stomping grounds. Toronto stormed out to a 4–0 lead before the Habs responded. Wendel Clark got the Leafs off to a good start on a shot Montreal netminder Patrick Roy flubbed. Doug Gilmour had the next Leaf tally and then set up defenceman Todd Gill for the prettiest goal of the night, before scoring another goal himself. Benoit Brunet scored for Montreal in the second to give the Habs some life. Mike Keane scored two in a row in the third to make it 4–3, and the Canadiens were pressing for the equalizer. Just when it looked like the Leafs were going to fold, Osborne beat Roy with a wrist shot from the slot that got by the goalie's pad to give Toronto a two-goal cushion. It turned out to be the winning goal. Ex-Leaf Vincent Damphousse scored for Montreal less than a minute later, but Toronto managed to hang on for a 5–4 win. When the siren sounded at the Forum to signal the end of the game, Burns celebrated by rotating his arm three times and got a handshake from captain Clark.

After the game Osborne was asked how the Leafs' coach handled returning to Montreal. "You could tell Pat was nervous about this game because he just wasn't himself for the last day and a half," Osborne said. "Usually he never goes to the back of the plane, but on our flight over he was

pacing up and down the aisle." Burns tried to keep the attention on his team and not on himself. "We're trying to gain more respect for our hockey team, and I think more Leafs fans are coming out of hiding," he said in the postgame interviews. Leaf fans did indeed come out from the shadows as the '92–93 season wore on, especially in the playoffs when the Leafs came within one game of the finals.

Osborne stayed with the Leafs until the end of the 1993–94 season before going back to the Rangers for one more year.

MAPLE LEAF CAREER HIGHLIGHTS

★ Scored 23 goals and added 50 assists for 73 points in 1989–90
★ Recorded 30 or more assists three times as a Leaf
★ Reacquired from Winnipeg in exchange for Lucien DeBlois in 1992
★ Totaled 254 points (94G, 160A) in 426 career games for Toronto

LEAF FACT:

Dave Keon (1963 against Detroit), Bob Pulford (1964 versus Detroit) and Mark Osborne are the only Leafs to score two short-handed goals in one playoff series. Osborne accomplished the feat when Toronto faced San Jose during the 1994 postseason. The Leafs beat the Sharks in seven games.

99 | BILLY
TAYLOR

BORN: MAY 3, 1919 IN WINNIPEG, MANITOBA
POSITION: CENTRE
YEARS AS A LEAF: 1939–40 TO 1945–46
SWEATER #: 7, 19 AND 21
MAPLE LEAF MOMENT: JANUARY 12, 1946

WHEN BILLY TAYLOR was just 10 years old he was playing hockey against boys as old as 13 in the Toronto area. He then played junior hockey, in Oshawa for the most part, and developed a reputation as one of the best prospects not yet in the NHL. He scored 22 goals in just 14 games during the 1938–39 season, plus another 11 tallies in nine playoff games when the Generals won the Memorial Cup. Taylor did not grow to be a large player (only 5´9˝ and 150 pounds), but he was very skilled with the puck, and that made him an exceptional playmaker. He split the 1939–40 season between Pittsburgh and Toronto, managing 10 points in 29 games for the Maple Leafs.

The following season saw the swift-skating Taylor make the Leafs on a full-time basis, recording 35 points in 47 games played. He scored 12 times in 1941–42 and upped his point total to 38, but he saved his best that year for the playoffs when the Leafs took their first Stanley Cup since 1931. Taylor recorded 10 points in 13 games and had the most assists of any player in the postseason with eight. In the seven-game final against Detroit, Taylor was especially outstanding in the final two games (one goal in game six, two assists in game seven) as the Leafs completed their remarkable comeback from being down 3–0 in games. The 1942–43 season saw Taylor enjoy the best year of his career with 60 points (18 goals, 42 assists) in 50 games. He then served in the Canadian army for the next two seasons (as his father had done in the First World War) but rejoined the Leafs for the 1945–46 season — his final year in Toronto. He was involved in setting a Leaf team record on the night of January 12, 1946, when Toronto played Detroit at Maple Leaf Gardens.

The Leafs had won the Cup in 1945 but would only win 19 games the following season and missed the playoffs with only 45 points (finishing five behind fourth-place Detroit). But the Leafs got off to a hot start against the Red Wings on the night of January 12 and whipped in six goals in the first period on the way to a 9–3 shellacking of the Detroit club. The scoring started early at 3:17 of the first when Gus Bodnar scored for the Leafs. Just over two minutes later, Taylor scored his first of two that night when he beat Detroit goalie Harry Lumley to make it 2–0 Leafs. Gaye Stewart, Syl Apps, Jackie Hamilton and Taylor all scored before the game was 11 minutes old to make it 6–0 for the Leafs. The six Leaf tallies, scored in 7:16, are still a team record for fastest six goals in one game. The Red Wings finally got one back before the end of the first period and one to start the second, but the Leafs scored the next three to give them a 9–2 lead. (Taylor earned an assist on the final Toronto goal of the night by Lorne Carr.) The game also featured a vicious assault by Jack Stewart on Leaf captain Apps and a fight between Toronto netminder Frank McCool and Joe Carveth of the Red Wings. The final Detroit goal was scored by youngster Harry Watson.

Detroit manager Jack Adams was impressed with the Leafs after the contest was over. "I'm not surprised," he said. "The Leafs have always been tough for us. I've maintained

[Leaf coach] Hap Day's club is much better than the records indicate. Our club was knocked off stride early in the first period and never recovered. Leafs were just too hot for us, that's all." Taylor (who finished with 23 goals on the season) must have made an impression on Adams, who traded for him once the season was over. In return the Leafs received Watson, who would go on to have a Hall of Fame career with the Maple Leafs.

Taylor would play just one year in Detroit (leading the NHL in assists with 46) before being moved to Boston and then to the New York Rangers for the 1947–48 season.

MAPLE LEAF CAREER HIGHLIGHTS

★ Member of Stanley Cup team in 1942
★ Recorded 35 or more points with the Leafs four times
★ Led the Leafs in assists for three consecutive seasons (1940–41 to 1942–43)
★ Recorded 184 points (66G, 118A) in 222 games as a Leaf

LEAF FACT:

In 1931–32, when the Maple Leafs won their first Stanley Cup, the team mascot that year was 12-year-old Billy Taylor. During intermissions at Maple Leaf Gardens, Taylor would entertain the fans with skating exhibitions.

BY THE END of the 1949–50 season the Maple Leafs sensed that the great career of goaltender Turk Broda was winding down. Finding a capable replacement was not going to be easy, but general manager Conn Smythe spotted a lanky six-foot-two, 175-pound netminder named Al Rollins playing in the minors. The Leafs brought up Rollins for a two-game trial in the '49–50 season, and he recorded one shutout victory (a 8–0 pasting of the Boston Bruins on March 25 at Maple Leaf Gardens). The Leafs sent a package of players and money to Cleveland of the American Hockey League to secure the rights to Rollins, who would share the Leaf netminding duties with Broda for the 1950–51 season. Rollins played in 40 games and put up a sparkling record of 27–5–8 during the regular season while leading the league with a 1.77 goals-against average. He also recorded five shutouts but hurt his leg during the first game of the semi-final series against Boston. The injury kept him out of the postseason until the third game of the finals on April 17, 1951, when the Leafs travelled to Montreal with the teams all tied up at one game each.

The game at the Montreal Forum did not start well for Rollins, who was obviously rusty after a long time away from the nets. Maurice Richard scored the opening goal for the Canadiens before the contest was three minutes old, but Rollins settled down quickly and gave the Habs nothing the rest of the way, making 26 saves in the process. He was especially strong in the first and third periods, and his teammates helped to scoop away a couple of drives that got past Rollins before they crossed the goal line. The Canadiens nearly blew the Leafs right out of the arena in the opening frame, but the Leafs withstood the offensive onslaught and got a goal from Sid Smith in the second period to even the score. Neither team could score in the final stanza, so the series went to its third straight overtime. (Each team had won 3–2 in the previous games.)

The 14,447 screaming fans watching the contest thought the Habs were going to win in the extra session, and they nearly did. But Toronto captain Ted Kennedy swept away the puck just before it was about to enter the Leaf net. Kennedy got the puck over to defenceman Bill Juzda, who lugged the puck back up the ice and into the Montreal zone. Montreal's Calum MacKay could not get the puck out of the Canadiens' end, and Kennedy picked it up in the face-off circle, drilling a 20-foot drive into the far corner of the net past goalie Gerry McNeil for the game winner. Rollins had certainly proved that he was back in a big way.

Afterwards, Rollins said he was not nervous about his first full playoff game in '51 but admitted to being a little tired. "I was so weak when the old captain shot that winner that I couldn't holler, although I wanted to shout and shout," he said in the jubilant Leaf dressing room. "And my [injured] leg didn't bother me a bit. I had an idea I was going to play tonight, but neither Turk nor I knew definitely until we got to the rink an hour before game time." In the Montreal dressing room Maurice Richard moaned about the missed opportuni-

ties. "I gave the game away when I missed three chances to score," the Rocket told inquisitors.

Rollins backstopped the Leafs the rest of the way during the series with the Canadiens, winning two more contests in overtime to give the Leafs the Stanley Cup in five games. He won 29 games the next season for the Leafs while playing in all 70 games, but in the playoffs the Leafs lost in four straight to Detroit. Smythe became enamored with Chicago goalie Harry Lumley and sent Rollins away in a trade with the Black Hawks. Rollins won the Hart Trophy with Chicago in 1953–54 despite a last-place finish in the league standings.

MAPLE LEAF CAREER HIGHLIGHTS

★ Named winner of the Vezina Trophy for the 1950–51 season
★ Member of 1951 Stanley Cup team
★ Recorded 11 career shutouts with Toronto
★ Posted a 57–30–24 record in 112 games as a Leaf

LEAF FACT:

When Al Rollins won the Stanley Cup in 1951 he became one of only seven goalies to be in net the night the Maple Leafs clinched the coveted trophy. The others are Lorne Chabot (1932), Turk Broda (1942, 1947, 1948, 1949), Frank McCool (1945), Don Simmons (1962), Johnny Bower (1963, 1964) and Terry Sawchuk (1967).

THE NEXT TIME . . .

IT WOULD BE INTERESTING to rank the top 100 Maple Leafs of all time once again ten or twenty years from now. What would change? Mats Sundin might move up in the ranking, and would the captain's teammates from 2006–07 also rank higher? It's possible that Bryan McCabe, Tomas Kaberle and Darcy Tucker could move up in the list, but that is not a given by any means. Might some of the Leafs' younger players from the '06–07 season play their way into the top 100? Alex Steen might be the best talent of the group, but Kyle Wellwood, Alexei Ponikarovsky, Matt Stajan or Ian White might develop into solid NHL players and earn a spot on the list. It will be a difficult task for any of those players to replace someone from the current top 100. NHL rosters will keep changing in a way they did not in an earlier era, with the salary cap thrust upon team general managers. But it's not beyond the realm of possibility. Might draft choices like Jiri Tlusty and Justin Pogge be considered as great Leafs some day? Is there a player who has yet to join the Leafs who could one day be a member of the top 100? All these questions are interesting to ponder as time moves on and players' careers and achievements are reviewed.

It is also possible that the next time the best Maple Leafs are ranked there will be some who are new honoured members of the Hockey Hall of Fame. Doug Gilmour, Dave Andreychuk, Ed Belfour and Alex Mogilny are potential inductees who spent significant time in Toronto. As well, Gary Roberts, Vincent Damphousse and Curtis Joseph should also get consideration for a plaque in the Hall someday. There is also an outside chance that the likes of Lorne Chabot, Carl Brewer and Rick Vaive might get recognized for their outstanding careers. Dick Duff finally got his just reward in 2006, and the six-time Stanley Cup winner finished his NHL career in 1971! Duff's election proves anything is possible, and changing membership of the selection committee means a fresh perspective on the careers of many players.

There is no doubt that the best way to ensure change takes place in the top 100 list would be for the team to win a Stanley Cup. Winning a major trophy, being named an All-Star or having an extended career with the Maple Leafs will still be important considerations, but as we have seen with the current list, membership on a championship team is the surest way to gain consideration. A twelfth championship will give everyone a chance to reconsider who are the best players in Maple Leafs history.

LIST OF SELECTORS

★ **MARK ASKIN**

Mark Askin spent 13 years as a producer for *Hockey Night in Canada* and then as senior producer for regional and national telecasts of the Toronto Maple Leafs. He is now in an executive capacity at Leafs TV.

★ **HOWARD BERGER**

Howard Berger is an 18-year veteran of Canada's first (and largest) all-sports radio station, The FAN 590. For the past 12 years, Howard has covered the Toronto Maple Leafs at home and on the road.

★ **JOE BOWEN**

Joe Bowen is the mid-week television and weekend radio voice of the Toronto Maple Leafs, having broadcast over 2,200 Leafs games. He called his first Leafs game on October 6, 1982, at Chicago Stadium, a 3–3 tie.

★ **MILT DUNNELL**

The former *Toronto Star* sports editor was simply Canada's top sports columnist for more than half a century. Integrity is a word associated with Dunnell, honoured in the writers wing of the Hockey Hall of Fame in 1984.

★ **DOUG FARRAWAY**

"The Deacon," Doug Farraway, is in his 29th year of broadcasting, having worked in many Ontario markets such as London, Hamilton and Toronto. He is currently the sports director of The FAN 590 radio.

★ **PAUL HENDRICK**

A native of Noranda, Quebec, Paul Hendrick has worked for years as a host/interviewer on Leafs TV. He also appears on Leafs television broadcasts broadcast by TSN and Rogers Sportsnet.

★ **LANCE HORNBY**

Toronto Sun hockey writer Lance Hornby is also the author of *Mats Sundin: The Centre of Attention* and was a contributing writer to *Quest for the Cup: A History of the Stanley Cup Finals 1893–2003*.

★ **JOHN IABONI**

John Iaboni has covered hockey for more than 30 years. He was the Maple Leafs' beat writer at the *Toronto Sun* from 1971 to '84. Since 1991, he has been executive editor of the Leafs game day program.

★ **MIKE LEONETTI**

Mike Leonetti has written extensively on hockey since 1985 and has done a variety of books on the Leafs, including *My Leafs Sweater* and *Maple Leaf Legends*. He also wrote Paul Henderson's autobiography *Shooting For Glory*.

★ **HARRY NEALE**

In addition to being the top analyst on CBC's *Hockey Night in Canada*, the former NHL head coach/GM Harry Neale was also hockey analyst for CBC's coverage of the Olympic Winter Games in 1998, 2002 and 2006.

★ **FRANK ORR**

Frank Orr spent 30 years as a sportswriter and hockey columnist for the *Toronto Star*. He has written numerous books on hockey and was honoured with the Elmer Ferguson Memorial Award in 1989.

★ **PAUL PATSKOU**

Canada's leading hockey-video archivist has possibly seen more Leaf games than anyone else. He is also a top researcher, and the long-time Leaf historian helped put together the Leafs' 75th Anniversary video.

★ **FRANK SELKE**

Frank was born in Toronto where his father, Frank Sr., worked with Conn Smythe and the Leafs in the 1930s and '40s. Frank Jr. was TV host of *Hockey Night in Canada* games from Montreal over seven years starting in 1960.

★ **BILL WATTERS**

Leafs Lunch on AM 640 Toronto Radio with former Leaf assistant general manager Bill Watters has quickly become "must-listen radio." Bill is also a member of the Hockeycentral panel on Rogers Sportsnet.

ACKNOWLEDGEMENTS

I would like to say a special thank you to my wife, Maria, and my son, David, for their support and understanding while I was writing this book.

I would like to thank the following writers for their books, articles and stories on the Maple Leafs and on hockey in general, which proved invaluable in helping to compile the player profiles: Jack Batten, Dick Beddoes, Howard Berger, Ross Brewitt, Stephen Brunt, Stephen Cole, Charles Coleman, Jim Coleman, David Cruise, Dan Diamond, John Devaney, Bruce Dowbiggin, Bob Duff, James Duplacey, David Dupois, Milt Dunnell, Gerald Ezkenazi, Trent Frayne, Stan Fischler, Ed Fitkin, Tommy Gaston, Ira Gitler, Burt Goldblatt, Alison Griffiths, Tim Griggs, Foster Hewitt, Zander Hollander, Lance Hornby, William Houston, Jim Hunt, Doug Hunter, John Iaboni, Dick Irvin Jr., Harry Kariher, Brian Kendall, Richard Lapp, Bill Libby, Alec Macaulay, Ron MacAllister, Roy MacGregor, Craig MacInnis, Ted Mahovlich, Brian McFarlane, John Melady, Scott Morrison, Andy O'Brien, Stan Obodiac, Frank Orr, Raymond Plante, Andrew Podnieks, Jim Proudfoot, Joseph Romain, Kevin Shea, Al Strachan, Tommy Smythe, Theresa Tedesco, Michael Ulmer and Scott Young.

I would like to thank the following Maple Leaf players, coaches and managers for their memoirs on the team and their careers: Bob Baun, Andy Bathgate, Johnny Bower, Carl Brewer, King Clancy, Brian Conacher, Ron Ellis, Billy Harris, Paul Henderson, Punch Imlach, Frank Mahovlich, Howie Meeker, Bernie Parent, Jacques Plante, Borje Salming, Frank Selke Sr., Eddie Shack, Conn Smythe, Darryl Sittler, Gord Stellick and Dave Williams.

The following publications were consulted: *Maclean's*, *The Hockey News*, *Hockey Digest*, *Hockey Illustrated*, *Hockey Pictorial*, *Hockey World*, *Sports Illustrated*.

The following record books were consulted: NHL *Guide and Record Book*, *Stanley Cup Playoffs Fact Guide*, *Total Hockey (2nd edition)*, *Total* NHL and *The Sporting News Guide and Register*.

The following publications, broadcasts and videos involving the Maple Leafs were consulted: Maple Leaf game day programs, Maple Leaf media guides, the Maple Leafs 75th anniversary video, and various Leaf games broadcast on Leafs TV and on *Hockey Night in Canada*.

The following newspapers provided game reports and quotes from players, coaches and managers used in the profiles: the *Toronto Star*, the *Toronto Sun*, the *Globe and Mail* and the *Toronto Telegram*.

Interviews conducted by the author with the following Maple Leaf players were used as reference material: Johnny Bower, Ted Kennedy, Dave Keon, Frank Mahovlich, Lanny McDonald, Darryl Sittler and Harry Watson.

I would like to thank the following people for their assistance in putting this book together: This book would not have been possible without the assistance of John Iaboni, who has provided me with much-needed guidance and support, not to mention access to his many contacts in the hockey world. A big thank you to Paul Patskou for his great help in securing the game reports needed to complete the player profiles and for his patience as needs changed. Thanks to Dennis Miles and Craig Campbell for their assistance in securing many of the photos used in this book.

Thank you to the entire staff at Raincoast Books, and especially to Allan MacDougall, Jesse Finkelstein and Teresa Bubela. Thanks also go to Brian Scrivener for his sharp editing work and his enthusiasm for this project.

— *Mike Leonetti*

JOHN IABONI is eternally grateful to Ken Arnold, senior director of communications for the San Jose Sharks. It was Ken who many years ago asked and inspired John to launch a "Legends" series in *Sharks Magazine*. That permitted John the opportunity to write about the many NHL legends who have affected his life. John's essays in this book are an example of his passion.

INDEX

235

PHOTO CREDITS

The photographs in this book came from the following collections:

Hockey Hall of Fame (Graphic Artists, Lou and Nat Turofsky Collection, Doug MacLellan, Paul Bereswill):
3 (Horner, Barilko), 4 (Jackson), 5 (Bentley), 6 (Sittler), 12, 14, 15, 17, 18, 19, 27, 28, 29, 38, 39, 41, 45, 60–69, 82, 83, 94–97, 100–109, 114, 115, 120–123, 127, 128, 129, 132, 133, 136, 137, 142–146, 148, 149, 150, 152, 153, 154, 155, 166, 167, 168, 170, 171, 180, 182, 183, 186, 187, 192, 193, 204, 205, 212, 213, 216, 217, 219, 224, 225, 228, 229, 230, 231

The Legendary Harold Barkley Archives:
3 (Kelly), 6 (Keon), 7, 8, 9, 11, 13, 20, 21, 23, 30, 31, 33, 34, 35, 37, 42, 43, 46, 47, 49, 54, 55, 74, 75, 76, 77, 80, 81, 84–93, 98, 99, 110, 111, 130, 131, 134, 135, 147, 169, 172, 173, 178, 179, 184, 185, 194, 195, 202, 203, 206, 207, 208, 209, 214

Dennis Miles Collection:
4 (Potvin, McDonald), 5 (Williams, Clark), 24, 25, 50, 51, 53, 56, 57, 59, 70, 71, 72, 73, 78, 79, 112, 113, 116, 117, 118, 119, 124, 125, 126, 138, 139, 140, 141, 151, 156–165, 174, 175, 176, 177, 181, 188, 189, 190, 191, 196–201, 210, 211, 215, 218, 220, 221, 222, 223, 226, 227, 232